MOTHER FATHER DEAF

. . . .

MOTHER FATHER DEAF

Mother Father Deaf

· · · · · · · · · · · · · · · ·

Living between Sound and Silence

P A U L   P R E S T O N

H A R V A R D   U N I V E R S I T Y   P R E S S

Cambridge, Massachusetts, and London, England 1994

Library of Congress Cataloging-in-Publication Data

Preston, Paul (Paul M.)
Mother father deaf : living between sound and silence /
Paul Preston.
      p.   cm.
Includes bibliographical references
and index.
ISBN 0-674-58747-2
1. Deaf—Family relationships.
I. Title.
HV2380.P73 1994
362.4'23—dc20   93-44895
CIP

Designed by Gwen Frankfeldt

For Mom, who encouraged me to take risks

. . . .

For Dad, who warned me not to run out of gas

CONTENTS

Preface

One of Michael's first memories is a hot summer day, standing outside the gate of his family's small home in Akron, Ohio. It was 1924; Michael was four years old. His father, a newly arrived immigrant from the Ukraine, yelled from the porch to close the gate. Michael ignored his father. His father yelled again, but Michael kept staring out the open gate. His father, Cossack eyes fiery with anger, grabbed him from behind and dragged him into the house. His older sister and brother could hear the sounds of their father whipping Michael.

A few days later, the source of Michael's disobedience was discovered. Michael had never heard his father's voice calling from the porch. Michael was deaf. Born hearing and never apparently sick, he had been stolen from the world of sound by some unknown thief. The change, invisible and profound, had not been noticed until then. Michael remembers his father grabbing him once again, but this time clutching him to his chest and rocking him quietly. It was the only time he ever saw his father cry.

Michael is now 74. He is my father.

. . . .

Although I have normal hearing, both of my parents are profoundly deaf. This book explores the lives of other people like myself—hearing children of deaf parents. I begin with my father's story because it is part of my family history. It is one of the pieces that I know about a hearing grandfather long dead, and about my father as a young boy. Three generations—my grandparents, my parents, and myself—represent a twist in our family Möbius strip: Hearing into Deaf into Hearing. As in most of the families described in this book, both grandparents and grandchildren are hearing—yet somehow different from each other.

The title of this book—*Mother Father Deaf*—is a commonly used identifier for children of deaf parents within the Deaf community.[1] Although used for both hearing and deaf children, "mother father deaf" remains a lifelong identifier for hearing children. Deaf children of deaf parents become known in the Deaf community in their own right as deaf persons. However, for hearing children and adult children of deaf parents, this phrase legitimizes their connection to an often separate and impenetrable land. It is how many deaf people explain the curious presence of a hearing person in their exclusively Deaf world: "Oh, you know him . . . mother father deaf." By the knowing responses of other deaf people, hearing children recognize their acceptance within the Deaf community.

During my fieldwork, I traveled to Israel. The political climate was particularly tense, and I was foolishly wandering alone through the streets of a nearly deserted Jerusalem. Unbeknown to me, tourists had been warned off the streets. I could feel piercing eyes watching me through closed shutters. I nervously scanned the streets and saw a group of ten tourists gathered in front of one of the Stations of the Cross. What caught my eye was that they were signing. They were deaf. I immediately moved over toward them. They were a group of German deaf tourists. Although sign language is not universal, we were able to communicate. Almost immediately, they wanted to know how I knew sign language. "Mother father deaf," I explained. They all nodded their heads and smiled. One woman came over to me and put her arm around me. "Same us," she nodded as she pulled me into their group.

When Cultures Collide

Introduction

In a small-town café, Peter sat across the table and paused after I asked him a final question: "So did having deaf parents make any difference?" In a quiet and deliberate voice, he said:

> I was so fortunate. You know, I saw a side of life that most people never see. I learned things that even today most of my friends still don't know. My life is just so much richer because my parents were deaf. In spite of all the hardships they had to endure, they kept going. Kept on. And, most of all, they loved each other, and they loved me. What more can you ask for?

Months later, I waited impatiently in a classroom. I had never met Doreen before she stomped into her interview:

> Boy! I can't wait to get this stuff off my chest! I've been holding on to all this negative bullshit for over thirty years! "Interpret what they're saying." "Sign this for me." "Don't listen to the radio, I can't hear it!" Yes, it's too bad you can't hear, but is it my fault I can? I'm not deaf. I'm hearing!

Thousands of miles from either Peter or Doreen, I sat in Angelique's kitchen. While her mother watched television in the next room, Angelique explained what it was like to have her mother live with her. Then she stopped and looked at me:

> You know, these frustrations are just part of human life. It doesn't really make that much difference that my mother is deaf. A lot of it is just

human nature, human interaction. My mother is deaf, but she's also my mother.

Peter, Doreen, and Angelique[1] represent a brief spectrum of the people interviewed for this book. They illustrate the range of emotional and reasoned responses to the overarching question asked of these informants: How have deaf parents made a difference in who you are today?

These men's and women's lives highlight two features that are central to all cultures: communication and family. Recalling a scene from her early childhood, Martha evokes the terror of not being able to communicate or be understood:

> I don't know if this really happened or I dreamed it. I was about three years old. It was absolutely dark all around me and I was afraid. I screamed out, but my parents couldn't hear me. They couldn't hear me. I kept screaming, Mamma, Daddy, why can't you hear me? I'm afraid! Why can't you hear me? Why can't you hear me?

Ricardo's assessment of his family role was both defiant and uncertain:

> Ever since I was little, people used to pat me on the head and tell me, "Now, you make sure you take care of your parents. You're all they've got." God! I hated it. I wanted to say, And who's supposed to take care of me?

Martha and Ricardo raise questions that cut across ethnic and geographic boundaries: How important is auditory language in any child's development? Are nontraditional family roles functionally adaptive or intrinsically damaging?

These informants' lives appear to be a laboratory of human behavior that only the most perverse researcher could have invented—such as the birth of a white child to a black family, or the discovery of a changeling child from fairy tales. Given the enormous cultural significance of language and family, how do hearing children of deaf parents make sense of their family history? Does it affect who they are today? And, reaching beyond the individual experience, is there any sense of a collective identity among these people? Or are these one hundred and fifty lives separate, momentarily corralled within the confines of a researcher's paradigm?

As I prepared to write this book, I sat down amid volumes of transcripts, field notes, maps, letters, and more than a few tattered scraps of uncertain decipherability. Overwhelmed by the accumulation of information before me, I remembered a woman who spoke to me briefly about my research. She sought me out and confided that she knew two people who had deaf parents. Then she shook her head. "They're nothing alike! I just don't see any connection between the two." Her voice had a tone of exasperation: "Maybe you'll find something I don't see."

I did find something—but not necessarily something that she or many others could see. Above all, what I found had to be felt. Previous studies on hearing children of deaf parents have been inconclusive, contradictory, or conjectural. Most of this research has attempted to document objectively how having deaf parents damaged these children: How severe was their language delay? How much were their family experiences like those of children of alcoholics? Hearing children of deaf parents have been bombarded by myriad questions which presume that they are, as one friend surmised, "like wounded fledglings raised by wounded birds." Yet researchers have rarely allowed these men and women to tell their own story. There has been no study that gives primacy to a broad cross-section of hearing children of deaf parents. Although there are many reasons to question the reliability and the validity of insider research, I make no apologies. It was our shared history that provided the key.

Fieldworkers are warned *never* to turn off their tape recorders: you might miss something. Generally, I followed this advice. Keeping the tape recorder on provided me with memorable quotes after an interview had apparently concluded or even as I was halfway out the door. Yet there were moments when informants asked me to turn off the tape recorder. Sometimes informants told me things about themselves that had little or nothing to do with having deaf parents. Sometimes I heard things that had never been shared with another human being.

While disclosures to strangers are not unusual in fieldwork, these remarks were made not just to a researcher, but to someone else with deaf parents. One woman asked me point-blank: "Which of our secrets will you tell?" From remarks like these, it was clear that informants often separated my two identities: the hearing son of deaf parents and the researcher. Higgins (1980) suggests that "a low refusal rate is only one indication that trust has been established" (p. 187). As I look back upon this study, trust, indeed, was a critical issue. It was undeniably our shared history that provided me entrée into many of these women's and men's lives. Our shared family experiences were a source of trust during the interview process itself—both in terms of what they could tell me, and in terms of what I would tell the world.

Researchers have noted that insiders are often able to get more information from respondents than outside interviewers can. In addition, interviews with insiders are likely to be more visceral and contentious (Sattler 1970; Phillips 1971). Higgins (1980) suggests that "the information a hearing researcher would obtain from the Deaf would be more idyllic and less militant than what a deaf researcher might obtain" (p. 186). As I look over my results, I find similar emphases. In comparison with other studies on hearing children of deaf parents, these informants generally described sharper and more frequent feelings—of anger, of joy, of sadness, of confusion. A carefully maintained equilibrium—often presented to both deaf and hearing people—was temporarily lifted during our encounters. As they talked to me, these men and women would say things like, "I wouldn't ordinarily say this," or, "Most people don't know this, but I know you do."

As other fieldworkers have observed, even explicit reminders of the researcher's identity (whether a tape recorder, video camera, or pen and paper) often recede during the interview process. Yet this population was quite familiar with the prying eye of outsiders (including researchers). To many informants, the tape recorder—not me—represented the outside world. Asking me to turn off the tape recorder or prefacing their remarks ("I'm not sure I want this taped, but let's keep going for now") allowed another type of interaction that shattered the distance a researcher's gaze invariably creates. Although I would remind these women and men that I was still trying to keep mental notes,

I also became aware of their trust. It was a level of trust based on our bond of having deaf parents. What informants told me during these times was rarely outside the range of other informants' experiences. Yet such moments of disclosure gave them an opportunity to step outside the interview. It also gave me an opportunity to be one of them.

Mitchell (1991) discusses the paradox of intimacy: "a high degree of trust achieved early in an investigation may actually curtail a researcher's freedom to look and ask" (p. 103). I often found just the opposite to be true. Informants were freer not only to tell me details of their own lives, but to ask me questions. Sometimes the two of us would talk *about* the research process itself. We could both momentarily step outside of our defined roles as interviewer and informant and be two adults who had deaf parents. We could acknowledge the misperceptions the Hearing world had about deaf people—and that researchers had not always helped in this matter. I could ask these men and women which secrets could be told and which should remain between us.

A sizable and distinguished cohort of anthropologists has focused on the intersection of culture and the individual, attempting to unravel the question of cultural transmission: How are people socialized to become members of their cultural group? Much of this research has focused on the family as the primary arena of socialization. Yet most deaf children are born to hearing parents, and therefore they learn Deaf culture from outside their family. Studies by Becker (1980), Meadow-Orlans and colleagues (1987), Padden and Humphries (1988), and others have shown how Deaf culture is transmitted to other deaf individuals primarily through deaf peers. Because deaf children are largely shut off from Hearing culture, Deaf culture represents one of the rare instances in which peer socialization is the primary arena of socialization, consistently exceeding or replacing that of the family. Complementing these findings, writers have also described how deaf children of deaf parents are the symbolic if not practical core of Deaf culture.

Although researchers have examined the issue of cultural transmission among deaf individuals, there has been a significant omission: What happens to the children of deaf parents who are not deaf? Deaf culture has developed around a particular functional condition. Is this culture transmitted to their hearing children—even though they are so evidently different from their parents? It is this fragile pattern of cultural transmission that lies at the heart of this work.

Examining the relationship between self and family has become a hallmark of contemporary life: who we are, who we were. In Western thought, parent and family experiences are generally assumed to surpass all other variables in shaping one's identity. Whether through unseen genes or remembered childhood, we lay considerable baggage at the feet of our parents. An enormous body of professional and popular literature unequivocally identifies the family as the source of how we came to be who we are. Unlike the Azande, we do not use witches to explain why things turn out the way they do. Unlike the Dogon, we do not point to the wind. We are the inheritors of our family: they have caused us to *be*. Yet, when we assess who we are in light of our childhood experiences, what informs this perspective? How variable and culturally dependent are the concepts of family, of parents, of childhood? If flawed or ethnocentric, why do these models remain so salient in Western thought?

My goal in this book is not only to examine the lives of a particular group of men and women who shared a common childhood feature, but to understand how they made sense of that experience. In piecing together the meaning of having deaf parents, informants held their family experiences against two cultural templates: the Deaf and the Hearing. These competing and contrasting perspectives not only illuminate certain features of Deaf culture but expose cultural assumptions that are shared with those whose parents are not deaf. It is this spectrum of behaviors and values—imperceptible to most, but distinctly "Hearing" to some—that permeates how most of us define and understand ourselves. Amid a kaleidoscope of memories, routines, and aspirations, this cultural lens shapes how the dreams and shadows of childhood become part of the fabric of our adult lives. It informs the questions we ask as well as the answers we give.

The cultural emphasis in this book frequently led to challenging and sometimes displacing traditionally held biomedical interpretations and psychological repercussions of deafness. This is not an absolute stance, however. Hearing loss is a very real condition with very real consequences. Yet a long history of explanations and responses to deafness has reflected biases of the dominant Hearing culture and continues to overshadow the understandings of deaf people themselves. Nor are deaf people immune to this cultural hegemony. As Ortner (1974) suggests, both those in power and those who are depreciated often learn the same version of truth which uplifts one group while condemning another.[2]

It is, ultimately, impossible to extract Deaf culture from Hearing culture. They exist in relationship to each other. Rather, my intent in this work is to focus on Deaf culture within the context of (American) Hearing culture. These informants' lives incorporate the conflicts and the resolutions of these two often opposing world views. Traditional anthropological constructs of culture as pristine and unchanging have been replaced by a recognition of culture as fluid and dynamic. What becomes important is not only an understanding of the characteristics and internal values of a particular culture, but multiple perspectives that consider what happens when cultures collide. In an increasingly complex and interactive world, these encounters have become the norm rather than the exception.

Within the narratives of these informants, this book examines myths and beliefs about hearing and deafness, about sound and silence. It also concerns the culturally relative nature of families, and the assumptions and expectations that all of us hold to be not just important, but vital to our well-being as individuals and as a society. The process of cultural transmission forms the link between the more immediate experiences within the family and the larger influences of society and culture. While writing this book, I struggled to balance these broader explorations of identity, family, and culture with a more focused ethnography of hearing children of deaf parents. At times, the voices and emotions of these men and women broke through my agenda. Hearing children of deaf parents have been used by researchers to explicate a host of questions—but who is to tell their story? Although these social and cultural dimensions are an integral part of the daily lives of hearing children of deaf parents, I am also keenly aware that they have entrusted me to be their voice.

Deaf people, per se, are not the focus of this book. This study concerns their hearing children. In presenting this material, however, it is impossible to avoid describing and discussing the historical, social, and cultural features of those who are deaf. I have chosen to disperse this information throughout the book as it relates to a particular issue—reflecting the ongoing and, sometimes, incidental nature of such facts. Similarly, although the discussions in each chapter are organized around a central topic such as grandparents (Chapter 4), communication (Chapter 7), or stigma (Chapter 9), these issues are neither isolated nor definitive. Individual chapters and themes are fluid and contingent upon other chapters. It is from the relationships among the various themes and ideas within this book that the full story emerges.

Through this research, I have learned much more about my parents' history and my own cultural heritage. My cultural perspective has affected how this book was conceived, carried out, and ultimately written. Shortly before completing this study, I was invited to give a keynote speech on Deaf culture at a national conference for more than a thousand deaf people. What I learned from writing this book was that it was important not only to give that speech in sign language, but to give it in the "Deaf way." This meant identifying myself through my parents, giving the speech in American Sign Language without voice, addressing the audience interactively and informally, asking questions, and drawing from a rich history of oral traditions. I have written this book as much as possible in the Deaf way—not in sign language but in interwoven stories, fragments of sharply drawn scenes, repetitions for emphasis, and the use of questions to create dialogue. Deaf storytelling does not, as one informant explained, "boil down to a punch line." It is in the telling.

Interpreting Our Lives

You would not recognize them on the street or even in your own home. Their appearance and dress are as diverse as their life-styles. They are gray-haired grandparents and earringed punk rockers. They include politicians and teachers, bartenders and doctors. Some are even insurance salesmen.[1] Their speech is unremarkable—except for the dialects and accents of their geographic home communities. Their demeanor can be shy and retiring, or boisterous and effusive. They are married, single, gay, and straight. Some are model citizens; some have criminal records. Hearing children of deaf parents appear to be any man and any woman. Indeed, informants often described themselves as unusually adept at fitting into a variety of environments. You might never know.

Some keep their family history guarded, while others are quite open about it. Disclosure might occur in casual conversation or on national television. When she accepted her 1975 Oscar for Best Actress, Louise Fletcher tearfully thanked her mother and father in sign language. When the family history is revealed, whether to a stranger or a fellow worker, reactions can include curiosity, pity, interest, or silence. Marilyn recalled a fairly common misunderstanding:

> And so he says, "Death? You mean your parents are dead?" And I said, "No, *DEAF,* my parents are deaf!"

Jeff described how mentioning that his parents were deaf would escalate into a major revelation:

> Like when I'm on a date and we're talking about our parents. We'll be laughing about something my father said or shake our heads about how our mothers are just alike . . . And then somewhere along the way she finds out that my parents are deaf. It just changes everything. They're not just a mother or father any more. They're these DEAF people!

When I talked with Anna, she remembered that such disclosures led to a shift with regard to herself as well:

> They think, Oh, deaf, deaf, deaf. Your parents are deaf. And then, after a few minutes, they look at you with this, Oh, and are you weird too?

Agar (1980) describes ethnography as "committed to an understanding of a given instance of the human experience—the environment that surrounds it, the history that precedes it, the intent of the persons who create it, and the pattern that gives it form" (p. 223). This ethnography begins at the intersection of two cultures: Deaf and Hearing. For hearing children of deaf parents, this intersection is both metaphoric and substantive, both childhood memory and adult life. This chapter provides an overview of hearing children of deaf parents, but it primarily concerns the narrower universe of my sample of informants. Because there is no available estimate of the population size or characteristics of all hearing children of deaf parents, the observations made throughout this study cannot be expected to apply to every hearing child of deaf parents, and the conclusions drawn cannot be extrapolated with complete confidence.[2] This research disclaimer is made not only for the benefit of a general audience; it is given for the hearing children of deaf parents. A recurrent theme throughout this book is how hearing children of deaf parents struggle to interpret their lives—often amid conflicting and sometimes coercive explanations. It is each hearing child of deaf parents who ultimately determines the patterns that give form and meaning to his or her life.

Deaf Culture

Three generations within a family history: unsuspecting hearing parents have a deaf child; that deaf child grows up and typically marries another deaf person; those deaf parents give birth to a hearing child.

It is estimated that almost ninety percent of the children born to two deaf parents are hearing.[3] This inversion appears to reinstate the normal order of things. Very few of these hearing children will have deaf children.[4] The generation of deaf parents represents a momentary disruption in a Hearing family history. The legacy of deafness remains suspended, and within another family, another pair of hearing parents begins the cycle again.

Although hearing children of deaf parents do not overtly share their parents' functional condition, they potentially inherit a sensibility and a cultural legacy which is unlike that of any other hearing child. This socialization pattern is even unlike that of their own deaf parents—most of whom were raised in hearing families. Hearing children of deaf parents have been raised on the peripheries and often within the heart of an exclusively Deaf community. As children and as adults, they are poised on the brink of this remarkable world, which is often only superficially accessible to those who can hear.

The condition of deafness creates a community with a separate language and a distinct culture.[5] Although the vast majority of deaf children were raised in hearing families[6] and although the careers and residences of deaf adults disperse them throughout the larger Hearing society, most lifelong deaf adults socialize exclusively with other deaf people. As children, deaf individuals develop close and lasting friendships with their deaf school peers—from whom they learn a sense of shared identity, a cultural heritage, and a means of communication. As adults, they participate in a wide variety of exclusively Deaf social organizations ranging from sports to religious groups. Schein and Delk (1974) estimate that deaf people have an 85 to 95 percent endogamous marriage rate.[7]

Sorting out the functional condition of deafness from the cultural experience of deafness has been problematic. Although an increasing number of studies acknowledge "Deaf culture," writers have often avoided clarifying what they mean by "culture." For some, difference from others is sufficient to merit cultural designation. Using difference as a criterion, however, bypasses an important component of culture: those aspects which are shared within the group. Many writers have emphasized the distinct sign language of deaf people. Yet equating language with culture overstates the relationship and ultimately provides a circular definition of Deaf culture, ignoring the variations in sign language fluency and usage within the Deaf community. Other writers have become bogged down in the issue of whether to describe the Deaf as a culture or a subculture. A few writers have skirted the conceptual issue by simply endorsing a political agenda: a cultural view of deafness is preferable to one that pathologizes.

Culture does not have the tidiness of cellular division or the definitiveness of a mathematical equation. Although most of the men and women I interviewed endorsed the concept of Deaf culture, many had difficulty articulating what it meant. Sandra explained her frustration:

> Usually I understand why a deaf person did so and so. I can understand why they did it. But I can't explain to hearing people. Like, when I saw it, it didn't look wrong to me. I understood just fine, but to hearing people it looks real strange. I don't even think about it, don't think anything about it. That's just how deaf people are, no big deal. And then they [hearing people] look at me like [signs *"gape"* and *"dumb"*]. They want an answer. But I don't have a black-and-white answer for them.

Researchers and informants have repeatedly acknowledged that hearing loss is *not* a satisfactory criterion or description of Deaf culture. What, then, is Deaf culture? Andersson (1987) notes: "Unfortunately, field or historical studies about the social life of deaf people which could provide evidence on the development of Deaf culture are still seriously lacking" (p. 261). This book is, in part, a response to this need.

As an anthropologist, my views on Deaf culture are informed by an understanding of "culture" that includes four components: (1) a system of shared ideas and behaviors, (2) which are distinct, (3) which are learned, and (4) which provide a template for personal and social interaction. Culture explains and restricts how things are known, affecting both the practical and the symbolic realms. The intensity and the flexibility of these cultural templates vary for individual members and are influenced by the history of the culture as well as by interactions with other cultures.

Although deaf people throughout the world often report feeling more kinship with each other than with their hearing countrymen, the Deaf culture described and explored throughout this book is a specific one: American Deaf culture. The political, historical, and social dimensions of a nation or region's Hearing culture create a particular context for deaf people. Such differences result in distinct characteristics among deaf people from the community to the national level. Thus far, researchers have paid the most attention to documenting and analyzing regional and national sign language differences.[8] In contrast, there have been almost no ethnographies of the deaf people in other countries. Without cross-cultural documentation, the underlying commonality or differences between the world's Deaf communities and cultures can only be surmised. Almost all the deaf parents and hearing children written about in this book reflect the interplay among three broadly defined cultures: Hearing, Deaf, and American.[9]

Most culturally Deaf people have moderate to profound hearing loss since birth or childhood. Yet cultural Deafness is not just about hearing loss. Being culturally Deaf is interdependent on the individual's identification with the group and the group's evaluation and acceptance of the individual. This assessment is largely based on a sense of cultural familiarity: having a breadth of life experiences associated with being deaf; routinely participating in social interactions with other deaf people; and sharing similar social behaviors, historical traditions, and a common destiny. American Sign Language (ASL) is regarded by many as an integral feature of Deaf culture.[10] Yet not all culturally Deaf persons are fluent in ASL—including a small minority who oppose the use of any sign language. Unlike most definitions of Deaf culture, the one proposed here includes deaf people who are oral— that is, deaf people who do not use sign language as their primary form of communication.[11] This inclusion is supported by interviews in which informants described a sense of cultural Deafness and community as characterizing non-signing as well as signing deaf parents.

A number of writers have attempted to distinguish individuals who are clinically "deaf" from those who are culturally "Deaf" by using either a lowercase or an uppercase designation.[12] The lowercase "deaf" describes a person with a moderate to profound hearing loss. The uppercase "Deaf" describes an individual—regardless of hearing status—who participates in and considers himself a member of the Deaf community. Analogous distinctions between clinical and cultural terms have been used to describe other groups, such as "homosexual" versus "gay." With the possible exception of hard-of-hearing individuals and hearing children of deaf parents, culturally Deaf people are usually functionally deaf as well. Although I find the distinction between "deaf" and "Deaf" conceptually useful, I have found it to be practically unworkable. Colleagues and friends have found the use of these two terms confusing in my own writing as well as in published materials from other authors. In part, the difficulty arises because the distinction uses the same four letters: *deaf*. More important, however, there is a range of both cultural and functional deafness, and the distinction between the two is not clear-cut. Ongoing concerns about membership and boundaries are important features of Deaf culture.

In this book, I reserve the use of the capitalized "Deaf" to refer to the more generalized group of persons who are culturally and usually functionally deaf: the Deaf community, the Deaf world, Deaf culture, and the Deaf. I use "Hearing" in a similarly generalized way: the Hearing world, Hearing culture, and Hearing people (as a group). Individual persons are designated by the lowercase "deaf" or "hearing" according to their grossly delineated auditory status; the use of the lowercase "deaf" or "hearing" does not indicate whether that person is a member of the Deaf community. At times, my decision to use lowercase or uppercase was a judgment call. Not surprisingly, the most difficult determinations occurred among these informants. Any one of them could be "hearing," "Hearing," "Deaf," and, in a few cases, "deaf."[13] When informants were referring to themselves (for example, "I'm more Deaf than Hearing"), I capitalized these terms because such references were almost always intended as cultural rather than functional descriptions.

Among the general population, there is a continuum of acute hearing to profound deafness. Yet within the Deaf community, ambiguity is rarely allowed: people are either *hearing* or *deaf*. Foster (1989) has demonstrated that this dichotomization is both reaction and assertion: deaf individuals seek out other deaf people in response to their sense of alienation from hearing people, as well as finding positive value in the affiliation with other deaf people. The polarization between the Deaf and the Hearing cultures is often increased by the use of two significantly different communication systems: English and American Sign Language.[14] While characteristics ascribed to either deaf or hearing people are not consistent, what has endured is the dichotomization—there is a Deaf world, and there is a Hearing world. As adults, most culturally Deaf people maintain a highly homogeneous world—until the birth of their hearing child.

The Search for Childhood

Although my fieldwork was conducted almost exclusively among hearing adults with deaf parents, I had opportunities to speak with several deaf parents as well. As I conversed with one deaf woman in ASL, she told me about the birth of her daughter:

> When Barbara was born, it wasn't until about three days later that I had this funny feeling about her. I started wondering if she was deaf or hearing. I was still in the hospital . . . There I was in the bed feeding her. My first child. I kept wondering to myself, Is she deaf or is she hearing? I was holding her in my arms near the metal food tray. I picked up a spoon and dropped it on the tray. I couldn't believe it! I was really upset. I did it a second time because I just couldn't believe it. I dropped the spoon again, and it was the same thing. I even did it a third time. I thought, Oh, my God, she's hearing! What am I going to do? I have a hearing daughter! My husband came in and I said, My God, our daughter's hearing! He was just as surprised, but he told me it was fine, it was going to be okay. I'm the third generation deaf. There was no question but that we would have deaf children. Then I find out that my daughter was born hearing! What on earth am I doing to do with her? I don't even know how to talk to her. ["So you never thought that you might have a hearing child?"] No, never! It never occurred to me that my child would be hearing. I was really surprised. I was scared. I wanted to be close to my children. I've always been very close to my family, and I wanted the same for me and my children. The Hearing world and the Deaf world are such separate worlds. I worried that we would never connect, or that we would drift apart.

This deaf mother's distress over having a child so fundamentally different from herself mirrors the reactions of many hearing parents who discover they have a deaf child. Like hearing parents, some deaf parents also expect to have a child who is the same as themselves. Because this woman is from a multiple-generation deaf family, she is atypical of most deaf parents: the majority of deaf parents can expect to give birth to a hearing child. However, her comments illustrate two significant themes which appear throughout many of these informants' narratives. First, this mother's reactions to having a hearing child vividly demonstrate that in a number of families, deafness—not hearing—was the status quo. Second, this woman describes a polarization between the Deaf and Hearing worlds, a pervasive dichotomy that has a profound impact on the lives of deaf parents and their hearing children. How is it possible that parent and child from two such different worlds can meet?

It is remarkable that deaf people have had children at all—not because they could not, but because hearing people often decided they should not. Out of fear that deaf parents would create more deaf children, the Hearing world has often espoused and even legislated various forms of eugenics. Some laws prohibited deaf people from marrying; others barred them from having children. Alexander Graham Bell, whose mother was deaf, became one of the most vocal opponents of marriage between deaf people. Bell reasoned that the chance of hereditary deafness would be minimized or eliminated if deaf people would marry only hearing partners. But Bell's genetic theories are unsound: most deaf parents have hearing children, and a few forms of genetic deafness are dominant and would be passed on to the child even if one parent were hearing. Although generally unfounded, genetic fears continue to shadow the lives of deaf people and their families. Yet the question of heredity taps into a far more fundamental concern that forms the basis of family and society: What does it mean to be a parent? How will deaf parents' hearing children learn to be members of the larger Hearing society?

Concerns about deaf parents do not end with marriage or childbirth, nor are they merely hypothetical. A number of hearing children of deaf parents have been taken out of their family homes because of allegations of child neglect and abuse (Charlson 1993). Have these parents truly failed, or has the larger society presumed failure because these parents are different? When I first spoke with Carl on the phone, he suggested why I might not want to talk with him: "I really don't remember my childhood." Carl's words are straight out of countless psychotherapy books and self-help groups. What unmentionable childhood abuse and terror could evoke such loss of continuity and memory? As I hung up the phone after Carl agreed to meet with me, I remember feeling a knot in my stomach. The researcher in me said to keep going; but as the son of deaf parents, I paused: What will I do if I find out that having deaf parents leads to disastrous personal consequences?[15]

During my fieldwork, I did hear stories of abuse from a few inform-ants—but the frequency of these incidents appears to be comparable to that in the general American population. In most of these cases, abuse was inflicted not by parents but by persons outside the home. It was, as one woman suggested, "as if deaf people and their children are easier targets." When I finally met with Carl, I came to a much different understanding of his "lost" childhood. Carl actually had fond memories of his parents and his childhood. Why, then, had he told me he could not remember his childhood? I had many turning points during my fieldwork, but one of the most profound was when Carl pointed out quite simply what this research was ultimately about:

> I always knew there were others like me . . . but I never got a chance to talk with them. I don't know anyone else like me, you know, with deaf parents. You're the first one . . . When I hear other people talking about their childhoods, I never hear my story. I don't know what to say.

Just before I finished this book, a colleague spoke with me about my research. "You know," she said, "problems with communication and family and identity aren't just peculiar to hearing children of deaf parents . . . we all have them." To some degree, she is right. But what she underestimates is the importance and the power of hearing one's own story. After listening to these men and women, I realized that some childhoods were "lost" because these adults had no frame of reference for their experiences. They were unable to see the parallels, to make the necessary translation from the prevailing cultural stereotypes to the specifics of their own lives. Among hearing children of deaf parents, this is not surprising. Having deaf parents has been a lifelong socially distinct variable that has often set these children apart and identified them as different from others. Is it possible that they are really just like everyone else?

As I continued my fieldwork, the specter of lost childhoods surfaced in another way. Most women and men remembered their childhoods quite well. However, as they measured their experiences against the dominant cultural norms, some felt as if they came up short. As Melinda said, "Sure, I was a child . . . but I didn't have a childhood." Like several other informants, Melinda described how too much childhood responsibility had eroded her sense of being a child. Indeed, there are myriad features of many informants' childhoods that fall outside the cultural expectations for what it means to be a child, a parent, or a family. Yet these prescriptions are based upon values derived from Hearing and American cultures. These assumptions are so entrenched and pervasive that it is often difficult to question their inevitability or their naturalness.

In the course of attending various workshops and conferences over the past twenty years, I have noticed a paradoxical stance among many professionals who work with the Deaf. Social workers, psychologists, and educators frequently focus on high-risk deaf individuals and families. These professionals are quick to point out that the deaf persons they work with and write about are not typical deaf people: they are the extremes. At the same time, these professionals caution that we must pay attention to cultural differences among deaf people—cultural as defined by African-American or Vietnamese or Native American. What is missing, however, are the cultural norms and patterns of Deaf people. Although we increasingly recognize cultural diversity, in one sense these differences—whether Irish or Hispanic—are all alike: they are all Hearing. What are the cultural practices and norms of deaf-parented families? In writing about and attending to only those who are most troubled, we present a dangerously flawed picture of deaf people and Deaf culture.

Previous Research

A small body of research has developed around hearing children of deaf parents. Using the same deficit model that has dominated studies of deaf people, researchers have frequently reinforced negative assumptions by their selectivity: many of the sample populations and individual case studies on hearing children of deaf parents were obtained from speech clinics or therapists' couches. As such, most of these studies are tautological, and have often alienated their subjects in the process. They have also missed a great deal. Aside from the research that is pathologically biased, comparative studies between hearing children of deaf parents and control groups of hearing children of hearing parents have been inconclusive (Charlson 1990; Chan and Lui 1990). Although these and other researchers report impressionistic differences between these two groups, they were largely unable to substantiate their findings using standardized psychosocial measurements.

As adults, hearing children of deaf parents have largely been passed over by researchers. Whether considering deaf individuals or those with deaf parents, researchers have often tended to focus on infants and young children, forgetting that both deaf and hearing children grow up. Exceptions to this are studies by Arlow (1976), Taska and Rhoads (1981), Wagenheim (1985), and others which generalize on the basis of a single case study. A few other researchers have concentrated on performance measurement in the areas of language acquisition and communication skills (Bellugi and Fischer 1972; Poizner et al. 1981). Neville's fascinating study at the Salk Institute (1990) compared brain activity in deaf and hearing individuals; her study also included a third group—adult hearing children of deaf parents who had acquired ASL as their first language. She found that these adult hearing children had certain left hemisphere activities more like those of deaf subjects than hearing subjects. In particular, both deaf individuals and hearing children of deaf parents had heightened attention to peripheral space and motion. Neville hypothesizes that this difference may be due to the early learning of a visual language (ASL) which necessitates enhanced peripheral vision skills. Bunde (1979) and Wilbur (1986) have each conducted large-scale surveys of adult hearing children with deaf parents. Their research represented an important first step in delineating some features of this population and in suggesting future research directions. However, their studies were limited by their research design—mailed surveys using a predetermined list of questions and possible responses—as well as by sample populations largely derived from persons who worked as interpreters.

A handful of researchers and writers have begun allowing deaf people to tell their own stories (Jacobs 1974; Becker 1980; Higgins 1980; Padden and Humphries 1988; Wilcox 1989; Lane 1989, 1992). These studies offer a remarkably different perspective—contrasting with previous observations that focused on the myriad problems or presumed characteristics of those affected by deafness. Through these more phenomenologically oriented studies, we learn how deaf people make sense of their world, and we begin to see a community that has developed not only compensations but unique cultural dimensions. These pioneering works have paved the way for this current exploration of deaf people's hearing children.

Researchers have often presumed certain characteristics about hearing children of deaf parents without adequately investigating or clarifying their assumptions. These suppositions are frequently found among the general public—and were even proposed by a few informants as well. I will elaborate on these characteristics in succeeding chapters, but a few generalizations can be made here. First, a number of informants did *not* sign as children—even if sign language was their parents' sole means of communication. Second, the amount of interpreting that any one hearing child did varied tremendously among informants—particularly among siblings within a single family. Third, more than half of these men and women did not work in a job related to deaf people (such as interpreting, counseling, or teaching). Finally, although they may have routinely interacted with other hearing children of deaf parents when younger, many informants had little or no

contact with other hearing children of deaf parents as adults.[16] Outside of their own siblings, several men and women had not met another hearing adult with deaf parents until they talked with me. This isolation changed somewhat over the course of this research as more and more people became involved in or aware of the organization known as CODA.

CODA (Children of Deaf Adults) is a ten-year-old organization with members throughout the United States and several foreign countries.[17] Voting membership is generally restricted to hearing persons who grew up with at least one deaf parent. Almost all of the current members are adults over 18 years of age. The organization's stated mission is to "address bicultural experiences through conferences, support groups, and resource development." At the time of my fieldwork, the majority of the informants had not heard of CODA. Slightly under one-third of the men and women interviewed were active members of CODA, and they were generally very positive about their participation. Other informants explained that, although they were supportive of CODA, they were generally "not interested in joining an organization." A few informants were adamantly opposed to CODA—insisting that members dwelt upon negative rather than positive interpretations of their childhoods.

There is a brief discussion of informants' disagreements about participation in CODA in Chapter 11, which concerns the various ways in which hearing children of deaf parents express and explain their present adult identities. Although CODA clearly centers on the experiences of hearing children of deaf parents, it raises separate research issues involving organizational dynamics and group interactions. Because these issues create an additional dimension of complexity, I will not discuss CODA in any detail in this book.

The Problems of Culture

Anthropologists generally confine themselves to the study of phenomena at the group level. But this broader view often overlooks the relationship between the individual and culture. Culture is not some external force that tells us what is important or what we should do; it

is a process in which we are an interactive and creative part. Accordingly, my study begins with the individual experience. Each of us with deaf parents has a unique story, and authors like Lou Ann Walker *(A Loss For Words)*, Carol Glickfeld *(Useful Gifts)*, and Ruth Sidransky *(In Silence)* have drawn from their family histories to create highly personal portraits of being the hearing child of deaf parents.[18] Although she did not have deaf parents, JoAnne Greenberg *(In This Sign)* convincingly depicts the life of a deaf couple and their hearing daughter engulfed by poverty during the Depression. Many of my informants had read one or more of these books, but there were strong disagreements about which author was best able to convey an informant's particular family experience. While these and many other works written by hearing children of deaf parents have given me rich insights into this research, my approach has been to move from these individual experiences to the broader cultural experiences of this group as a whole.

The theories I draw from and discuss throughout this book are taken from several disciplines besides anthropology. I use them advisedly. Although theory can give people a structure they can use to step back and begin to understand their experience, I reject the notion that it is the observer rather than the observed whose perspective approximates some greater truth.[19] I use theoretical constructs as long as they fit with the experiences of these women and men. There are occasional loose ends. The problem of interpreting is central to anthropology, yet no single theory prescribes how to interpret what is observed. However, a central tenet of anthropology steers the course: listen to what people are saying; observe what people are doing.

The transmission of culture from deaf parents to their hearing children unfolds somewhat differently in each family. As I traveled across the United States, informants shared their personal histories as well as explaining how they have made sense of their lives. These individual and collective accounts provide what Gergen and Gergen (1983) have called "narratives of self." These men and women have constructed explanations and stories around one variable in their lives: having deaf parents. Many of those I spoke with were ideal informants

in that they had long considered the very question I was asking: What did all this mean? Zelda, a retired schoolteacher in her late sixties, explained how certain events triggered an understanding of her family and herself:

> Anyway, for years and years I never dealt with it. And there's a lot of shit there. But I remember seeing a list of classes at the college. And I kept looking at the ASL classes. And I didn't know ASL from a hole in the wall. That was what I used, but I didn't know it . . . So, I kept looking at these classes and that was about 10 years ago. And then I finally said, OK, it keeps coming up. I'll do it. I went into the class. And doors would start flinging open. Memories of things came flooding back. The teacher would do a sign and I would understand finally not what the sign meant—which I already understood—but what it *meant,* who my mother was when she used it.

Informants' interpretations—individually and as a group—were not always consistent. Yet, as I attempted to reconcile the sometimes conflicting explanations that informants gave, I recognized one underlying commonality: these women and men struggled with and were making interpretations. Fate has given these individuals a socially significant variable to make sense of. As one stranger inquired only moments after she found out I had deaf parents, "Oh, what did it mean to have deaf parents? What did it *really* mean?"

The cultural view presented in this book is not without its biases. A cultural emphasis may overstate the sense of a shared perspective among these men and women. A few informants reported that they saw their experiences as unique or isolated, and did not identify themselves as part of a larger group:

> I don't really think I have that much in common [with other hearing people whose parents are deaf]. Maybe a little bit, but it's mostly history. Our lives are so different now. Besides, when I was a kid I had to deal with things on my own. It was just me and my parents. There wasn't anybody else involved.

Deaf parents, too, while recognizing differences between themselves and their hearing children, often did not see hearing children of deaf parents as sharing a cultural identity. Jill described this scene with her mother:

> I was trying to explain to my mother about getting together [with other hearing children of deaf parents]. She looked at me and said, You mean they're deaf? [Signs *"No, they're hearing, but their parents are deaf . . . Like me."*] So she nodded, but I could tell that she was thinking, Why on earth would you want to do something like that?

Outside researchers have grouped the hearing children of deaf parents under several clever names and awkward acronyms.[20] These labels were generally for the convenience of the researchers and did not reflect actual usage among deaf parents or their hearing children.

In choosing a name to identify a group of people being written about, anthropologists have traditionally relied on the term(s) used by the people themselves. With the establishment of CODA, an increasing number of hearing children of deaf parents have begun referring to themselves as "codas."[21] Although many deaf people as well as other professionals working with the Deaf have also adopted this term, there is considerable dissension—as these two informants attested:

> [Mel:] What is that they're calling us? Codas? What's that supposed to mean? Coda! Who makes up these names anyway?

> [Bill:] I don't like the name "coda." I don't mind being called a child, but I object to being connected to deaf adults. It's not just deaf adults that I am related to, it's my deaf parents. It should be something like CODP (Children of Deaf Parents) . . . I'll always be a child in relation to my parents, but I am an adult in relation to other adults, deaf or hearing.

Other informants familiar with CODA felt that the organization represented a particular philosophical or political stance and dissociated themselves from the term "coda." Several were concerned about the potential for confusion because the term "coda" is also the acronym commonly used for Co-Dependents Anonymous. In this book, I have chosen not to impose my own label on hearing children of deaf parents; nor do I wish to alienate some who do not want to be called "codas." I do make use of anthropologists' perennially favorite term:

"informants." In fact, these men and women have had lifetimes of being informants—to the Hearing world about the Deaf, to the Deaf world about the Hearing.

The pseudonyms that I use to identify individual informants reflect a Hearing bias. These pseudonyms are spoken and written English names. Although the informants were indeed known by such names, within the context of their deaf families they were known by other names as well. Like most individuals within the Deaf community, more than half of all informants had sign names—a unique sign for that individual. Moreover, almost all informants' spoken names were pronounced differently by their deaf parents. To outsiders, deaf people's pronunciation of spoken words often appears to be guttural or high-pitched sounds unrelated to spoken words. Informants, however, recognized their deaf parents' voiced names for them with familiarity and, often, with special fondness.

The illusion of researcher omniscience remains an inescapable construct of written discourse. Although I have attempted to give primacy to the voices of these men and women, I recognize the danger of commodification of others' narratives. Jackson (1987) suggests that the fundamental goal of an anthropologist is to let those studied reveal themselves "so we can better see what the world looks like through their eyes" (p. 82). While sound advice, this approach is more often an ideal rather than an achievable goal. My insider status further complicates the dilemma of postmodern anthropologists: Whose voice does the reader hear?

I address these concerns in two ways. In writing this book, I used at least one representative quotation from each person interviewed. Although this multitude of voices may burden the reader with a staccato effect, this approach forced me to include the perspectives of all these men and women—no matter how disparate any one individual's account might be. I also kept a daily journal of my own perspectives and family history, and constantly checked my perceptions with friends and colleagues. There is, ultimately, no way for me to extract or separate myself from those I have studied. My life, as well as theirs, is under the microscope.

Anthropology's strength and also its Achilles' heel is the concept of cultural relativism. Understanding behaviors and values within a cultural context can provide a much greater understanding of others and ourselves. Yet certain issues test the limits of tolerance (for example, clitoridectomy, infanticide, wife-burning). Can such practices merely be observed and described without intervention? Deaf people have seized upon Deaf culture as a way to reject the presumption of pathology and dysfunction. But is this cultural view of deafness merely denial? How can that deaf mother possibly have wanted to have a *deaf* child? Even hearing children of deaf parents do not agree on the nature and impact of deafness. Before I even began interviewing one woman, she immediately asked me, "You're not gonna say that our parents weren't handicapped, are you?" No, I'm not. But I will at least question whether deaf people are handicapped because not hearing is an intrinsically pathological human condition, or whether deafness becomes handicapping because it runs counter to certain dominant social and cultural norms.

Research Methods and Parameters

In the final scene of the movie *Blade Runner,* a dying android describes how he has seen sights in the universe that most humans can only read about because of the immense distances in time and space. He remembers distant galaxies, erupting supernovas, and swirling nebulas. As I finish this work, I feel a similar joy and frustration. I, too, have heard and seen stories that I can never fully convey. This is not merely the angst of postmodernism. It reflects the limits of research that was designed from a Hearing perspective. I had anticipated interviews that could be tape-recorded. I foresaw interactions that would be impersonal and time-limited. I expected that *they* would do all the talking.

When contact sheets were returned from potential informants, I was pleased at how many men and women agreed to be tape-recorded during the interview. I anticipated that a tape recorder would make taking field notes much easier. After the first few interviews, however, I realized that I was missing a great deal by having an auditory but not a visual record. What about informants' faces, their eyes, their looks, their gestures, their signs? Time did not allow a revision of my interview schedule; money constraints did not allow the purchase of video equipment. More important, many potential informants acknowledged that they would be reluctant to participate if the interviews were videotaped. A tape recorder, perhaps because it so clearly belonged to the Hearing world, would be paradoxically less intrusive than a video camera. As it turned out, I was left to write down notes as the tape recorder ran—and even this method created problems. My active listening meant keeping almost constant eye contact with informants. Informants repeatedly acknowledged an increased comfort level when I did this ("I know you're paying attention to me"), and they invariably stopped talking or lost their train of thought whenever I glanced down to take notes.

Selecting these informants was both a random and a systematic process. Initially, potential informants were randomly drawn from a compilation of names and addresses throughout the United States that I had collected over the two years prior to the interviews. Most of these names came from three sources: various agencies, organizations, and schools working with the deaf; CODA; and referrals by potential informants to other childhood or adult acquaintances.

I sent out letters of request to a randomized list of one hundred persons throughout the United States. In asking for their consent to be interviewed, I promised confidentiality and anonymity. My only initial stipulation for participation in this study was that the person be hearing, 18 years of age or older, and have two deaf parents. I did not spell out any criteria for hearing or deafness. My targeted sample population was to be fifty persons.

I had to revise the sample size for this study twice—from fifty to one hundred, and finally to one hundred and fifty. These increases reflected an unexpected outpouring of interest and support for this project. I received letters and phone calls from people who had heard about the study. Other potential informants told me they had a childhood friend or a sister or a brother who might be interested in participating. Deaf parents sent me the names of their children. I had not anticipated such enthusiasm; it had not been reflected in previous studies or in my own initial pilot study, which indicated that hearing children of deaf parents would be reluctant to discuss their family histories and their lives. The informants themselves offered several reasons for their willingness to participate. Many were eager to tell their own story. Dave told me:

> Oh, you got me when you said I could talk as long as I liked. [Laughs.] You wanted to hear my side of it, my story. I don't know that I get many opportunities to really talk about it. Not now.

My shared history provided me entrée into a family life often off-limits to outsiders. One informant, Vera, explained why she decided to participate:

> You know, at first I wasn't going to do this. I've been through this my whole life. People always wanting to know, always wanting to look at me and my parents. It's like, What makes you tick? I'm tired of all that. At least maybe now, I'll get to say what I think . . . And, even though I don't know you, I know you. You know what it's like. Partly, I don't have to do so much explaining. But, I guess, it's also that I can trust you. Because it's not just my family we're talking about, it's yours too.

Finally, in addition to my pledges of confidentiality, the large and nationally diverse sample size itself convinced several people concerned about anonymity that they would not be recognizable in this study.

My initial fieldwork indicated that no single set of criteria could be used to identify an adult hearing child of deaf parents.[22] Although hearing adults whose mother and father were both deaf consistently identified themselves as "adult hearing children of deaf parents," some other adults also identified themselves within this group: those with only one deaf parent, those whose parents had mild hearing losses, and those adult children who themselves had developed some degree of hearing loss. These inconsistencies reflect similar difficulties in estimating the number and demographic characteristics of deaf people. Ultimately, however, this complexity raises a critical issue: variation is part of what creates the Deaf community. When they are among other deaf people, individual characteristics and personalities can emerge.

These people who cannot hear are no longer faceless deaf people: they are gossips and poets, lawyers and peddlers. Paradoxically, deaf people must maintain a certain allegiance to their community by identifying themselves as Deaf—despite variations in actual hearing loss or speaking ability.

In an effort to balance a preliminary clustering of potential informants with geographic diversity, I selected eight regions across the country as my main interview sites. As time went on, I struggled to broaden the demographic variation without creating a logistical nightmare. I stepped up my efforts to find informants who did not work with deaf people, who were older or younger, or who belonged to ethnic and racial minorities. I also solicited for a variety of perspectives. I asked people, Do you know anyone with deaf parents who seems totally unlike you? Anyone who has an entirely different take on her experiences? Some people suggested their own siblings, and although this affected the randomization, I concluded that information about siblings from the same family would be an important dimension of this study. I interviewed six sets of siblings.

In compiling a broad sample of adult hearing children of deaf parents, I began by matching, as much as possible, certain features of the U.S. population. I randomly selected informants within certain parameters, focusing on adequate representation of gender, age, and racial groups as reflected in the current U.S. census: a roughly equal number of men and women; a gradient from young to old, with the majority between 25 and 55; and a majority of European whites with decreasing numbers of African-Americans, Hispanics, Asian-Americans, and Native Americans. Although I was able to match informants according to these features, it became difficult to prevent the final sample population from being skewed in other characteristics—characteristics that ultimately reflected the demographics of the Deaf world.

Although deafness usually occurs without regard to any particular demographic variable,[23] by the time deaf persons become adults and have families, their demographics have undergone considerable delineation. In certain features, the sample population reflects the social, cultural, and economic impact of deafness on the parents: a majority of the informants' parents were educated in residential schools for the deaf (81.6 percent), married another deaf person (94.0 percent), and socialized almost exclusively with other deaf people; and a majority of the informants' families of origin were described as poor, working class, or lower middle class. Despite my efforts to maintain a broad cross-section of the sample population, informants were highly represented in two areas: a majority (85.3 percent) considered themselves middle class, and a significant number (43.3 percent) were employed full-time or part-time in jobs working with deaf children or adults. Since there is no demographic information on the entire population of adult hearing children of deaf parents, it is impossible to establish whether these two features are characteristic of this population as a whole.

There were a few people who did not want to talk with me. Fewer than one-fifth of those initially contacted by letter did not respond, and the reasons for their reluctance can only be surmised. Other potential informants were contacted by third parties, but did not want their names given to me. One of them, I was told, was "not ready to talk about all this." I spoke directly with only five people who declined to participate. Three of these cited concerns about confidentiality. Another felt that the time commitment would be too great. Finally, I was unable to convince one woman who told me that "my story isn't that interesting . . . Just the usual stuff. You probably have a lot more interesting people." Two people who initially declined to be interviewed agreed to participate as long as I did not tape-record the interview.

Although almost all of these interviews were conducted in spoken English, many informants spontaneously used occasional to frequent signs during the interview process. When I quote informants who spoke in sign language, translation becomes a linguistic and an artistic challenge. Authors have responded to this challenge differently. Some writers have used a more literal translation from sign language to spoken language. While this method conveys the sense of difference between sign and spoken language, it creates a false impression of sign language as an ungrammatical or disjointed language. Many writers have used variations on the more traditional approach to translation by treating sign language like any other spoken language and have given conceptual equivalents in grammatical English. A few authors, such as Sidransky (1990), have experimented with a more figurative style that attempts to convey the distinct visual and metaphoric richness of sign language while approximating English grammatical order. Because the informants themselves used varying forms of sign language during the interviews—including some who gestured, others who were fluent in sign language, and still others who spoke and signed at the same time—I have attempted to reflect this diversity in my translations.

Ablon (1977) points out that a potential hazard of fieldwork among one's own social and economic peers is an inability to escape completely your informants' gaze. Indeed, my study roused the attention and curiosity of many other adult hearing children of deaf parents, deaf people, and hearing professionals working with deaf people. My methods and my progress were often under the scrutiny of informants as well. This visibility, however, proved to be an ongoing resource. Informants and others offered me insights and opinions not just about their own lives but also concerning the larger group, and this input into my own creative process has been invaluable.

The Sample Population

The data for this book are based primarily on interviews and life histories of these one hundred and fifty women and men. The youngest informant had just turned eighteen; the oldest would celebrate an eightieth birthday a few months after our interview.[24] The interviews lasted from just under an hour to seven hours, averaging a little over two hours per interview. I met with eighteen informants more than once. With three exceptions, all interviews were tape-recorded. I also collected additional data at local, regional, and national meetings of CODA. Forty-three of the one hundred and fifty informants had been or were currently participants in this organization.

During the eleven months when I was conducting fieldwork, my life was a revolving door of packing, unpacking, and repacking—and driving. Unlike most anthropologists' field sites, mine were fluid and changeable. Within the eight geographic sites, I would sometimes drive between one and three hundred miles each day in pursuit of that elusive ultimate informant. By the time I had completed my fieldwork, I had met with informants in twenty-four states.[25] My time alone in the car allowed me to spin my own webs of significance—to ruminate on the previous interview while preparing for the next one. Although these men and women were dispersed throughout the country, my immersion into their separate lives sometimes created the illusion of a single community. As my fieldwork progressed, I would often create dialogues between informants who had never met: "Someone I interviewed told me this . . . What do you think?"

I almost always interviewed people alone—usually in their homes, sometimes at work, and a few times at places of mutual convenience. These environments provided an added dimension to the interview itself, allowing me to observe the rhythms and contexts of informants' daily lives. We were not restricted just to using our voices or signing; several informants showed me photographs, artwork, writings, and a variety of mementos which they felt conveyed their experiences. Before or after our interviews, I was frequently introduced to informants' spouses, children, co-workers, neighbors, and friends, who helped to enrich my sense of these men and women by broadening my focus. Many of these family members and friends also shared their own perspectives and opinions on the meaning and impact of having deaf parents.

This study began as a series of interviews with one hundred and fifty separate individuals. Although I emphasize the shared cultural experiences among these men and women, there were many differences—among informants as well as in their family backgrounds. The individual personalities of grandparents, parents, and informants each contributed to distinct family histories. Economic and educational factors affected each informant's childhood experiences, along with family composition, the informant's gender, and birth order. Although parental deafness tempered ethnic and racial family heritages among almost all informants, these features still had an impact. Most notably, informants who were also minorities reported that their parents had far less access to economic and educational resources than the already restricted opportunities available to European-American deaf people.

Other than their parents, many informants had no or very few other deaf relatives. In contrast, a few informants were the only hearing child in a long line of deaf grandparents, parents, and siblings. The proximity to and interaction with other deaf people in the community strongly affected the family's sense of isolation and uniqueness. Communication methods and styles varied considerably among individual deaf parents and their hearing children. Although most parents used some form of sign language, a few parents disavowed sign language and used lipreading or speaking.

In addition to idiosyncratic family and personal variables, historical and developmental cohorts developed among informants. Historical groupings reflected educational and technological changes which affected the available methods and styles of communication.[26] Some older informants reported that their parents had gone to schools in which sign language was an acceptable part of the school curriculum. The parents of most informants—especially those between the ages of 30 and 65—had experienced educational policies that prohibited or denigrated sign language. Many younger informants felt the growing public acceptance of sign language and awareness of deaf people made their own childhoods somewhat less stigmatized.

Technological innovations—whether for hearing people or for deaf people—affected routine family interactions. Many older informants (those over 65) had rarely interpreted phone calls or television shows for their parents because this technology had not been available. This contrasts with the situation of most informants (those between 30 and 65) for whom telephone and television interpreting had been regular features of their home life. Since the development of adaptive equipment such as the TTY and decoder,[27] younger informants generally had to do far less interpreting for their parents. In addition, with the availability of professional interpreters, younger informants were more likely to have parents who had occasionally used such interpreters instead of the informant.

The age of informants also affected how they interpreted their childhood experiences. This follows Erikson's lifelong process of identity development, in which each stage of the life cycle has particular features, crises, and developmental resolutions. Certain themes were more prevalent among a given age cohort of informants: younger informants were much more concerned with identity and role confusion; older informants were generally more resolved about such issues. In addition, younger informants were more likely to be actively involved with their families, while many older informants' parents were deceased.

An inherent limitation of this study concerns the artificiality of examining a single human variable. Although having deaf parents was and is a significant feature in the lives of these informants, it is only one part of their lives. No one is just a child or just a parent. Whether a person is deaf or African-American or male, human lives manage to be far more mercurial than any laboratory construction. We are not only more than the sum of our parts; each part, each role is itself fluid and contingent on other parts and other people. Veronica, one of my last informants, reminded me of my own research blinders:

> I get tired of having to explain myself to everyone. To explain about deafness, to explain about my parents. Sure, I think it's important that people understand, but sometimes I just want to be myself. I don't want to be connected to all this. Yes, they're different, yes, I'm different, but so what!

The men and women in this study provide a window of opportunity, a time when the Hearing world and the Deaf world come closest together. Unlike most of their grandparents and parents, these informants were raised within a deaf family and often within a larger Deaf community. Yet, unlike most of their parents, they also had access to the Hearing world. Their lives encompass unique features with regard to language, family, and cultural transmission. Although not all of these men and women were interpreters for their parents, these informants were interpreters in another sense: most actively considered the relationship of their parents' deafness to their present adult lives. Many even considered how they were affected as a group. Informants would propose various hypotheses to me: "I think that children of deaf parents are more insecure." "Do we have a higher divorce rate?" "I think we're more sensitive to difference." Although many of these premises were not substantiated for the group as a whole, they highlight an important feature that the informants did share: that their experiences meant something. As David got up to leave, he shook his head:

> So, my parents are deaf. And, I'm hearing. I grew up with deaf people. People looked at me and made fun of me just like they made fun of them. I always felt a part of the Deaf world. When I started working with the deaf, it really seemed right. Then some deaf people would tell me I wasn't deaf, I was hearing. So I asked my father and mother and they said, Oh, you're Deaf. And some deaf people keep telling me I'm not. I don't know. Deaf, Hearing. Hearing, Deaf. This world, that world, in-between. There must be a reason for all this. There just must be. It's got to mean something.

Contemporary life has become synonymous with the search for self, the relationship between our past and our present. The term "identity" has become a lightning rod for interdisciplinary scrutiny and squabble, mirroring the ethereal and composite views of self. DeVos (1975), Alba (1990), and others have described Americans' preoccupation with a particular facet of identity—ethnic origins and cultural affiliation: whom to include, exclude, accept, or reject. My hunch when I started this research—which may have been as much subconscious as conscious—was that cultural affiliation and identity were important issues for this population. During these unstructured interviews, informants spontaneously raised this concern within a broad spectrum of topics and issues. Their narratives of self went beyond what Gans (1979) has described as "symbolic identity"—a primarily abstract affiliation which has little content or bearing on everyday life. Among many of these informants, the question of identity and cultural affiliation was not abstract or inconsequential. These women and men shared a vision of identity and culture that often had real consequences in their personal lives and in their everyday interactions.

PART II

Family Albums

Sarah's Story

My father was born deaf to deaf parents. So there was a lot of pride in being deaf. My mother was born hearing to hearing parents. She became deaf at an early age. My mother always wished she could be hearing again. And my grandparents wished she could be hearing. When I was growing up, my grandfather—who was well into his eighties at that time—was still sending hearing aid salesmen to our door, even though my mother hadn't heard a thing since she was five years old. My mother would calmly send the salesman away. And my grandfather would still cry because his daughter couldn't hear.

I was the first grandchild on both sides of the family. So I was really this wonderful happening—sort of. On my father's side, I think everybody, not my parents, but my grandparents I think would have regarded me much higher if I had been born deaf. They would have valued me more if I had been born deaf.

On my mother's side, when my mother married my father, her parents told her, "Don't you ever have a child. Stop it right here, don't have a child!" When my mother got pregnant, my grandmother wouldn't speak to my father. Then, when my mother got pregnant with my brother a year and a half later, my parents were not spoken to at all for daring to chance having a deaf child.

When I was born, it was like the miracle of the ages. I know that my grandmother on my mother's side saw me as her second chance. As the golden baby doll girl that could do no wrong, that could have anything she wanted. I could have anything I wanted if I asked it the right way and wore my little white blouse like she wanted, say the right things, do the right things.

My grandmother had a beautiful diamond wedding ring, my maternal hearing grandmother. She would show me her ring, and she kept saying, "Sarah, this is yours! This ring is yours." And my mother put up with years and years of being skipped over. When my grandmother died, we were all at the funeral home. The entire family knew that ring was mine. So, they brought the ring to me in a little manila envelope and tried to put it in my hand. And I looked down the aisle at my mother. She was watching everything, and she knew. She knew that ring was always meant to be mine. And I said to my uncle, "Please, take this ring. Give it to my mother." But he tried to argue with me. He shook his head and said, "Your grandmother wanted you to have this. This is your ring." I looked at him and I said, "No, not yet." I took the ring and [cries and signs, *"gave it to my mother"*]. And she held it so tightly.

About five years ago my mother gave me the ring. She laughed and said, "I don't want to die for you to have this ring." I don't allow myself to think about the pain my mother must have felt about that ring. And how did she feel about my grandmother, who thought that I was the end of all miracles? This woman who was her own mother?

Like the accounts of other men and women in this study, Sarah's story draws from memories and perspectives over several generations. Grandparents, parents, and children—each contribute to their family narratives. The task of separating out and isolating informants' stories from those of other family members is illusory at best. Their narratives are inextricably embedded in a family tapestry which, like all histories, is neither stagnant, nor complete, nor resolved. And the stories of these men and women are inherently biased. In all but thirteen of the interviews, a single informant was providing an undisputed version of the family history. (I interviewed five pairs of siblings; in another case, I interviewed three siblings from one family.) But this study is not an attempt to render complete and accurate family portraits. Instead, it places one family perspective at center stage: that of hearing children of deaf parents. By their very selectivity and bias, informants reveal central beliefs about themselves and their family heritage. As Shengold (1989) observes: "There was a past, however imperfectly we have registered it and however impossible it is for us to communicate it or recapture it completely" (p. 32). Informants' family narratives not only form the basis for an ethnography of hearing children of deaf parents, they provide a framework in which their present adult identity is given shape and meaning.

Although interpretations and outcomes differ from family to family, many of the milestones and features of informants' lives are remarkably similar. Homans (1961) has described studies of social behavior as moments frozen in time: snapshots. Each of the four chapters in Part II is organized around principal characters in the informants' childhoods: parents, grandparents, family friends, and siblings. Although deaf parents appear to be the most visible figures in the childhoods of these hearing men and women, these other immediate or extended family members are integral to the question of cultural transmission. Each represents a particular facet of cultural identity and conflict, and, by their presence or absence, these family members create a dynamic intersection of Deaf and Hearing cultures.

These family portraits are an amalgam of childhood recollections and present adult interactions. Informants selectively open their family albums, dwelling on certain memories, passing over others. The emphasis here, as it is throughout this book, is on the informants' narratives of self: their perception of their experiences and how this history informs their present adult identity.

Invisible and Profound

There are times when I get so filled with rage, helplessness, I don't know, all these feelings. Like when I'd be talking to someone about my parents. But I couldn't make them understand or maybe they refused to understand. I felt like I was throwing my parents to the wolves. I'm thinking about my neighbors and my friends. I didn't realize until now, but I sort of hate them. I hate them because they don't care enough to ask me. [Starts to cry.] It just means so much to me when somebody cares enough to ask me, you know, what it's about. To get past saying how neat sign language is, or aren't your parents sweet. Not many people do that. It's so different from their lives. My life, my parents, it's all so far away from hearing people. And my neighbors and friends, I feel like, I really do, I feel like, fuck 'em!

Most informants shared similar feelings of frustration and anger at trying to or even needing to explain—about deafness, about their parents, about themselves. Explaining that deaf people can drive, or that deaf people can read. Explaining that deaf people can have hearing children, and that their hearing children learn to talk. As one informant noted, "Sometimes I just don't bring it up—I get tired of explaining." As was true of several other informants, one woman agreed to be interviewed only after learning that my parents were also deaf: "I wasn't going to do it [the interview] because I always get asked so many dumb questions. It's a lot better knowing that you understand, that I don't have to explain everything." A lifetime of explaining. Given the opportunity to talk about their lives without the burden

of explanation, what did the informants talk about? Their deaf
parents.

These women and men talked at length about their parents. This
was partly a result of the informants' narrative style: a temporal pro-
gression of family history from past to present. Talking about their
deaf parents also reflected a stated focus of my study. Yet the emphasis
was unmistakable: the intensity and the drama of their parents' stories
frequently overshadowed their own. Even in the most unstructured
interviews ("Tell me about yourself"), informants generally followed a
familiar pattern: they began by telling me about their parents. I found
myself entranced with stories about their deaf parents. Mothers and
fathers who were tenacious, ingenious, vibrant. Mothers and fathers
who tangled with oppression, negation, and failure. Often I had to
remind myself and the informants that I was primarily interested in
them, not their parents. In group gatherings as well—when adult
hearing children would meet for the first time—many would introduce
themselves by describing their mothers and fathers: where their parents were from, which schools they had gone to, which organizations
they belonged to.

The intense presence of informants' unseen parents underscores a
significant dilemma for hearing children of deaf parents. Much of their
childhood identity has been highly associated with one equation: their
parents are deaf; they are hearing. This equation has represented a
tenuous balance—counterpoised both to being deaf and to adult
status. As informants leave their childhood homes to take their place
in the Hearing world, this paradoxical heritage becomes increasingly
problematic. In this chapter I consider informants' deaf parents—undoubtedly the central figures within these family albums. Yet this
exploration is not primarily concerned with a deaf mother's history or
a deaf father's character. The discussions here investigate how these
descriptions and explanations of their parents reflect the informants'
own feelings of identity and cultural affiliation. Four interrelated
themes emerged from informants' narratives about their parents: the
meaning of deafness; accountability; protection and advocacy; and,
finally, similarity or difference. Other family members modified or
amplified these issues; they also raised additional concerns. Yet, be-

cause most informants' sense of deafness and of Deaf culture was substantially informed by their parents, these four themes represent fundamental aspects of the unique heritage of hearing children of deaf parents.

The Meaning of Deafness

After nearly four hours, I was preparing to leave Jim's house. Jim was my sixty-seventh informant. We had spent an evening discussing a wide range of topics. I remember feeling confident that his family experiences fell well within the parameters of my emerging ethnography. Among my informants, Jim's life was nothing out of the ordinary. Both of his parents were deaf, had gone to residential schools, socialized almost exclusively with other deaf people. Jim shared stories of his childhood, of his feelings of difference, of communication and cultural conflict. As I thanked him for his time, the phone rang. He answered it and began talking. Jim momentarily turned aside and said, "It's my father." I was dumbfounded.

Using the telephone is increasingly commonplace among deaf people. There are now several options for conversing over the phone: teletype machines, interpreters, and relay services. Yet Jim's father used none of these. He spoke with his own voice, and heard with only minor amplification. Despite his understandable speech and his ability to hear, Jim's father considered himself a *deaf* person—not just culturally Deaf but functionally deaf as well. Jim's own childhood experiences were little different from those of most other informants whose parents were profoundly deaf.

A consistent observation made by almost all informants was that their parents' degree of hearing loss or age of onset made little difference in how their parents functioned as adults. No informant used the term "hearing-impaired," and only three consistently used the term "hard-of-hearing" to describe a deaf parent.[1] Sam explained:

> Well, when people ask, I tell them that my parents are deaf. I don't tell them, oh, you know, that my father can hear a little bit or that my mother has a 100-decibel loss in both ears. They're both just deaf!

This monolithic functional label—"deaf"—runs contrary to the variations expected from such features as the etiology of deafness, the degree of hearing loss, and the age of onset. These synergistic factors—particularly severity of loss and age of onset—have routinely been used to assess a deaf child's educational and audiological needs, and are presumed to determine the eventual impact and outcomes of deafness. Profound hearing loss usually begins at 80 to 90 decibels—a threshold that eliminates most of the range of a human voice. The degree of loss is compounded by the age at which it happened, and the most common age-thresholds use language development as a point of reference: "prelingual" or "postlingual" deafness. Both markers are based on cultural assumptions: that it is the ability to hear a human voice which determines the ultimate severity of the loss, and that the acquisition of language means acquiring a *spoken* language. These thresholds reflect an often unequivocal standard of hearing and speaking against which a child must perform or fail. Yet, a generation later, informants questioned the rigidity and the significance of these norms.[2] A few informants felt that if circumstances had been different, their mother or father could have functioned as a hearing person. Most informants, however, described how much of their parents' childhood had been lost in an effort to learn how to hear and speak.

Being "deaf" not only includes a wide range of hearing and speaking abilities; it also demands certain attitudes and social obligations. Informants described the importance of coming to terms with one's deafness, of making the transition from deaf to Deaf. These women and men generally evaluated their parents' feelings about being deaf both by their personal attitude (whether they were ashamed or bitter, or not) and in terms of how much the parent interacted with other deaf people. Barbara compared her mother with her father:

> She never really accepted it [being deaf]. . .not like my Dad. I guess it has something to do with her parents not accepting it. She would always sign small in public, or not at all. She didn't want anybody to know. To see her different from them. She almost never went to the Deaf club. My Dad was there all the time. A lot of the time he just went by himself. But he does just fine. He's proud of being Deaf.

The signed expression "strongly deaf"[3] was used by several informants when describing a parent (or other deaf acquaintance) who had a positive, often activist stance about being deaf.

From informants' descriptions of their deaf parents, two interrelated perspectives emerge on the meaning of deafness: first, one can be deaf regardless of speaking or hearing abilities, and second, being Deaf ideally includes an attitude of self-acceptance and social interaction with other deaf people.[4] The subjective nature of deafness is a pivotal feature which relates to informants' own cultural identity. They, too, can be Deaf or Hearing—apart from their functional status. Yet, because being Deaf also includes participation in the larger Deaf community, cultural affiliation was problematic for many informants. As I will discuss in later chapters, hearing children's interaction with other deaf people was often limited by their language skills. Even those who actively participated in the Deaf community as children faced an uncertain adult identity: How could they be Deaf when no longer living within a deaf family or a Deaf community?

Identifying oneself as Deaf or Hearing also involves significantly different cultural expectations: an orientation toward the group, or an emphasis upon the individual. Such conflicting norms create a lifelong tension for a hearing child of deaf parents: does he find refuge in a group like himself, or remain apart as a distinct individual?

Accountability

Considering the contemporary Western (particularly American) propensity to probe and analyze one's family of origin, several informants wondered at their lack of questioning about their childhoods. Eileen shook her head as she asked why she had never talked about this with her own siblings or with other hearing children of deaf parents: "You'd think we would've talked about all this, but we never did . . . It never occurred to me."

As children, many informants felt their situation was unique—even if they had hearing siblings or knew other hearing children of deaf parents. They described a highly personal sense of deafness—despite situations and environments that were frequently parallel to those of other hearing children of deaf parents. Only as adults did many informants feel that they were motivated to examine their experiences, to learn about deafness, or to talk with other hearing children of deaf parents. Gloria explained:

> When we were at the Deaf club, or when it was just me and my sister, we didn't need to talk about our deaf parents. I mean, that's just the way it was. And we certainly didn't want to talk about it with hearing people. They were the ones who kept making us feel different.

Like many other hearing children of deaf parents, Gloria conveyed her intrinsic sense of her family as normal and her desire to exclude external suggestions of negative difference. It was often a change in the anticipated life course of these men and women (such as a divorce, a career change, or the death of a loved one) that prompted them to reevaluate their childhood experiences. In keeping with Western cultural beliefs, which strongly correlate adult outcomes with childhood environment, adult hearing children now began to question the long-term impact of their childhood experiences.

Without adequate comparisons or a sense of shared history, many informants found it difficult to evaluate the impact of their parents' deafness on their life. Five different informants used identical words to describe this quandary: "I don't know what's the deafness and what isn't." Yet informants often disagreed over whether it was possible or even worthwhile to separate out these factors. Several informants told me that they were interested in my research because they hoped for answers to their own life questions. For almost all these men and women, the issue was not whether having deaf parents had made any difference in their lives—it was a matter of defining and evaluating these differences. Informants described a personal version of the nature-nurture controversy: Were the benefits or disadvantages of growing up with deaf parents primarily dependent on the personalities of the parents, or were there certain features that were intrinsic to being deaf? Who was accountable for those childhood experiences which some informants judged to be difficult or even harmful? Their

deaf parents? Their grandparents? Hearing people? Or are such outcomes simply unavoidable in the clash between two distinct cultures?

For many informants, it was their family's economic situation rather
than their parents' deafness that caused the greatest family hardships.
Despite considerable variation in the economic status of the informants' grandparents, their deaf parents earned their livelihoods within
a much narrower income bracket. Deafness—like many disabilities—
proved to be a great economic leveler. Upon completion of school,
many deaf parents confronted a society that emphasized their difference and overlooked their marketable skills. Informants reported that
their parents were frequently underemployed. Although in recent
times deaf people have had better career options, job opportunities
were historically limited for many deaf parents. Even when they were
hired, job security was often tenuous, promotion virtually nonexistent.
Martin describes his father's situation:

> My Dad was a carpenter. He traveled a lot. He always said he didn't feel
> like he could change jobs. I had a hearing uncle who was also a carpen-
> ter, but he wouldn't work anywhere except within a small radius from
> his home so he could be home at night. He could change companies if
> a job was finished, he could go work for some other company that had
> a job nearby. My Dad felt as a deaf person he didn't have that option.
> Once you go to a new company, you've got to sell yourself all over again.
> So he got with this company that was very good to him and he followed
> them wherever they went with a job. He would go to Kentucky for a
> while, then he went to Virginia. Once in a while he would be close to
> home. Most of the time he was all over the Southeast. He could only
> come home maybe every two weeks or sometimes once a month for two
> days or so. So we didn't see much of him when I was a teenager . . . He
> always worked for an hourly wage. He never did get into the supervisory
> position where he would have gotten a guaranteed salary. He would have
> definitely gotten that if he had been with a company that long as a
> hearing person.

Martin's recollection is precariously perched: an acknowledgment of
the social inequities his father had confronted, and an admission of
the negative impact of his father's absence. While conceding that his

father probably had little opportunity to alter the situation, Martin later stressed to me that one of the most important changes he made with regard to his own children was "not being an absent father."

Overall, informants were least likely to find their own parents accountable for whatever difficulties they as hearing children had experienced. These women and men offered several alternative explanations: a lack of choices, social oppression, their parents' poor relationships with their families of origin, economic limitations, and communication barriers. Edward explained his philosophy about deafness:

> It's like deafness created certain kinds of situations that wouldn't be there otherwise. It changes the family dynamics. But it's not like the deafness itself caused this or caused that. It's what people do, how they react to being deaf that makes the difference.

Edward clearly absolves deafness from blame and places any adverse reactions squarely at the feet of the outside Hearing world. Like most children, Edward identified with his parents—despite their functional differences. His arguments reveal a strong loyalty to his parents and indicate what will become a central dilemma for hearing children of deaf parents: It is hearing people who make deafness problematic.

A Legacy of Protection and Advocacy

This book opens with Peter's description of how rich his life has been made by his deaf parents. After our interview, Peter drove me to the area where he grew up and, with justifiable pride, he pointed to the house his father had built by hand many years ago. His hand swept across the panorama of a large brick house surrounded by acres of rolling pastures, and he shook his head. "People would never think a deaf man could do that." Months later, when I first sat down with Della, she began telling me about something that had happened when she was eight years old. Della described a May Day celebration when her mother had sewn dresses and vests for every girl and boy in Della's grade school class. Della looked straight at me and said, "That's the kind of thing that people need to know about our parents. They need to get beyond this idea of deaf people as helpless and broke... words reiterated strongly felt opinions from an overwhelming majority of informants.

Although almost all informants acknowledged some difficulties in their families, in retrospect most felt that these problems were comparable to those of other families. Yet, as children and as adults, informants remained concerned about public reaction and interpretation. During our interview, Louise leaned toward me and said:

> You think I'd tell anyone that there were problems? Can you imagine what they would say? "Oh, it must be because your parents are deaf." It doesn't matter that other families have problems too. What family doesn't have problems? But, if my family had problems, then it's all because my parents are deaf.

Another young man exhorted, "There's so much negative stuff out there about deaf people. We have to fight back." As a listener but also an insider, I was often pressed to pursue a role of advocacy in my research. How does this legacy affect cultural transmission from deaf parent to hearing child?

Goffman (1963) and others have described various ways in which discredited persons manage information and situations in order to control the impact of stigma. (See Chapter 9 for a broader discussion of stigma and difference.) While the management of stigma may have been important for both deaf parents and their hearing children, hearing children have access to the speaking world. Speaking provided them with opportunities to promote their parents' normalcy or confront negative criticism:

> I would see these people staring at us. Making comments about us. I just wanted to run over to their table and say, "What the fuck you looking at?" I don't know these people! What do they want from us?

Yet advocacy could underscore informants' ambiguous identity. By using spoken words, informants identified themselves as hearing—simultaneously demonstrating their parents' difference from other people, and their own difference from their parents. Those informants who overheard negative remarks but chose not to respond were left with a different predicament. Barbara explained: "I never knew if I should tell them [parents] what I heard. I usually didn't. I figured it would just hurt them." Others, like Richard, reported that even when they told their parents what others were saying, their parents often dismissed it:

> He [father] just told me to ignore it. Well, I guess that's probably the best thing, but still, he wasn't the one who had to keep hearing all that. I did. And I'd get really pissed off!

Whether responding or not responding to outsiders, the hearing children of deaf parents were caught within a web of difference—different from hearing people because they appeared deaf, different from their deaf parents because they could speak and hear. This increased their sense of uniqueness as well as their sense of isolation from others.

Informants described a style of stigma management in which they often portrayed their deaf parents as very much like hearing people. A number of women and men, however, confessed that they "weren't always sure how hearing parents behaved." In their attempts to normalize their parents, informants frequently created a veil over deafness that downplayed negative features as well as diminished culturally distinct aspects of deafness. Informants cited numerous occasions in which they altered their parents' words or disguised their actions in order to create a positive impression or avoid unpleasantness. This childhood censorship was frequently remembered with humor. Don's story was typical:

> One time he [father] was just furious at this [store] clerk. My Dad told me to tell the guy to shove it up his ass! I remember saying something like, "Well, my father doesn't think this is a good idea."

Informants saw these alterations as necessary to offset the prevalent negative stereotypes of deaf people. Deaf parents, too, often minimized their differences from hearing people (by not signing, by mouthing words, by nodding even though not understanding), as well as stressing only positive aspects or outcomes of being deaf.[5] However, these modifications, whether by parents or by children, created a distorted sense of deaf people—not only for outsiders but for insiders as well. Denise, in describing how she protected her family from stigma, reveals how she also sacrificed a fuller understanding of her parents:

> I really worked at it [signs *"vague"; "cover-up"*]. You know, not letting others see them being deaf. I mean, people knew that they couldn't hear. But I never let anyone see that they were different. It's like I washed them out. And now all I have is this faded idea of what being deaf is all about.

Stigma management that emphasized how much deaf people are like hearing people precluded an acknowledgment of difference. This frequently discouraged discussion by the informants of family concerns or issues with others (even others like themselves) and ultimately diminished their sense of Deaf culture and identity.

While most informants felt that some degree of advocacy and protectiveness was inevitable, many questioned whether these responsibilities were appropriate for children. Shaking her head, Margaret evaluated her childhood experiences:

> They tried their best. And they did a lot for me, they really did. But, sometimes now I think, who was looking out for me, who was protecting me?

Margaret's words echo those of Ricardo in the Introduction: "And who's supposed to take care of me?" Their concern reflects a popular sentiment in American culture: the family responsibility of protection is immutably that of the parent (Demos 1986). One fundamental tenet among the multitude of "Adult Children" groups[6] is that the parents have failed to let children be children—which includes burdening children with too much responsibility and not sufficiently protecting them (Black 1982; Gravitz and Bowden 1985; Elkind 1988). These popular values create another dilemma of identity for adult hearing children: they must either accept the norms of the broader (Hearing) culture, which conflict with their deaf family's way of life, or align themselves with their deaf parents and remain outside mainstream culture.

Most informants balanced any sense of compromised childhoods with the benefits of their experiences—including being more mature, being more sensitive to others, and having a greater variety of life experiences. Others, like Mark, suggested that their childhood responsibilities could not be judged by adult Hearing standards:

> Sure, I had to do things that other kids didn't have to do. It was part of my role. But that was then. I don't do it now. You do what you have to do in the situation. I don't have any hard feelings about it. I might if I still had to do it now, but I don't.

Attempts to resolve the contradictions between their deaf family experiences and how the Hearing culture interpreted those experiences were evident even in extreme cases, such as those few informants who described abusive childhoods. Although Ella described her father as a violent-tempered man who showed little affection, she also pointed out reasons for his behavior:

> A lot of other people would say, Well, he's just terrible, he's evil! But what kind of upbringing did he have? I mean, where was the love and support he should have had? If he didn't learn it or have it, how could he give it to me?

Most men and women continued to be advocates for their parents as adults—whether in more direct roles on behalf of their parents, in careers related to deaf people, or merely in day-to-day interactions with friends and acquaintances. These adult interactions often renewed issues of identity and alignment, further complicated by a growing militancy within many Deaf communities. Deaf people have increasingly rejected hearing people as spokespersons. But what about their own children: Are they Hearing or Deaf?

Similarity and Difference

The evaluation of one's similarity or difference to others is a recurrent theme that underlies the family life of many informants as well as their own identity. Hearing children's ambiguous identity within a dichotomized environment will be explored further in Chapter 10, which examines the segregation between the Deaf and Hearing worlds. However, without an acutely felt need to belong or to evaluate one's similarity to (or difference from) others, the motivation to choose among these polarized worlds would be lacking. Although compari-

sons and contrasts to others are standard features of identity development among most people, they are especially salient for these women
and men whose parents were deaf. This section focuses on the question
of marriage partners[7] among informants and among their parents.
Options and choices of marriage partners have long been regarded as
significant indicators of cultural values, ethnic boundaries, and social
structures.[8] As reflected in their discussions of marriage options for
their parents and for themselves, informants' perceptions of similarity
to or difference from others create a powerful paradigm within which
informants search for a resolution of their own identity.

Among the informants' parents, historical and social factors contributed to seeking marriage partners whose backgrounds and experiences
appear highly homogeneous.[9] In addition to the factor of deafness,
informants' narratives reveal their parents' history as emphasizing differences from others and similarities to each other. Adult Deaf social
environments frequently maintained this tradition. Although deaf people generally prefer the company of other deaf people regardless of
citizenship or racial differences, marriages among deaf people generally maintain racial boundaries. This was true among the sample population: out of 141 informants with two deaf parents, 139 had parents
from the same racial group. Regional, educational, and age differences
were often minimized between informants' parents: more than half of
all informants' parents had been classmates at the same residential
school. Only those parents who attended a multi-state residential
school or college were more likely to marry a person from another
state.

Some informants described educational, status, or temperamental
differences between their mother and father, occasionally questioning
how well matched their parents actually were:

> I can't believe my parents got together. They're both so different from
> each other. I mean, they're both deaf, but that's about it. Like night and
> day!

Yet even in cases where the parents' marriage was a difficult one or
ended in divorce, informants generally viewed their parents' marriage
options as constrained by the need to find another deaf partner.
Among the nine informants with one deaf and one hearing parent,

only two felt that their parents' marriage was successful. All seven other informants felt the hearing-deaf difference contributed to their parents' marriage problems or divorce. In contrast, 112 out of the 141 informants with two deaf parents felt that their parents' marriage was successful.[10] Although similar communication was routinely cited as a critical factor in successful relationships, many men and women felt that it was the overall similarity in their parents' perspectives and life experiences that contributed the greatest solidarity. For example, although Barry had been explaining how mismatched his mother and father were—in their family backgrounds, their education levels, and their different types of sign language—he conceded that their common bond of deafness united them against a confusing and sometimes hostile environment:

> It's a wonder they're together. But, you know, when I go back home now, I see how their deafness has pulled them together. With so much to deal with, they help each other out, in different ways. It's like fighting a common enemy.

The barometer of similarity continued to be an important measure of informants' present relationships, including marriage partners. Many informants felt that a critical feature in their present or potential life partner was his or her similarity to themselves. Yet this concern with similarity raises a fundamental question: similar to whom? Few men and women saw marriage to a deaf person as a viable option.[11] The majority of informants remembered one or both of their parents cautioning them against marrying a deaf person. Many women and men reported that they themselves had never even considered dating a deaf person.[12] But these informants frequently saw themselves as more like deaf people than hearing people. Michelle explained her options:

> I would never marry a deaf man. My God! Can you imagine? It would never work out . . . Well, I guess some day I'll marry some hearing guy, but I'm not sure. I don't think I have much in common with hearing people. I don't know where that leaves me. Who knows?

Michelle's concern with finding a partner epitomizes the dilemma of identity for hearing children of deaf parents. A few informants felt that the ultimate solution would be to find someone very much like themselves: someone who also had deaf parents.

Although Tom did not feel that he actually had to marry another hearing child of deaf parents, he hoped that his adult relationships would correct childhood imbalances:

> It's like I had too much difference in my life. Like all I ever knew was how it felt to be different. So, now, I'm starved to be like other people. I don't want to be different anymore.

Acknowledgment of difference was not consistent among all these men and women. A few informants insisted that their childhood experiences and their adult lives were no different from any one else's. Karen argued:

> My life was just like any other kid's. Just because my parents were deaf didn't make any difference. I'm just like anybody else. . . . . Really!

Yet Karen's adamant assertions of similarity belie her concern with difference. Overall, assessing similarity or difference in regard to others was a salient and pervasive template within which these informants developed and constructed their image of themselves.

. . . .

As informants remembered and described their parents, they repeatedly stressed the inherent normalcy they felt about their parents and about deafness. Parent and deaf: indelibly linked and carefully separated.

> My parents love me because I'm their son, not because I'm hearing or deaf.
> We fight because he's my father, not because he's deaf.

> Whenever I think of my mother, I remember her eyes. She had these wonderful clear eyes that were always glistening and watching everything. She could catch two conversations at once.

> My father had these gnarled old worker hands. And when he talked, his signing was kind of stiff and rugged, just like me. [Laughs.] And I never realized it until a few years ago when someone said, "You know, you sign just like your father."

This chapter is not about the normalization of a handicapped parent. It concerns the emergence of a cultural reality: a vision of deafness as viable, as normal, and sometimes as preferable. This version of deafness is not understood as a functional limitation but as a way of life. Yet such a stance is continually eroded by a Hearing majority who impose not only standards of communication but definitions of family. The realization that deaf people can have children raises significant issues about communication and family responsibilities: How can that helpless deaf child grow up to nurture and raise a family of his or her own? How can a mother sing lullabies to her infant if she cannot hear? How can a father protect his child when he cannot speak out? From within their family experiences, informants have the resources and the motivation to challenge such assumptions.

Yet the wages of advocacy come at a cost. In crusading for those who are deaf, informants often must point out the oppression by those who speak and hear. Baroe (1975) asks, "Is it inevitable in social life that a sense of moral value can be secured by individuals or groups only at the expense of others?" (p. 188). Because they are hearing, these informants can be both advocate and oppressor. This paradox continues to unfold as part of their own adult identity and cultural alignment. Can one be hearing and still be (culturally) Deaf? The expected developmental processes of separation and individuation may create a separate Hearing identity apart from family and deafness, but relinquish a cultural one. Yet, connected to their parents, these men and women remain a child-adult in the eyes of the cultural majority. In these narratives, there is sometimes a feeling of parents who were almost too powerful. In their family histories, informants have become shadows of their parents. It is a paradoxical legacy for these hearing children of deaf parents. Parents who were invisible within their own families and society have now passed on the mantle of invisibility to their own children.

Views from the Other Side

Sometimes with tears, sometimes with rage, one of the most emotional and often unsettled themes expressed by the informants was their feelings toward their grandparents. Many informants had at least some direct contact with one or more grandparents. Just as often, however, informants had to piece together the lives of phantom grandparents— lost through death or family dissolution.

Sarah's story at the beginning of Part II was one of many narratives about grandparents infused with anger and sadness. Only a few women and men expressed feelings of gratitude. As a whole, the informants shared many similar childhood experiences and issues of adult identity. Yet one striking difference in the tenor and the drama of informants' narratives was between those informants with hearing grandparents and those with deaf grandparents. Here, their family narratives take separate turns. As Sarah's story illustrates, informants' heritages from their hearing grandparents and from deaf grandparents were very different. Family narratives of informants with hearing grandparents often reach a dramatic crescendo as they herald the arrival of deafness, a time of upheaval when their family histories were changed forever. In contrast, the narratives of informants with deaf grandparents portray a more routine sense of deafness, underscoring that being hearing was what was considered different.

In this chapter I examine the separate issues that develop within the narratives of informants with hearing grandparents and those with deaf grandparents and relatives. I conclude with a discussion about the family gatherings of deaf and hearing relatives—occasions that succinctly epitomize the informants' divided heritage.

Hearing Grandparents

The vast majority of informants' grandparents were hearing. In only three cases were all four grandparents deaf. Like Sarah, several informants had both hearing and deaf grandparents.[1] For most informants, the critical moment of transformation in their family history occurred between grandparents and parents—a time when deafness came from unknown regions to become a permanent fixture in the family legacy. Through depictions of their hearing grandparents, informants captured the often inseparable rift between the world of the Deaf and the world of the Hearing. Here, the informants' family perspectives became the most divided: they expressed both their grandparents' sense of loss and bewilderment over this non-hearing child, and their parents' frustration and isolation within a family of ghosts.

As their narratives turn to that moment of change—the origin of their parents' deafness—informants pieced together conflicting meanings of deafness from their parents and their grandparents. Whether the causes of deafness were known or unknown, embedded in each family's explanation were historical and cultural beliefs about hearing people, about deaf people, and about families.[2] Although public reactions to their deaf parents were also an important part of informants' childhood experiences, their parents' families of origin provided the first critical arena in which the meaning of deafness was explored. Informants frequently cited their parents' families of origin as the single most important factor which affected their parents and, ultimately, themselves. For many informants, the interactions and reactions between their grandparents and their parents tested the bonds and the meaning of family. Martin linked his grandmother's devastation about her daughter's deafness to wider sociocultural beliefs and attitudes:

> My mother's relationship with her mother was really impacted by the deafness. My grandmother was uneducated. I think maybe she went

through second or third grade in school. She didn't have a whole lot of ways of dealing with that. The old folks in those days thought this maybe was a punishment from God or whatever. They didn't give a whole lot of thought to how to deal with a handicapped child. One that couldn't talk was even more handicapped than anything else. It was like she didn't have much in her head.

Through their hearing grandparents' reactions to their deaf child, informants often learned a version of deafness that equated it with loss, with the condition that caused it:

> Daddy was real sick then. They thought he was going to die. And one time I heard my grandma say that she thought maybe it would have been better if he died. That being deaf is like being sick your whole life.

The perfect child, the hearing child, became the broken child. Illness, accident, defect—all became synonyms for deafness. This time of change was stressful for the hearing family, and isolating for the child:

> My father had spinal meningitis when he was 6 or 7. He's not sure how old. He was in quarantine for anywhere from 6 months to 2 years. He was put into a hospital and not allowed to see his parents or anything. He remembers looking out the window and seeing his father looking in the window at him and waving at him. He remembers his aunt being in the bed next to him, and then waking up again and she was gone— finding out later that she had passed away because of spinal meningitis. And immediately after being in the hospital and being quarantined, he was taken to the state school for the deaf. So he thought he was just removed from the family, gotten rid of.

Although most informants distanced themselves from feelings of grief or rejection over deafness, many accepted their grandparents' initial feelings of confusion. Eva—while generally critical of her grandparents—empathized with their situation. When asked what her grandparents or any hearing parents who have a deaf child could do, Eva shook her head:

> I feel bad for them! I really do. Because I think it's so hard. You get so many second opinions and different options. I know they're inundated with all this information and how do you know what to do? I'm just not

sure. Giving your child *a* language is really important because that's how you're going to communicate with them. Whatever that may be. Beyond that, it gets really hard!

Other informants, like Louis, described grandparents who divorced themselves altogether from any responsibility for their child's deafness and, ultimately, any connection to their deaf child:

My Daddy was sent off to school once they found out he was deaf. He never had contact with his family again, so he never knew. Never knew how come he was deaf.

This version of deafness as brokenness continued to haunt informants even as adults. Whether on a first date or when meeting potential in-laws, informants were confronted with the shadow of their possible legacy: "Will my children be deaf?" "Will my grandchildren be deaf?" These concerns persisted despite the fact that the risks of most inform- ants' having a deaf child were no greater than those of the general population.[3]

In contrast to their hearing grandparents, informants' parents often regarded the circumstances of becoming deaf as unimportant. When informants recalled their parents' perspectives, the causes of deafness were frequently minimized. Such descriptions were brief, tentative, and sometimes dismissing:

[Jill:] My father had meningitis. My mother, scarlet fever. [long pause] That was all there was to it.

[Dwight:] The way my mother signs it [signs *"Fell. Finished."* Shrugs shoulders]. Like, well, one minute it was there, the next it wasn't. No big deal. Life goes on.

In comparison to their grandparents' reactions, most informants ech- oed their parents' limited tolerance for grief over or denial of being deaf—sometimes with sympathetic chiding:

My grandmother was just heartbroken. It was really hard for her. I think my grandfather didn't know what to do. And I could understand feeling that way at first, I guess, but it never stopped. They still feel bad. They still don't know what to do.

Sometimes with humor:

> My grandparents took my mother everywhere, you know, one doctor
> after another. Always the same thing. "She's deaf." "She can't be!"
> Another round, same thing. "She's deaf." "She can't be!" Thank God
> they ran out of money! They might still be dragging her around.

While recognizing their grandparents' sense of loss and confusion,
informants identified their grandparents' views of deafness as inalter-
ably Hearing. Many of those interviewed expressed a sense of exasperation at their grandparents' inability to cross the line, to become
like them: part-Hearing, part-Deaf.

A number of researchers have examined families' emotional and
behavioral responses to a child with a disability.[4] Many writers describe
how families negotiate personal and social expectations of normalcy
in the day-to-day interactions with their child. Often, these descriptions utilize a stage-reaction format to characterize family responses—
including grief, shock, denial, acceptance.[5] Regardless of the number
or sequence of stages, writers characterize the family's trajectory as
moving toward a resolution based on the reality of their child's condition. Deafness, however, presents a critical obstacle in this process
because the intrinsic condition frequently prevents the communication
needed to arrive at any sense of mutual understanding. Ron described
his father's family in this way:

> My [paternal] grandparents still don't sign. My grandfather's passed
> away, never knowing how to sign. And my grandmother's still alive, and
> the only way they communicate is passing notes. And I kind of look
> down on that, and plus the way she [grandmother] talks to us. My father
> still doesn't know how she talks to us. She'll say, "It's really amazing how
> your father's kept a job, and has a house and raised fine kids." And I'm
> thinking, Why are you so shocked? I can't understand why they're so
> shocked. To me they're just as normal as anybody else. But even their
> own parents look at them and think it's a big deal if they can drive or
> walk down the street.

Deaf parents who were oral were no more likely to have good
communication with their hearing parents. Whether through signing,
speech, lipreading, or writing, informants considered only 37 out of a

total of 288 deaf mothers and fathers as able to communicate well with at least one parent. This lack of family communication usually extended to their parents' hearing siblings and other family members as well, interfering with routine interactions and an overall sense of their own family.

The lack of communication and interaction among the parents' family of origin frequently screened out other cultural and religious heritages. Whether Catholic or Jewish, African-American or Polish, family traditions often dissipated between these generations. When I asked Polly if she felt that any of her grandparents' ethnic traditions had been passed on to her, she shook her head:

> I really noticed it one day when my son came home from school and had to do this project. And he wanted to know all this stuff about his grandparents and his ethnic background and all that. So we were all sitting down to eat and his father [Polly's husband] was explaining about the kind of food his family ate and what they wore. And all these sayings they had and how they acted. And my son turned to me and said, "Well, what about your family?" And I looked at him and said, "I don't know. We were just deaf." And the funny thing is my husband is like a third or fourth generation American. My grandparents came here off the boat.

Only a handful of informants felt that their family histories were unbroken, and this was always explained by the fact that one or more of their parents' family members could communicate with them. Nick stressed the continued significance of his grandmother's efforts:

> It wasn't easy for her [grandmother] but she tried. She knew how important it was. And I know it made a difference in how things turned out for me.

In a few instances, hearing grandparents and deaf parents developed a positive and interactive relationship. Most did not. Most never developed a way to bridge the world of silence and the world of sound—except through the informant. These women and men were able to listen to both voices: that of their parents, that of their grandparents. Often, the informants were literally interpreters between these two generations.[6] Often, they heard the anguish which neither side could express to the other:

> My grandmother sat me down one day and said, "You know, I would have given anything if your Mamma could hear. We tried to get her well, but it was too late. I just can't tell her how sorry I am."

Deaf parents, too, shared their family histories with their hearing children. Eva stopped several times before finally explaining:

> It's hard to talk about . . . There was just so much pain . . . My Dad was so separated from his family. He thinks he was rejected. He used to tell me [signs *"I cry cry every night until 11 years old"*]. Sometimes you just don't want to hear it, there's so much pain. Like when he tells me how frustrated he is because his Mom still can't talk to him. All she can do are the nurturing signs like *"food"* and *"love."* That's it. God, I see how much it hurts him!

The sense of guilt, of loss, of separation between the grandparents and the parents often persisted over the years as the informant grew from child to adult. As repositories for their grandparents' and their parents' untold stories, informants often chose to keep this realm of sadness and anger hidden.

A number of women and men questioned how their parents could suppress or ignore these feelings:

> My father was never really angry about that, but it makes me angry. I have a hard time understanding how come my father's not really mad at all this. I guess he just counts it as experience. Huh! Some experience.

Often it was the informants, not their parents, who confronted hearing relatives and strangers alike:

> My Dad would always tell me to just ignore it. But one time I'd had it. I just blew up and let them have it. "Who the hell do you think you are? You think because you can hear, you're special? Well let me tell you, hearing doesn't mean shit! And, my Dad is a lot more of a human being than any of you will ever be!"

As adults, many informants continued their mandate to protect their parents against the Hearing world, and for many this included their own relatives. Craig's anger erupted as he denounced his hearing relatives:

> On my Mom's side there's nine or ten brothers and sisters and we were always left out. Everybody had a motor home, everybody had money, everybody would go traveling. And we never got invited. We'd hear about it later, we'd see the pictures later . . . Now, my aunt invites me out to lunch and says, "Don't tell your parents, we don't want your parents to feel hurt." How on earth are they supposed to feel? It's so typical, the Deaf are always left out.

Blood ties to their parents' relatives were overridden by a glaring mark of identity: these people are hearing. They do not understand. They do not belong. Judith's definition of family was clear:

> So that's the kind of total fucking exclusion I feel. Not only did you [hearing relatives] do that to my father, you've also done that to me. I don't have any family. I mean, that's how I feel. I don't have a family. All I have is my brothers and my sister, and my Mom and Dad. That's all the fuck I got!

Alignment with their deaf parents was not always straightforward. Like their grandparents, the informants were hearing. Many informants' descriptions portray an uneasy relationship between their grandparents and themselves. Despite earlier criticism of the way her grandparents treated her father, Olivia also felt the allure of a shared perspective:

> I used to love to just sit and listen to her [grandmother]. It was like I remembered that I could hear.

Some informants described how earlier childhood alliances with their hearing grandparents often humiliated their parents and undermined their authority:

> When I was a kid, it seemed to make sense. My grandparents could raise me and tell me what to do because they're hearing. [sarcastically] How can deaf and dumb people raise a kid? Only *hearing* people know how to be parents.

Both grandparent and grandchild looked into the world of deafness, and yet both could hear. Both were indelibly linked to deafness through the birth of another. Yet even though the hearing grandparents mirrored many of the issues and concerns of their hearing grandchildren, such perspectives were rarely shared. Lisa explained why she was so angry with her hearing relatives:

> At a very early age—when I was probably three or four—I really began to conduct business for my parents. I think that's probably typical. I really think that my grandparents and aunts and uncles were almost relieved of the burden. They passed the mantle onto me. And at the same time, they were very—I don't know how to explain it—they made sure they didn't share with me how difficult it was going to be. Nobody ever said, Gee, Lisa, we had to go through this too, or how's it going? Instead, it was always, "Make sure you take care of your parents." And that is something that I think I'm extremely resentful about. One of my aunts was in town recently and I went to dinner with her. And during the course of dinner she made a comment to me: "You know, your parents really were very different. I never knew what to do or how to communicate with them. They just see the world differently." I thought, if only somebody had said this to me thirty or forty years ago. But nobody said anything to me when I was a kid. If somebody had said to me, "You know, we understand that your parents really don't see things the way everybody else necessarily sees them." It would just have made it a lot easier.

Lisa's criticism of her hearing relatives focuses less on sharing family responsibilities than on sharing the sense of difference. Here, her hearing relatives failed her most. They failed to acknowledge their own struggles with these two worlds, and thus failed to validate Lisa's perspective. Nor was it enough to be merely sympathetic. John explained why he resented his grandparents' comments:

> They always said things like, "You poor thing with your mamma deaf."
> I used to hate it. Hate that tone. It was like they were feeling sorry for me, sorry for my mother.

His response was not a desire to have grandparents confide to their grandchildren what they wanted to say to their deaf child. It was a plea for a sense of shared identity between grandparent and grandchild: two generations both touched by hearing and by deafness.

Although many of the issues between deaf parent and hearing child parallel those among first- and second-generation immigrant groups, stories about the informants' hearing grandparents reveal one significant difference. The gradual acculturation of immigrant groups often alters language and customs in such a way that grandparent is dissociated from grandchild. In those family histories, it is the parent who serves as the bridge between two worlds. Among the hearing children of deaf parents, however, the sequence changes. Here, it is often the grandchild who links these two generations—one hearing, one deaf—each belonging to lands far more separate than can be imagined.

Deaf Grandparents

In her family history, Sarah described a different set of expectations between her hearing and her deaf grandparents. Although brief, her depiction of her deaf grandparents leaves an unequivocal impression. "My [deaf] grandparents," she said, "would have regarded me much higher if I had been born deaf. They would have valued me more if I had been born deaf." In the narratives of those with deaf grandparents, the "different center" that Padden and Humphries (1988) describe among the Deaf community is most evident. Within these families, deafness was the norm. To be hearing was to be the outsider. Hearing—a forgotten feature now suspect. Hearing—a reminder of difference.

Although only a minority of informants had a deaf grandparent, the legacy of multiple-generation deaf families extends beyond their immediate families. Becker (1980), Padden and Humphries (1988), and others have noted the cultural importance of these deaf-of-deaf. Although atypical in their family histories (fewer than 10 percent of deaf children are born to deaf parents), multiple-generation deaf people occupy a pivotal role in the Deaf community. Because schools for the deaf historically kept the language and customs of the Deaf shrouded in secrecy and shame, it was deaf-of-deaf children who provided a crucial link between their Deaf home environments and deaf children from hearing families. Among their deaf school peers, they were the principal transmitters of Deaf culture. Meadow-Orlans (1987) and others have shown that deaf children of deaf parents outperform deaf children of hearing parents by all standards: intellectually, socially, and psychologically. As adults, these deaf-of-deaf frequently emerge as leaders and spokespersons within the Deaf community.

This legacy of strong Deaf culture and identity was often an advantage for their deaf parents, and informants from these multiple-generation deaf families often developed a heightened sense of a Deaf identity. Compared with informants with hearing grandparents, informants with deaf grandparents were much more likely to be fluent in sign language. Informants' immersion in the Deaf world was even more complete if they had deaf siblings—a genetic feature more likely among multiple-generation deaf families. Many of these informants served as the bridge between the Deaf and Hearing worlds not only for their deaf parents, but for an entire clan of deaf relatives. George noted matter-of-factly:

> One day it was [interpreting for] Mom, the next day it was GrandDad. Or maybe my brother. Sometimes I felt like I was one big ear and mouth for the whole family!

Informants' exposure to deaf grandparents and other relatives gave a broader sense of deafness and Deaf culture, a perspective not confined to one's parents. Because deaf-of-deaf parents were more likely to be core members of the Deaf community, informants' interaction with this community was even more commonplace. It was these informants who were most likely to overtly identify and conceptualize their family experiences as "Deaf culture."

Just as these informants were more likely to perceive themselves as culturally Deaf, these men and women were also more likely to be estranged from a sense of themselves as Hearing. Within these deaf-of-deaf families, the cultural normalcy of deafness often engulfed the occasional hearing relative. As Dan explained: "I was surrounded by deafness. It was all I knew." Although most informants reported being loved and accepted by their deaf grandparents, being hearing brought conflicts that had been kept outside of the family back within the walls of home. Mary Ann saw herself as a reminder to her deaf family of that "other" world:

It's as if they forgot about hearing people. Forgot that you needed to hear to be quote "normal." And then I come along.

Informants' alignment among their relatives as hearing or deaf was difficult to avoid. Dan remembered a childhood in which his hearing grandparents favored him, but his deaf grandparents favored his deaf sister. Other informants completely identified with their deaf parents and grandparents, keeping their hearing identity separate from their family. Although most informants described participating in the Hearing world as an experience that was often separate from and outside of their deaf family, these perceptions were even more marked among those informants whose extended family members were deaf.

Deaf grandparents' attitudes toward deafness or having a deaf child were not clear-cut. Overall, informants with deaf grandparents described a less problematic and closer relationship between their grandparents and parents. Elaine explained: "My deaf grandparents knew about deafness, knew about communication issues, knew which schools to send their deaf child to." Yet, despite this shared experience of deafness, deaf grandparents were not immune to the broader Hearing culture's views on deafness. Like hearing grandparents, a few deaf grandparents grieved because they did not have the perfect child: a hearing child. Deaf grandparents offered no uniform answers or responses to dealing with a deaf child. Often, cultural biases about signing and speaking, about deafness and hearing persisted:

You'd think they [deaf grandparents] wouldn't send him [deaf father] off to oral schools or try to force him to speak since they never learned how to do it either. But I guess they just bought the party line. You know, Speak first, sign later. If you don't learn how to speak, you'll never amount to anything. All that negative bullshit they had to live through themselves, but then they put it on their own kid as well. I don't get it.

Despite varying attempts by deaf grandparents to mirror the Hearing world, most of these informants credited their deaf grandparents with normalizing deafness for their parents. Unlike informants with hearing grandparents, these informants were rarely confronted with blatant cultural biases. Kevin's description of his hearing grandmother would have been unthinkable in a deaf-of-deaf family:

Sometimes I would hear my [hearing] grandmother telling people that her daughter was *not* deaf. Something like, "You know, she's just a little hard-of-hearing." My mother is deaf! [Signs: *"Deaf, closed." "Hears nothing!"*] I even remember my grandmother saying things to my mother while her back was turned. But when my grandmother really wanted to talk to my mother, she would come to me and ask me to interpret.

Even if the grandparents were hearing, informants reported that a parent's deaf sibling (or other deaf relative) often reduced the parent's sense of alienation and isolation within a hearing family. But neither deaf grandparents nor deaf relatives could guarantee an idyllic family life. Although Regina came from a large extended deaf family, she pointed out that conflicts within the family still existed:

You know, there were years that my grandparents didn't speak to my parents. And every now and then, my aunt and my mother get into these huge fights. Just because they're all deaf, doesn't mean they get along. They're just like anybody else. They just don't have that extra thing to deal with.

It is this very sense of routine family interactions—including disagreements—which often made these informants feel most secure. The conflicts in their family narratives were not between the Deaf and the Hearing, but between Aunt Mary and Dad, or between Grandma and Uncle Bill. Informants with hearing grandparents were often uncertain how to determine what effect better communication would have had within their families.

Among informants with deaf grandparents and relatives, it was often hearing, not deafness, that was the stranger. Many issues concerning informants with deaf grandparents and relatives are not restricted to this chapter. Their feelings and stories are threaded throughout this book—along with those of informants with hearing grandparents. However, among those from extended deaf families there is an increased intensity—a more confident sense of cultural Deafness and a greater uncertainty about being hearing. It is as if these deaf-of-deaf relatives provide a more distilled version of what it means to be Deaf. Through them, the richness and the biases of Deaf culture become most apparent.

Family Gatherings

Whether informants' grandparents were deaf or hearing, one event described by many women and men captures the essence of their divided households: family gatherings. Whether Christmas or Chanukah, birthday or anniversary, these occasions placed lifetimes of separation and misunderstanding literally within arm's reach: at the dining table. Two informants offered the following tableaus:

> [Russell:] The deaf relatives would sit in the living room, eating on TV trays. And the hearing relatives would be in the dining room. And every now and then someone from one room would get up and go into the other room and look around and nod and smile. Then they'd come back and sit down. Who knows what they were doing. Maybe they wanted to make sure everybody was still alive.

> [Liz:] One Thanksgiving my mother had this great idea, to have all the deaf and hearing relatives sit alternating, you know, one deaf, one hearing, one deaf, one hearing. Like that. They all got along just fine. The deaf people [signs: *"signing," "talking across the table"*] and the hearing people [pantomimes mouth movements] with the hearing people.

Although a few deaf and hearing relatives were able to communicate, in most cases it was no more than the "nod and smile" described above.

During these family gatherings, many hearing children of deaf parents were the principal bridge between these two worlds. Informants remembered intense conflicts of loyalty and of identity. For some, these situations provoked exasperation and anger when deaf parents were slighted by hearing relatives. At other times, it was an opportunity to experiment with being hearing:

> I remember one time stuffing my face and trying to talk to everybody. I wanted to see what it was like. I always had to be so careful when I was talking with my Mom or Dad. You know, "I can't read your lips because your mouth is full."

Informants often felt caught between facilitating the family's communication and still wanting to enjoy their own experiences:

People wanted to sing Christmas carols, and I didn't want to sign them. I wanted to just sing along with them. But then the Deaf would have said [signs: *"What say?" "What say?"*] I tried doing it both [signing and singing] but it got too complicated, so after a while I just signed them.

Family gatherings heightened strained interactions: deaf relatives who were careful not to sign too much because it left the hearing relatives out; hearing people who either stopped talking or began talking inordinately loud because they worried about the deaf people. Bob described his predicament: "I would try to sit back and just ignore everything. But it was so uncomfortable it was suffocating." Jean summarized her feelings with a wry smile: "Holidays from Hell!"

Family gatherings continued to be of concern to informants through adulthood. The chasm between hearing and deaf relatives had often become a routine and permanent feature of the family landscape, and informants continued to feel torn in their affiliation and in their sense of obligation to bridge these two worlds. Gary described the efforts he and his fiancée made to make sure that neither his deaf parents nor her hearing parents would feel left out at their wedding rehearsal dinner. An interpreter was hired. The hearing parents were given a crash course in sign language. The deaf parents were supplied with paper and pens. Yet, in the end, Gary found himself on familiar ground:

> My parents kept circling back to me. Like a magnet. They didn't want the [hired] interpreter. They wanted me. I guess I can understand it. This was family business. Not stuff you wanted to share with an outsider. But, there I was, right back in the middle of things.

Several informants resolved these conflicts by keeping the two worlds separate. During holidays, Art arranged two gatherings: one for his deaf family and friends; one for his hearing friends. Other informants like Maureen drew the line:

> Oh, I don't do it any more. I talk with the hearing people, I sign with the deaf people. And if anybody asks me to interpret, I tell them, "Hey, that's my job. I'm off work today! You go figure out how to talk with each other."

In addition to depicting the fissure between deaf and hearing relatives, these family gatherings illustrate two important issues of affiliation and identity that will be discussed in later chapters. First, most informants found it impossible to be both deaf and hearing at the same time. This is most evident in their family's communication difficulties. Although popularized as a solution, "Total Communication"[7] (signing and talking at the same time) was generally rejected by informants as an artifice that sacrificed the fluency and integrity of both languages. Second, within settings that accentuated the division of these two worlds, the one role that offered refuge from the "suffocating" discomfort was that of interpreter. It was a role that potentially robbed informants of a sense of themselves while reiterating their chimerical identity—as neither deaf nor hearing, as both deaf and hearing.

The Alternate Family

During the year my fieldwork took me throughout the United States, I took advantage of the hospitality of informants as well as the wide network of my parents' friends. One time I stayed a few days with Hazel, an old family friend I have known since childhood. One evening after dinner, Hazel led me to a framed picture in her hallway. It was a drawing of her school, long since destroyed by fire. This residential school for the deaf had been an imposing multistory building with two towers. She pointed to the main entrance, where her parents had brought her as a young girl. Hazel explained that the left tower was the girls' dormitories, the right was for the boys. She smiled as she remembered her adolescent years, looking across to the other tower and flirting with the boys. During the rest of the evening Hazel told me of her many years at the school through stories of discovery, adventure, and camaraderie.

For many informants, schools for the deaf were as much a part of their heritage as specific family members. Even though the "School"[1] may have wrenched a deaf parent from his or her childhood home, it remained a significant and cherished homestead for many deaf adults. Within these schools, deaf peers transformed experiences of alienation and isolation into one of community and culture. These schools not only dominated much of the parents' childhood, they continued to be an important social arena for many deaf adults as well. Lifelong school friendships often formed the basis of a highly interactive social network. Deaf clubs, microcosms of the Deaf world, provided ongoing activities within a uniquely Deaf environment. In this chapter I examine how their parents' peer-based environment—the deaf school, deaf family friends, and the Deaf club—became part of informants' own family histories.

The Deaf School

The overwhelming majority of informants' parents attended a residential school for the deaf.[2] Frequently supplanting absent or diminished family interaction, schools for the deaf became *the* significant environments of socialization and cultural transmission—concerning deafness as well as family life.[3] In their pioneering cross-cultural study of childhood socialization, Whiting and Whiting (1975) concluded that it was the setting in which a child was raised (for example, the arrangement of space, who was included and with what frequency, how much the child participated in the activities around him or her) rather than specific methods of child-training that had the greatest socializing influence on the child. Schools for the deaf literally created a separate cultural space.[4]

Residential schools modeled a family life considerably different from a deaf child's family of origin, contradicting the widely held observation that boarding schools routinely divorce minority children from their native language and culture. For deaf children, these schools were where they *found* their native language and culture. Residential schools favored a communal rather than an individually oriented nuclear family environment, paralleling other child-rearing collectives such as those set up in kibbutzim. For many deaf children, these schools were their total life—daytime and evening, weekday and weekend.[5] Regimentation was often the norm. Informants described idiosyncratic, occasionally humorous parental behaviors that originated within these early school years:

> My Mom's thing is she hates overhead lights. Her whole life in the dorms there were glaring overhead lights. Whenever we go someplace with overhead lights, she looks at me and I know exactly what she's thinking. Turn them off!

Regimens of school life often became part of the informant's upbringing as well:

> Well, when you get raised in an institution, you don't get to choose what you eat. You just eat everything on the plate. That's it. No arguments. That's how my parents were raised, and that's how they raised me.

Although informants shared many anecdotal stories of school life which their parents had passed on to them, they also discussed more serious consequences of residential life—both for their parents and for themselves. Catherine explained:

> My mother went away to a residential school when she was four and I think that affected her. Well, I know it did . . . I remember she never gave me any guidelines, I just had to make my choices. But when I made choices, they were wrong. "You're naughty." "That's not nice." "Be polite." "Be a good girl." Give me some guidelines! But I'd get no direction. When I got married, my mother-in-law would give me advice all the time. Probably too much. Like telling me not to get pregnant because it might be born deaf. But my mother never gave me any advice. Ever. My parents were there for me when I needed them, but I always felt I raised myself.

Catherine touches upon a central concern among informants with regard to residential schools: a limited world view. Although many informants favored residential schools as the best available option for deaf children, they also criticized these schools for limiting a deaf child's access to a variety of information and experiences. Ted complained that school personnel were often no better than most hearing parents at being able to communicate with a deaf child:

> Everything boiled down to rules. You did this, or you didn't do that. We all get that, I guess, but at least we get other information. But how on earth were these deaf kids ever supposed to question rules? Most of the teachers and principals couldn't carry on a conversation with a deaf kid to save their life. All these kids knew was if they didn't do something, they would get punished.

While several informants agreed with Ted's assessment of educators' communication skills, others focused on how these schools unavoidably separated the deaf child from the outside world. The residential school's physical isolation was seen as accentuating the communicative isolation of deafness.

Although many informants were respectful of the strong attachment and loyalty their parents had toward their schools, they also questioned how their parents' separation from their families and these institutional environments affected their family history. What part of informants' own family heritages had been indelibly altered by these transplanted homesteads? Howard shifted from discussing the effect residential school had on his parents to how it had affected him:

> Deaf people always seem like they're a generation behind in social awareness. Our parents, because they were institutionalized, didn't make the proper transitions between childhood and adulthood. I guess we did. Or, maybe we missed them as well.

A number of informants like Howard attributed social and informational delays among their deaf parents to their life in the residential schools. Several men and women felt that their parents learned through their hearing children, as Howard later explained:

> Sometimes I watched other people just to learn how you were supposed to do it. Like, sometimes I just didn't know. Then sometimes I just fumbled my way. You know, now when I look back, I realize I was bringing in a lot of information to Mom and Dad. It was like I had to pave the way for them.

An article written by Linda Konner (1987), the hearing daughter of deaf parents, captures this sense of being an information ambassador by its title: "I Was My Parents' Radio."

By their very nature, residential schools created a paradoxical environment: both a normalizing experience with others of a similar condition, and an emphasis on being different from others. Economic, social, and geographic differences often receded in this communal environment. Two informants offered complementary evidence of how their family histories had been altered:

> [Fred:] You know I always sensed this hostility between my Mom and her hearing sister. I found out that my aunt had a lot of resentment like

when my Mom went away to school during the Depression. Any money that the family had went to get her uniforms. And she had nice clothes and three meals a day. That was my aunt's perception. And she resented that because she got shit. She was stuck at home with a crazy grandmother and two brothers. My aunt had to quit school so she could help work. And here my mother is off getting a good education.

[Harriet:] God, I remember when I first met my Dad's brother. Talk about money! He's this upper class, big business, the whole nine yards. I suppose it's not that surprising—my grandparents were wealthy. But, my Dad was never really a part of it. Not really. I mean, they left him money, but it was different. He never grew up in that environment. It's like the money dropped in out of the blue. He might as well have won the lottery.

Family routines, ethnic traditions, hometown communities, poverty or wealth—all were diminished, in many cases lost.

A few informants like Alice described the synergistic effects of residential schools and noncommunicative families:

You know, Barbara [another adult hearing child of deaf parents] and I were talking about how our parents don't react, or don't seem to show a lot of feeling when we have a lot of pain. And then she started crying and said that it's just like common sense. They should nurture us. They should just do that. But they come from a residential school. They didn't have much to do with their families. What role models did they have for nurturing? And I think we were raised the same way. We feel the loss but it's also understandable. We never got it because they never got it.

Although not everyone agreed with Alice's concern about being nurtured, many men and women did attribute various deficiencies in their upbringing to a combination of their parents' families of origin and their parents' school environment. This was true whether or not the parent had attended a residential school. Informants whose parents had attended regular public schools[6] or commuted daily to special schools were often just as critical about these school environments. Although their deaf parents had lived at home as children, these informants frequently viewed this arrangement as forfeiting a shared peer culture and access to other deaf adults. Living in a hearing home was also little guarantee of improved social interaction or information:

> My Dad never went to a residential school. Some people might think he was lucky, but living at home was no great shakes. He mostly just stayed in his room . . . It took him a long time to become comfortable with being deaf, with being with other deaf people.

In addition to creating a regimented environment, schools for the deaf also promoted an unalterable differential: those who were in power, those who determined a deaf child's fate, were inevitably hearing. Until recently, many schools for the deaf throughout the United States would not allow deaf teachers in the classroom, or restricted them to certain subjects or older students.

Despite their criticisms of residential schools, most informants generally endorsed them. Often, this support developed from what many saw as a lack of better options. Diane put herself in the situation:

> I keep thinking what would I do if I had a deaf child. This is awful. I keep thinking what I want to do is live near a residential school, have them go to residential school during the day—if they're really bright and residential school doesn't challenge them, mainstream half day and residential school the other half day. And I'll be obviously [laughs] in my car driving back and forth making sure all their social needs are met, all their educational needs are met.

Others were dubious that most hearing home environments would ever meet a deaf child's needs. Robert warned:

> Sure, you can keep saying that parents should learn to communicate with their deaf child. Oh, it sounds great! Terrific! But in the end, they never do. They didn't do it back then, and they're still not doing it now. And all those years are wasted. It's better to at least give the kid a chance.

Many informants like Diane and Robert acknowledged the one strength that these residential schools had offered their parents: not being alone—either as children or as adults. Despite variation in deaf children's geographic home territories, isolation from the Deaf world, and persistent opposition to Deaf language and identity from the

Hearing world, deaf children who attended various residential schools emerged with a remarkably unifying language and culture. It was the residential school's opportunity for social participation that overrode its other failings. And, a generation later, being exposed to the Deaf community and culture is what many informants agreed was one of the more significant benefits of having deaf parents.

Deaf Friends

The continuing legacy of these schools for the deaf is epitomized by deaf people's adult network of friends—many of whom date back to these early school years. Within many informants' childhood homes, their parents' deaf friends were more like extended family members, in some sense substituting for the infrequent and often problematic relationships with hearing relatives:

> My parents imbued us—my brother and I—with the beauty of their friendships. They loved their schoolmates, their friends. They were so valuable and so loved that I grew to love them too. Their friends are all gone now, but that was a long lifetime of friendships. But it was never ever at the expense of our family. We were all loved, equally.

The routine presence of deaf friends within the family provided hearing children with an increased immersion into the Deaf community and culture, establishing an important dimension to the experience of deafness: peer-based relationships united by shared communication and an interactive community.

Very few informants remembered their parents as having hearing friends. Several informants mentioned an occasional hearing neighbor or co-worker, but these relationships were usually circumstantial and not characteristically intimate. Gerald described one of his father's hearing acquaintances:

> This one guy John would always try to talk with my father [here he used exaggerated mouth and lip movements]. But, you know how it goes, he [father] would just nod and pretend to understand it all. He didn't understand half of what the guy was talking about.

For Gerald, the lack of communication between his father and this hearing man constituted a major obstacle to friendship. Indeed, most informants reported their parents' friendships were exclusively among other deaf people. As informants described their parents' deaf friends, two communication issues stood out—one by its absence, and one by its repeated presence. In contrast to the persistent communication difficulties that characterized interactions with most hearing family members and acquaintances, informants almost never mentioned communication problems when talking about their parents' deaf friends. Instead, informants typically described their parents' friends by mentioning various memorable incidents, their sense of humor, their eccentricity, their long history with the family. Paradoxically, communication was a major focus of activity among their parents and their deaf friends. Jeannette reminisced:

> It didn't matter whose house they were at, or whether they got together morning, noon, or night. They got together and they all sat around and they talked. And they talked and talked.

The chance for fluid and interactive communication among deaf friends sharply contrasted with its absence in most other social situations.

Although sometimes disparaged as "gossip," talking with other deaf people—about each other and about the world at large—is a critical source of information for most deaf people. Until the more recent development of adaptive telephone equipment such as the TTY, deaf people were limited to face-to-face communication. Access to most forms of information was often haphazard.[7] In spite of substantially increased media options for the Deaf, face-to-face communication remains the preferred form of interaction and information for many deaf people. Considerable value is placed on frequent social interaction, as Sally's description illustrates:

> Sometimes we'd come home and they'd [deaf friends] be waiting on the porch. Sometimes they'd be sitting outside in their car. They'd wait all day. They'd just wait until we got home. They couldn't wait to tell us some news.

The irony of friendships that valued face-to-face communication is that a number of informants were unable to talk with their parents' friends. With the exception of those men and women who signed, whatever idiosyncratic combination of speech or homemade pantomimes was used between hearing child and deaf parent rarely carried over to deaf family friends. Although Carla's parents and many of their friends were oral, she found communicating with them difficult:

> Basically I couldn't communicate with these people. Most of my parents' friends could speak, but that was not their comfortable element of communication. They preferred a combination or just sign.

One time while still heavily medicated after surgery, Carla's mother imagined this scene from her hospital bed:

> She kept telling me that her friends were there. All her friends were there. And they wanted to talk to me but I wouldn't talk to them. "Why wouldn't I talk to them?" she kept asking. "You always embarrassed me, you always do this to me, you always make me feel this way." And I just sat down and I cried and I cried and I cried. I realized what she was saying was, "We didn't teach you sign language but we want you to talk to our friends." When I was a kid around these deaf friends, I didn't understand a thing they were saying. Well, they didn't understand what I was saying either. I would have talked to them, but I couldn't. It was kind of a double bind.

Thus, although many informants felt comfortable around their parents' friends and frequently identified them as kin, the interaction between hearing children and deaf family friends was often constrained by how well they could communicate with each other.

In contrast to informants like Carla, a few women and men who could communicate with family friends encountered a different problem: family friends who depended on the informant to be their interpreter. Thelma's fluency in sign language contrasted with other hearing children of deaf parents in her local Deaf community. Her role as "community interpreter" was an important part of Thelma's childhood memories and was intimately connected with her assessment of having deaf parents. Her mother's friends exacerbated Thelma's sense of being overburdened as a child:

I hated it when her friends came over—who had children, children my age, older or younger—and wanted me to be their interpreter for them to go to the bank, take care of their business. My mother would [signs: *"You interpret (for) them"*]. I was the community interpreter. I was put in situations I didn't know I could say no to. I was very bitter, I was a very bitter child growing up, having deaf parents.

The childhood and adult implications of disparate language skills among informants are explored further in the following chapter, which examines linguistic asymmetry in its most intimate setting: among siblings.

Another characteristic illustrated by family friends is the tendency among deaf people to interact as a group—whether sitting around talking, playing cards, or going to the Deaf club. An emphasis on the group rather than the individual underlines a key feature of the Deaf experience: loyalty to deaf friends and the Deaf community. Whether particular parents were core members or on the periphery, the Deaf community was the critical reference group for most deaf parents. Historical traditions of communal life in the schools complemented external and internal social pressures to belong to a Deaf group. When one compares Deaf and Hearing cultures, the different emphases on group solidarity versus individual autonomy are values second only to their contrasting views on communication.

The tension between belonging to a group and striking out on one's own was felt both by deaf parents and by their hearing children. Those few men and women whose parents did not live near other deaf people or were not active in their local Deaf community often described their parents as "isolated," "lonely," or "missing out." In contrast, among informants and their parents who grew up within an active and visible Deaf community, feelings of alienation and difference were far more likely to be minimized. The communication and support that deaf friends and the larger Deaf community provided deaf parents were seen as an enriching experience by most informants. However, deaf friends sometimes competed for parents' attention and loyalty. Several informants were critical of the way their family life lost out to their parents' friends. Julian assessed his childhood experiences:

My trust was broken because my parents said we'd go do this, but then they would decide they wanted to do something else with their deaf friends instead. So, they went out with them. Their deaf friends were more important than the family . . . I had to fight my alternate family. My parents' best friends were always their number one priority.

Although she was similarly critical of her parents' friendships, Wanda proposed an alternative explanation:

My parents always used to stress the importance of family. Always think of your family first. Yet, they did more for their friends than they did for their own family. I always hated that. But, maybe it's like teenage culture, that your friends are more important than family.

An imbalance between friendships and family could also favor the family. A few informants felt that their parents sacrificed their Deaf life for their hearing children. Brian explained:

I see it now more clearly. They gave up a lot of being with their friends to be with us. To give time for me and my sister. It must have been hard for them, to go to all those hearing things at school and all that. I mean there weren't any interpreters back then. They just went to show that they supported us, that they loved us . . . but they gave up an awful lot.

The presence of deaf friends and their involvement with the family enhance the degree of hearing children's contact with other deaf people. This network of family friendships also represents a much larger commitment to the values of the Deaf than to the Hearing world—one that emphasizes frequent communal interaction rather than isolated autonomy. As these informants entered their adolescent and young adult years, their development toward self-sufficiency also moved them toward the values and ideals of the dominant Hearing culture. This trajectory raised the issue of abandoning deaf parents; it also conflicted with a fundamental pattern of social obligation and interaction within the Deaf community. Thus the question of informants' identity not only fell along the axis of whether one was deaf or hearing, but, even more important, it encompassed which behaviors and values one espoused and embraced.

The Deaf Club

The Deaf club embodies key features of Deaf culture: an arena of frequent interaction among those with a shared identity.[8] Individual Deaf clubs demonstrate less homogenous aspects of the Deaf community: many clubs are segregated according to age, class, race, or method of communication. Some focus on a particular sport, religion, or school attended. Yet the boundaries of each Deaf club are rarely rigid. Many Deaf social events draw from all of these seemingly exclusive clubs in spite of their conflicting affiliations. Although there are subgroups within the Deaf community, an underlying sense of shared identity and common destiny cuts across these differences. The various social and political activities are united by the cornerstone of this culture: the interest in and the opportunity to communicate.

Accompanying their parents to the Deaf club was a routine part of childhood for many informants. Particularly as young children, almost half of all informants went to a Deaf club as often as once a week. Hearing children's interaction at the Deaf club was sometimes limited by their communication skills, sometimes by their age. When asked what they did at the Deaf club, informants remembered participating in club-wide activities (such as listening to deaf storytellers or watching captioned movies) as well as pursuing separate activities by themselves or with other hearing children of deaf parents. Jack fondly remembered playing with other hearing children at the Deaf club:

> I can just picture all of us kids running around all the time screaming our heads off! Sometimes we had to be careful depending on who was there. [Here Jack described a few deaf people who had some hearing.] Sometimes one of them would hear us and yell at us to be quiet. But mostly, nobody cared. We just had a great time!

Deaf clubs were organized and attended by deaf people. Hearing children of deaf parents were the one regular exception to this exclusively Deaf environment. Viewed as an extension of the network of deaf friends, the Deaf club embodies many themes previously discussed: a normalizing and supportive environment; communication as a central activity; and a commitment to the group. A few informants were critical of the amount of time parents spent at the Deaf club. Yet, considering the dominant presence of deaf people and the lack of sign-language skills among many informants, it is remarkable how positively the Deaf club was remembered by most informants. Although several informants regretted that, because of their language skills, their level of participation had not been greater, no informants described feeling ostracized because they were hearing. While a few men and women saw themselves as peripheral members of the Deaf club, they still felt included as part of the larger group.

One of the more common terms used by informants to describe the Deaf club was "safe": "I felt safe there"; "you got this feeling of being safe." For many informants and their parents, venturing outside their homes meant chancing stigma and miscommunication. The Deaf club provided a normalizing environment outside the home for deaf parents as well as their hearing children. Because interacting with the Hearing world was generally unnecessary within the Deaf club, many informants' routine responsibilities such as interpreting or telephoning for their parents could be temporarily abandoned.

Goffman (1955, 1963) has pointed out the risk of losing one's individuality in exchange for the support of the group. Paradoxically, within a community of shared identity, individual differences can emerge—identities that are not restricted to a single, all-encompassing feature. In an environment like the Deaf club where deafness was the norm, informants could be less focused on deafness or on thinking of themselves as hearing children of deaf parents.[9] This minimized feelings of difference as well as the need to filter information or comments. This attitude was most evident when informants shared stories about various eccentric people at the Deaf club or remembered with humor the sound of certain deaf people's voices. Art described one such woman:

> She had one of those voices, you know, that just pierces. God, I felt sorry for her daughter. Every time she'd call her daughter she'd go [here Art imitated a high-pitched "Lu-lu-lu-lu"]. And her daughter's name was something like Becky! Of course, my old man, his voice was something else too. When he called me, boy, did I come running!

When I asked Art if he had ever shared these observations with anyone else, he shook his head:

> Well, all us kids did crazy silly things, you know, at the Deaf club. Nobody thought about it. But, we never did it 'round hearing people. And the deaf people didn't know. I mean, people'd think we're making fun of them. But, it's not that, it's just like, well, they made funny noises and it was okay.

Art's reference to "us kids" raises the question of children at the Deaf club: deaf children, and other hearing children of deaf parents. A few informants remembered playing with deaf children; most did not.[10] Even among informants with a high degree of contact with the Deaf community, their interaction was almost exclusively with deaf adults. Where were all the deaf children? Their absence was explained by a number of factors. Many deaf children attended a residential school away from their home community. Even when it was possible to go to the Deaf club or other Deaf events, a number of deaf children were discouraged from going by their parents. Most hearing parents (and a few deaf parents as well) were ambivalent about these Deaf activities—either because they themselves were uncomfortable among deaf adults or because they perceived the Deaf club as encouraging their child to identify herself as Deaf and not Hearing. The lack of childhood deaf peers among informants contrasts with the prevailing peer-based relationships of their parents. For most informants, the primary reference group of deaf people was adults—and not just any adults, but their *parents*. Informants' hearing status created both functional and hierarchical differences between themselves and other members of the Deaf community. These features form the basis of a condition of cultural marginality that I explore further in Chapter 11.

Although most informants remember some childhood contact with other hearing children of deaf parents—children of their parents' friends, or children at the Deaf club and other Deaf events—many commented that they had failed to form independent friendships with these children outside Deaf events or to maintain friendships as adults. Several informants found themselves wondering what had happened to other hearing children of deaf parents. If deaf people banded together because of shared history, culture, and identity, why didn't their hearing children? What explains this lack of coalescing among a group which otherwise shared similar life experiences and perspectives?

Within the normative environment of home or the Deaf club, deafness was often removed from the focus of attention. Selma explained:

> We didn't need to talk about having deaf parents. [Laughs.] We could do other things . . . like just be kids.

In contrast, informants' most intense memories of being a hearing child of deaf parents generally emerge from the dichotomization between being deaf and being hearing. The Deaf social events that brought hearing children of deaf parents together rarely provided this contrast. In those situations, hearing children could be hearing ("screaming our heads off") at the same time that their deaf parents could be deaf (talking through signing or lipreading). Although parallel, informants' experiences with public stigma or family responsibilities usually remained highly encapsulated within their individual families. The need to seek out or belong to a supportive group came at times when they were most separated from others like themselves. In addition, the spirit of protectiveness among informants was a powerful force that frequently disparaged acknowledging differences. Walter explained his actions:

> I didn't hang around with Bill [another hearing child of deaf parents] even though we were in the same class. It was like, well, we each need to make it and show them. ["Show them what?"] Show them that we're just like anybody else. Just because our parents are deaf, doesn't mean anything . . . ["So, did it mean anything?"] Sure, but I wasn't gonna let anybody know that.

For most informants, adolescence and adulthood heralded a shift toward the Hearing world. Attending Deaf functions and socializing with their parents' friends decreased for most informants, as Deborah described:

> When I was 13 or 14, I got to that age. I didn't want to go to the Deaf club. I didn't want to go to the Deaf social gatherings any longer. I

wanted to go out with my friends and do my thing. And my Dad would say, [signs and voices: *"You think deaf nothing! Hearing better than me?"*] No! But I never could explain that and I'd get real angry and we'd have these fights. I felt guilty because I'm trying to leave this Deaf world and go off and do my own thing. It was just like, I can't win for losing!

As informants became adults in the Hearing world, the paradoxical turmoil of their split identity often subsided in favor of the Hearing world. Although several informants continued attending Deaf clubs and events, most informants' contact with the Deaf world became increasingly restricted to the circle of their immediate family. When I asked Selma how going to the Deaf club differed as an adult, she explained:

When I was little, I was with Mom and Dad. I mean, what were they gonna do with an eight-year-old? It was okay. But now, well, I'm an adult. I'm hearing. Don't get me wrong. I feel like I belong all right, but only for a while. Like I'm a visitor or something . . .

Although many informants similarly described being welcome within Deaf clubs and the Deaf community as adults, they were also more conscious of their uncertain identity. Selma continued her thoughts about being a "visitor" in the Deaf world:

It's like, you have to come to terms with the fact that you're really a hearing person. You can't be deaf any more.

For some informants, the resolution in favor of a "hearing" identity precluded interest in participating in Deaf activities or contacting other hearing children of deaf parents. Steve shared the sentiments of a few other informants:

I know. I feel some connection to them . . . I mean, I wouldn't be talking to you if I didn't feel like we have something in common. But that was all in the past. You know, like getting together with your old high school buddies. I have my own life now.

For most men and women, however, their paradoxical identity lingered and swerved between these two worlds. And, despite their apparent assimilation into the Hearing world, many informants confessed that it was within the world of the Deaf that they were most at home.

CODA (Children of Deaf Adults) has developed largely around an exploration of shared history and identity among hearing children of deaf parents. Participation or non-participation in the organization among informants often reflected the tension between individual and group orientation. Because of the diversity of individual members' family backgrounds (including differing communication methods, family members' personalities, and overall family histories), informants who had attended at least one CODA meeting or conference reported varying degrees of "fit" with other participants. Most informants who participated responded the way Agnes did:

> The first minute I got there [CODA conference], I felt like, I'm home. These people are like me. They understand me. I'm one of them.

Many of these informants felt that even if their particular family experiences differed, they nevertheless shared a history of Deaf culture—including the frequent oppression and stigmatization by hearing people, as well as the sense of not quite fitting into the Deaf world. Several other informants who chose not to continue involvement with CODA felt that the organization was primarily interested in resolving psychodynamic issues. Jonathan explained:

> Oh, you know, it's just another one of those finding-yourself-groups. I don't need to find myself. I know who I am.

A few informants felt that their family experiences were highly personal and not to be shared outside their own family.

. . . .

After our interview, Sam sent me a few thoughts he had written. He began by telling me that our interview had sparked all sorts of forgotten memories, and the most vivid of them all was his recollection of the Deaf club:

> All those bodies in motion, the sharp voices, the lively animation. Small groups of two, three, or four. Each one different. One with everybody riveted to a storyteller. Another group with everybody all talking at the

same time. Some who stood and glanced from one group to the other. Scattered couples, standing or sitting in folding chairs, nodding or talking. It was so vibrant. All us kids yelling and screaming about the monsters while racing up and down the stairs. I remember the windows there. They were these special windows, the kind of glass they use in bathrooms to blur the vision. When I pressed my eyes up to the glass, the red and yellow and green flashes of the stoplights outside became colored snowflakes. I remember sometimes we would take time out from our relentless screaming and running and game playing and look out the windows, especially when it was winter cold and too dark and bitter to go outside and play in the parking lot. I can hear the strangely pitched and modulated voices of the deaf adults in the background. I remember how safe I felt. It was the safest place I can ever imagine.

The Deaf School, Deaf friends, and the Deaf club: Despite some feelings of rivalry for their parents' attention, these alternate families were remembered by many informants as more of a family than their own blood relatives. In this reconstituted family, informants and their parents could be themselves. Here the mark and the significance of being deaf receded to reveal gossips and storytellers, pranksters and organizers. Schools for the deaf began a lifetime of shared community and refuge from social alienation—while implicitly incorporating many of the broader cultural beliefs that set deaf people apart. These schools and friends represent a paradox of identity for deaf parents as well as their hearing children: to be separate from others because of your difference, and to seek out those who are similar so you can be yourself.

Imperfect Mirrors

Greta was one of five hearing children. Although all of them took turns interpreting phone calls or interpreting for an occasional visitor, each child developed a particular area of interpreting responsibility within the family. One dealt with the car, another with household repairs, one with finances, another shopping, and one with doctors. When I asked Greta whether these various areas of expertise correlated with any adult careers, she laughed and shook her head:

> No, but at least we all pitched in together. My sisters and brothers and I are so close. Both as kids and even now. I talk to them all the time . . . And when we wanted to know something, when something wasn't right, we didn't go ask Mom and Dad. We sat down together and we talked about it. "Well, what makes that weird noise?" "Well, I don't know." We would talk about it. [Laughs.] We came up with some really strange ideas.

Roger was the younger of two hearing children. He had been explaining why he never learned sign language very well and how his relationship with his sister was strained at best:

> I feel like my sister always stood between my parents and me. It's like she tried to be my mother. She would always tell me what to do and how to do it. She did all the interpreting, all the calling, everything! And you know, I figured, well, if she wants to do it all, let her. I've got my own life!

Erica's sister was deaf. I asked her how having a deaf sibling differed from having deaf parents:

Oh, in some ways, sure, I had to do some of the same things like interpret. But, my sister was like me. Like a mirror image of me, or me of her. It's like I was what she could have been if she had been hearing. And she was what I could have been if I was deaf.

Of the 150 informants, 123 had at least one other sibling. Informants' siblings represented opportunities to share childhood experiences as well as adult reflections. The sign for either "brother" or "sister" is a compound sign: "male" + "same" or "female" + "same." For myself, as a researcher but also as an only child, siblings suggested a shift in direction. This would be not only a chance to consider how individual informants interpreted their family experiences, but a way of comparing interpretations: Were siblings telling the same story?

In this chapter I explore variations among informants: communication skills, interpreting responsibilities, gender differences, and the presence or absence of deaf siblings. Each of these features altered the pattern of cultural transmission between deaf parent and hearing child. Such differences were most evident among siblings, and I consider how sibling relationships were affected by these imbalances.[1] Finally, I examine the issue of interpretation itself.

Ellen, one of three hearing children, expressed dismay at trying to resolve her family's divergent perspectives:

I can't believe we all sat around the same table and now we can't even agree on anything: what we ate, what we said, what went on. Nothing!

An Elusive Link

Differing family histories shaped parental attitudes toward deafness and toward using an identifiably different means of communication such as sign language. Informants' birth order, temperament, and gender all had an effect on their communication skills and uses. Although all siblings in some families could communicate equally well with their parents, this was not typical. In over half of the families with more than one child, one sibling became what a number of informants referred to as the "designated family interpreter." This child interpreted not only between parents and hearing outsiders but often between parents and other siblings. This feature occurred whether the parents' principal communication method was sign language or lipreading.

Not unexpectedly, the role of family interpreter often fell to the eldest child. Of the sixty-three informants who described one sibling in their family as the principal interpreter, thirty-seven identified this person as the eldest sibling. Many first-born women and men cited their hearing status as their parents' first real opportunity to interface with the Hearing world. Among the remaining twenty-six families in which the principal family interpreter was not the eldest child, seventeen identified the designated interpreter as the eldest daughter and four others identified another daughter (not the eldest).

The discrepancies in communication skills and interpreting responsibilities among siblings raise several questions: Why were all children in the family not equally fluent in sign language? How did one particular child become designated the family interpreter—and why was it more likely to be a daughter than a son? How did parents communicate with their other children before the "designated interpreter" came along?

Many informants were keenly aware that hearing children of deaf parents often lacked effective ways to talk with their parents—whether in other families, among their own siblings, or, in some cases, themselves. Adam spoke wrenchingly of lost opportunities:

> I mean, I had to go and take a [sign language] class when I was 24 years old. 24 years old! Just so I can finally start having a conversation with my parents. Damn it! All that time wasted! Why? Why?

Adam later explained that as a child he could, in fact, communicate with his parents; yet, like many other informants, Adam felt that his interactions with his family had been severely hampered and often superficial.[2] Several women and men who had opportunities to work with or observe other deaf parents and their hearing children noticed a recurrent pattern:

> I see this thing of the brokenness. It keeps going on and on. When I have to interpret for juvenile court, I see it all the time! And it's like, Well, what can we do with this kid? I mean, he's thirteen years old, he

can't talk with his parents. He's angry, he *hates* his deaf parents. But nobody thinks, Maybe we should work on communication issues in the family. But, no, they decide, Let's put 'em in day care . . . Hell, why doesn't anybody ever stop to ask, Why can't this kid communicate with his parents?

Even among informants whose parents were described as primarily oral, most reported that their parents preferred using some sign language between themselves or with close friends. Most men and women felt that lifetimes of denigration of sign language inevitably led to such family communication fissures. Deaf parents themselves often had no other communication options. Yet, like many immigrant groups, deaf parents often encouraged their children to use the dominant language—even at the expense of intra-family communication.

Not all deaf parents or their hearing children were equally affected by this linguistic hegemony. Nor did all children who were fluent in sign language become the family interpreter. Several women and men separated their communication skills from actual interpreting responsibilities. Despite being fluent in sign language, Maureen rejected the responsibilities her older sister took on:

> There's a big difference in where you are in the family, too . . . My oldest sister, she was with my Mom and Dad at a time when they were real young and they didn't know how to deal with the world as well. I think a lot of people grow up with their kids. So, she was the one that helped Mom and Dad when they were growing up, so to speak. Financially, there's a lot less money when the first child is born than there is on the second or third. I mean, I was spoiled rotten. By the time it was my turn, I wouldn't take my turn. I said, Forget it! I'm not doing what you did. I was the one that rebelled . . . I learned a lot from my older sisters. In just general life stuff. They made mistakes that I learned from and I didn't have to make the same mistakes.

The personality, temperament, and linguistic skills of a particular sibling sometimes overrode birth order. In describing his own signing ability as "fairly good," Norman explained why both his sister and brother were better at it:

> My sister [the oldest] was good [at signing], but she had a better rapport
> with our parents. So you might say rapport had a lot to do with it . . .
> My brother was more fluent. He was the most talented you might say
> with the sign language. He went into interpreting for the deaf, he was
> a teacher for the deaf, he went into more areas for the Deaf. He was
> more fluent. I have to admit, he was pretty good.

The availability of other siblings also affected how much any one
sibling had to take on interpreting responsibilities. In several families,
the role of primary interpreter shifted to another sibling as one child
grew older or left home. Other informants reported that even after the
primary interpreter left home, that person continued to act as their
parents' main interpreter—even though other siblings were still living
at home.

If the oldest child was not the main interpreter, was there *no* communication between that child and his parents until the interpreter
sibling came along? Although it is possible that some children were
severely deprived of language exchange with their parents, it is also
possible that initial communication existed. Informants who did not
remember signing as children may have used (some) sign language
when very young; social pressures or the presence of other siblings
may have diminished this usage as well as their memory of ever having
used sign language. Grosjean (1982) notes that language maintenance
is dependent on need:

> Children will become bilingual when psychosocial factors create a need
> for communication in two languages, and . . . they will revert back to
> monolingualism just as quickly when such factors disappear or are no
> longer considered important (p. 179).

The actual extent of language use or deprivation in early childhood
remains uncertain since informants could only speculate about their
earliest childhood years.

However uncertain the origins of communication differences among
siblings, a number of women and men did remember childhoods in
which one sibling emerged as the interpreter between other siblings
and parents. Harry explained how he talked with his parents:

I'd get my sister to interpret what I was saying. I'd go, Tell them this or explain this to them. I mean, I could talk to them, but it was just easier to have Mary do it. I guess I was just lazy.

These communication imbalances among siblings frequently continued into adulthood, and these differences underscore the unique family dynamics between each hearing child and his or her deaf parents. These differences also raise a question about cultural identity: If sign language fluency and interpreting responsibilities among hearing children of deaf parents were so varied, are all hearing children of deaf parents truly culturally Deaf?

Daughters before Sons

Although the eldest child was most likely to be the primary family interpreter, this was less true if the eldest child was male. When I asked Scott who did the interpreting in his family, he was somewhat sheepish:

Oh, it was mostly my sister. ["So, you never interpreted?"] No, she was the main interpreter. ["So, what happened if your sister wasn't around?"] Oh, I'd do it, but I was never as good as she was. She was really good at it. She still is.

Like many other male informants with a female sibling, Scott deferred to his sister as the identified family interpreter. This gender bias was true regardless of birth order or age difference between siblings. I asked Thelma about interpreting in her family:

I'm the middle child. But I'm the only one who does the interpreting. ["How did that happen?"] Good question! You know, I really don't know how that happened. I was always called to do the interpreting, and I always wanted my brother or sister to do it, but it was always for me to do. Well, I'm the oldest daughter. Maybe that's why.

Indeed, women in this study were much more likely to have had childhood interpreting responsibilities and to remain actively involved in interpreting for their parents as adults. Women were also far more likely to become professional sign language interpreters. Even among informants who did not consider themselves fluent in sign language, it was invariably the daughter who took on interpreting responsibilities. Why were daughters more likely than sons to be the family interpreter?

Informants' narratives suggest that the practice and the meaning of interpreting often reflected a larger pattern of socialization and status differences between women and men. As described by hearing children of deaf parents, interpreting entailed behaviors and skills often culturally ascribed to women: "helping," "connecting," "mediating," "bridging," "caretaking." Such responsibilities reiterate findings from other studies which have noted the propensity for women to be the family caretaker (Hooyman and Lustbader 1986; Sommers and Shields 1987). Nurturing roles have been socially defined and internalized as women's work, a concept that is reinforced by lifelong patterns of socialization and structural constraints (Gilligan 1982). Like other forms of caring, interpreting becomes inseparable from feelings of love and ties of obligation (Graham 1984), and this concern for others rather than self represents a defining aspect of femininity (Lewis and Meredith 1988).

Nurturing and connecting with others are not the only aspects of interpreting that evoke feminine associations. Many informants spoke of needing to be adaptable, invisible, and even subordinate when assuming the role of interpreter. These characteristics coincide with the generally tentative or inferior status traditionally available to women and, as such, contrast with the more fixed, visible, and dominant roles available to men. Informants repeatedly pointed out that a highly desirable skill in interpreting was the ability to shift roles. This adaptability sometimes had negative implications. Several informants described how interpreting made them feel invisible, pointing out that interpreting situations often required them to suppress their own identity: "If everyone forgets I'm there, then I know I've done a good job." Celine, who was a professional sign language interpreter, remembered the time when she interpreted for a deaf jury member. The judge legally certified Celine as a "non-entity" so there would be no more than twelve people on the jury. Other informants emphasized how interpreting meant assuming a more subordinate role. One woman who worked as an interpreter in an elementary school said:

It doesn't matter that I'm forty years older than these kids. My job is to be their voice. I have to give up having a college education and being a wife and mother. When I'm the interpreter, I'm just the voice of an eight-year-old kid.

As a consequence of their restricted or even devalued status in the wider culture, women may have fewer options but, at the same time, may have less to lose by assuming the interpreting role.

Although the negative associations of diminished identity and status were true for several women and men, a few other informants stressed that interpreting provided them with a much greater degree of visibility and control. While she sometimes felt burdened by interpreting, Helen underscores her pivotal family role:

I didn't just interpret. I had to make the decisions. I would be nine or ten. I would interpret like at the bank or something and then it got too hard. I'd tell my father, "I'll explain later." It was easier. You know, it's funny, many times now I can look back and say, I wasn't the interpreter, I was the decision maker. I'd go to the bank and the man would explain. And I would nod or ask questions. And all the while I was telling my father, "I'll explain it to you later."

Rather than being a passive and objective translation, interpreting could also be understood as authoritative and dynamic cultural brokering. In this sense, interpreting could be an expansive rather than a delimiting opportunity which offered the possibility of breaking out of socially restricted roles.

The generally feminine associations of the nature, mechanics, and status of interpreting appear to fit the experiences of many of these women and men. However, there were a few families in which this pattern was turned on its head. Matthew was a middle child with both an older and a younger sister. Yet he—not either of his sisters—was the family interpreter. I asked Matthew how this happened:

Oh, that's easy. My father always believed the men should do the work, not the women. He told us, "Interpreting is a *job*." And, in our family, interpreting *was* a job.

Matthew's family history points to the need for a more encompassing perspective. His explanation underscores a significant dimension of interpreting: its function, value, and meaning vary from family to family. Gwen described how signing and interpreting became an expression of sibling rivalry in her family:

> My sister and I would fight over who would get to go and interpret. It's like it was a chance to do something different, to be somewhere else. And so we'd both say, Oh, I'm better than you are. People understand me better. My fingerspelling is better than yours.

The importance of considering each family's meaning system helps to explain apparently contradictory examples of parental favoritism. Some informants felt their parents favored the sibling who was the main interpreter, while others felt that their parents favored siblings who did not interpret. Sharon explained it this way:

> My brother got away with murder. He never had to do anything . . . But, whenever they wanted anything, I was the one they called, I was the one that got dumped on.

Sharon's perspective sharply contrasts with that of a number of male informants who did no interpreting as children and, in retrospect, felt cheated out of participating more fully in their parents' lives.

A Brother's Keeper

Discrepancies in language use and interpreting responsibilities within the family often complicated relationships between siblings. In addition to interpreting, older siblings were more likely to assume roles frequently identified by both older and younger informants as "parental." Laura explained: "I, being the oldest, I pretty much told them what to do and how to do things. It's like I was the mother hen." Frank spoke of the strained relationship he had with his two younger brothers because they resented the fact that he—not their parents—raised them. Rita felt more positively toward her older sister:

> My older sister is my mother. She is like my mother. We've always been close . . . She would come to my school activities instead of my mother . . . It was wonderful having her as a mother. I didn't know that's what she was at the time, but it was nice.

Like many informants, Rita's description of her sibling vacillates between one which is more metaphorical and one which is indistinguishable from identifying her sibling as her parent.

The use of parental terms to describe oneself or one's siblings appeared throughout many informants' narratives. In some ways, this is not remarkable. Older siblings—whether their parents are hearing or deaf—have often assumed certain kinds of family responsibilities. Yet the informants' interpretation of these responsibilities is clear: they are those of a parent. Why were certain activities necessarily identified as parental? What makes an activity that of a mother but not of a child or sibling? In the previous example, Rita characterized her sister in retrospect: "I didn't know that's what she was *at the time*." Rita's assessment was informed by her adult perspectives. Like many other informants, Rita explained that as an adult she learned "the way families are supposed to work."

Many other men and women—regardless of their birth order—assessed their childhoods using similar descriptors:

> [Tony, an only child:] Sometimes I feel like I was the parent and I helped raise them [parents].

> [Gloria, the youngest of four:] We all did our part. Probably Maria [oldest child] had to do the most. But I did my part too, I did my part to help out. I got to learn how to be a mother real early.

In explaining their family relationships and roles, informants frequently used the terms and models of the dominant Hearing culture. Although this represents a satisfactory explanation of their childhood experiences for a number of informants, others felt coerced by its implications. Pam explained:

> Oh, the kids used to say things like, "Well, do you have to go home and change your mother's diapers?" And I'd say, "No, but at least I know how to change a diaper. You probably still have your mother changing yours!"

Pam's retort suggests alternative ways of considering the parent-child relationship. The dominant cultural view presumes a hierarchical structure: the caretaking parent and the care-requiring child. Such views do not, for example, consider families in which responsibilities are assumed by appropriate family members as part of the family's resource system. In Chapter 8 I expand this discussion of family roles and responsibilities and consider the cultural models used to explain them.

Deaf Siblings

Although only eight informants had a deaf sibling, their narratives provide important perspectives. For most women and men, the experiences of being a deaf child were learned through their parents' stories. Informants with deaf siblings saw the developmental, social, and educational issues of deaf children first-hand. Like any siblings, deaf and hearing brothers and sisters fought, played together, and learned from each other:

> I taught my sister how to dance . . . I gave her a sense of the music. And my sister is one of the best partners I have in terms of dancing. [Laughs.] And when I see her, we periodically will do it and we get such a kick out of it.

Informants with deaf siblings were far more likely to meet other deaf children. When they interpreted for their deaf sibling, hearing children were exposed to interactions and situations that differed from those they encountered when interpreting for their deaf parents. Informants with deaf siblings were more likely to develop sign language that included the vocabulary of a younger generation, compared with informants whose main interaction was with their parents' peer group. These women and men also experienced the family disruptions that frequently occurred when their deaf brother or sister left home to attend a residential school.

Like deaf grandparents, a deaf brother or sister intensified the family connection to the Deaf world and often heightened an informant's sense of being the different one in the family. Unencumbered by the usual generational differences between parents and children, deaf siblings could more clearly illustrate the cultural contrasts between the Hearing and Deaf worlds:

My parents didn't understand a hearing child. They had my [deaf] sister, and she did things as they expected. And they knew the people she was doing things with. And they were part of her world, or she was part of their world—however you want to look at it. I wasn't. I never was going to be. I wasn't deaf. I had a whole different world that I dealt with. And they didn't understand that world other than through me. And so I became the symbol for this whole other world which they didn't understand. And they didn't understand me.

Sibling relationships within the family often became shaded by whether one was deaf or hearing:

I always think of her [deaf sister] as being my parents' pride and joy. And my sister, I think, thinks that I was given a lot because I could hear. That my parents were easy on me. And I think my parents were much harder on me because they really expected that much more of me.

Another informant, Monica, described how she and her other hearing siblings always ended up leaving their deaf brother out—no matter how hard they tried to include him:

I don't know what we could have done. [Pauses for a long time.] Probably nothing. We just belonged to such different worlds.

The presence of a deaf sibling also emphasized the power differential between being hearing and being deaf. Even younger hearing siblings were often given responsibilities toward their older deaf brother or sister:

The other thing is my parents wanting my brother to speak. And because I could hear, they put me in the position of trying to teach my brother how to speak. And my brother hated it, to this day will not wear a hearing aid . . . And I'm sure my brother just resents that to this day. Because part of that is trying to make him like me. Which I don't think my parents meant. I just think that they thought because I could hear and because I could say things that I could help my brother.

Hearing outsiders also endorsed a preferential hierarchy:

People would always say, Oh, you're so lucky, just think, instead of him [brother], it could have been you. You could have been the one born deaf.

Yet sometimes the status of being hearing was undercut by the sense of being different from the rest of the family. And, as Lisa observed, the sense of childhood ostracism could continue into adulthood as well:

> My [deaf] brother married a deaf girl and they had a baby boy. The baby is profoundly deaf. And my brother wrote me a letter saying, "I was so happy to find out that he was deaf because he will always be one of us" . . . They really do believe that if you're hearing, you're never part of them and you're part of a different world and you don't belong. You're not theirs.

Outcomes and Validation

The informants' descriptions of different family members were most varied when they were talking about their siblings. Four men and women offered these observations:

> My sister is my closest friend.

> I haven't spoken with my brother in years. I don't care if I ever do.

> We fought all the time as kids.

> We were each other's support network.

The variation in intimacy or enmity between these siblings appears no different from that among the general population (Bank and Kahn 1982). Yet sibling relationships illustrate an important dimension of the cultural identity of hearing children of deaf parents. Whatever the combination of birth order, gender, temperament, and historical context, each child had a distinct relationship with his or her parents. Within each family as well as among all these men and women, each informant developed a highly personal system of meaning. For some, having deaf parents also meant taking care of other siblings. For others, having deaf parents meant talking to them through another sibling. Some were compared with deaf siblings and elevated because they were hearing, while others were distanced because they were not deaf.

There were few actual contradictions in the overall histories of siblings from the same family. Yet emphases and interpretations of these histories did vary. Informants themselves often prefaced their remarks by recognizing the potential for variation in any one sibling's perspectives: each one had a different personality, had grown up at a different time, and had a different family role. Sharon offered this insight:

> My brother thinks everything was pathological. And I don't feel that way at all. And we're looking at the very same experiences, the very same situation, the very same people . . . but I don't feel that there's any way to put a label on it and say, That's the right answer. A lot of it is just up here [points] in our own little heads.

Despite these disclaimers, most informants continued to express concern over discrepancies between their stories and those of their siblings. Like many informants, Ben needed validation of the family history that he remembered:

> Sometimes I just can't believe that we remember things so differently. There are some things that I remember so clearly, but they can't even remember at all.

Ben's uneasiness and sense of urgency lie at the heart of identity. In understanding and defining who we are, we rely on our own sense of our histories as well as available explanatory models. What did deaf parents have to do with how these men and women turned out?

Siblings provided one way for informants to explore their own hypotheses and validate their interpretations. In effect, comparisons and contrasts with siblings created early explanatory systems:

> All three of us [sisters] are so different, we have totally different issues. My oldest sister will drive down the freeway and she'll say, "Oh, I feel so bad because there's a deaf guy in jail and I didn't have time to interpret for him on Friday so he has to stay in jail all weekend." And my attitude is, He committed a crime, who the hell cares? It's not your responsibility to take care of deaf people. And my middle sister's different too . . . My middle sister always feels like she has to make sure everybody's included. And that's totally different from the way I look at it.

Ken and Shelly explained how their parents' deafness propelled them both to succeed. They also described how their other two siblings developed low self-esteem because of this same family feature. In assessing how family responsibilities affected her, Barbara continually referred to her sister as "the rebellious one" and herself as "the good one." Siblings underscore informants' dilemma of interpreting their family history. Whether first-born, last-born, or only child, the singular perspective of each informant was often undermined by its very uniqueness. The opportunities for comparison with others—whether siblings or other hearing children of deaf parents—could potentially invalidate a long-held system of beliefs and explanations about having deaf parents.

. . . .

During the interviews and during group meetings of adult hearing children, I often observed these men and women attempting to find common explanations for their lives. For many, it was the first adult opportunity to consider what having deaf parents meant. Many hypothesized outcomes fit particular individuals but conflicted with the experiences of others: "I don't trust anyone"; "I trust everyone." "I have low self-esteem"; "I feel very self-confident." When these men and women failed to find consensus, they frequently considered possible explanations for these divergent outcomes. One of the most common explanations informants offered for these differences was family composition: only child, eldest child, youngest child, deaf siblings, middle child. Although these subgroups did have common themes, contradictions continued to arise. Only children were generally very responsible, but some turned out to be fastidious while others were slobs. Informants and subgroups reshuffled their explanations and often subdivided again.

This categorical narrowing does suggest distinguishing features among these men and women. As the past four chapters have shown, family members and family histories provide one framework in which to understand these informants' experiences: how each parent dealt with and experienced his or her deafness; whether grandparents or siblings were deaf; an informant's birth order; isolation from hearing people or interaction with other deaf people. Yet attempting to correlate individual family factors with particular outcomes often leads to an intellectual quagmire of contradictions. Rather than continuing to pursue an elusive family feature that will explain all outcomes, I will turn in Part III to the day-to-day experiences of being a hearing child with deaf parents. The next four chapters include not only routine features of daily life but informants' childhood and adult emotional responses. Despite the variation in individual circumstances, these descriptions provide a much more unified tone and perspective on the lives and the identities of hearing children of deaf parents.

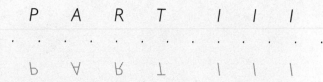

Childhood Landscapes

Arlene's Story

When we'd go shopping, I got lost I don't know how many times. Man, when I got lost, I got lost! People would come up to me and say, "Can I help you? I'm sure we can find your Mamma and Daddy." And I'm thinking, well just you try. Let's see you call them over the P.A. system. And knowing my mother, the way she shopped, it would be a while before she found out I wasn't there.

This one time, we were traveling and we pulled up at a filling station and I was asleep in the back seat. My mother was looking at this road map while my father was in the restroom. I woke up and I told my mother I was going to the bathroom. So, when I came back from the bathroom, the car was gone. I was only five or six and I was scared to death. I just started crying and the gas station man said, "What's wrong?" I said, "My Mamma and Daddy drove off!" He said, "Oh, they'll be right back soon as they notice things are so quiet and you're not talking with them." I said, "But you don't understand. They don't hear anything, they're deaf."

It turned out they didn't get that far, maybe five or six miles down the road before they noticed. They said it was a good thing I had rolled down my window because it was the air that made this wind in the car and my Daddy finally turned around to see what it was and saw that I was gone. Otherwise, who knows how long it would have been.

I got lost lots of other times too. [At this point Arlene sighed, her eyes filling with tears. Her voice began to break.] And I know when my parents are gone, I know I'm really gonna feel lost again.

. . . .

Since beginning this research, I have traveled more than 58,000 miles—almost 9,000 miles of them driving alone across the American countryside. For nearly twelve months, I crisscrossed a landscape altered by geography and by season. I met informants at home, at work, and on the run: at a punk café on the north side of Chicago; a rocky beach on the Pacific; a tavern in the rural South; a sprawling suburban mansion in the northeast. Vygotsky (1978) proposes that each child "grows and develops in an extremely individual cultural-social environment which reflects the complex path of the historical development of the given people and the complex system of economic and cultural conditions of its present-day existence" (p. 27). Considering the diverse lives of these men and women, are there unifying features within their childhood landscapes?

In the previous four chapters, informants' narratives about their family members provided glimpses of the historical contexts and social forces that contributed to the experience of being a hearing child of deaf parents. Part III shifts from reflections of identity in others to informants' own remembered experiences. These chapters focus on the routine yet distinct landmarks of their childhoods, and on the emotional threads that connect these childhood experiences to their present adult lives. As Arlene's story illustrates, many informants' feelings about their childhood and their parents were not merely lodged in descriptive memoirs of the past. These ongoing responses were very much a part of their adult life, often emerging during the interviews as well.

Sumner, Bateson, and others have used the concept of "ethos" to describe what Clifton (1976) calls "the dominant emotional aspects of consciousness which color and give quality to different behaviors observed in a community" (p. 152). Each of the four chapters in Part III is organized around a major theme that is both evocative and persistent: communication, family roles, difference, and dichotomization. The intensity as well as the response to each of these issues varies among informants. Yet it is the recurrence of these themes—despite the diversity in informants' age, locale, or family circumstances—which demonstrates a remarkably consistent topography and a unifying ethos among this population.

A Song You Never Heard Before

Sure, everybody's different than their parents. But there's this one thing—I don't exactly know how to describe it. It's like we [signs *"look into"*] like we see into the Deaf world because of them, but we're also hearing. And, no matter how hard either of us tries, they can't ever be hearing and we can't ever be deaf . . . I don't know, it's like when I try to explain music to my parents. My Mom is always wanting me to explain music. And if your parents aren't deaf, you can't understand. It's like me telling you about a song you never heard before. I can try all sorts of ways, but until you hear it, you can never really know what it's like. Not really. [Shakes his head and signs *"can't"*.]

Rafael sat cross-legged on the floor of his living room trying to explain the difference between being deaf and being hearing. Imperceptibly, he shifted to trying to explain his own life. At the heart of Rafael's narrative is his concern with communication—trying to express feelings, convey information, share experiences. What does it take to communicate with others? Is there some inevitable wall that exists no matter what the subject, no matter how skilled the presenter, no matter who the audience? Must each of us acknowledge that all communication is ultimately flawed—is it, as Rafael describes, like trying to explain "a song you never heard before"?

It would be easy to overestimate the significance of sign language among hearing children of deaf parents. One-fifth of all informants did not use ASL or any other sign system; this group included not only those whose parents were oral, but several informants whose parents' sole form of communication was ASL. Yet, despite varying language competencies and uses among informants, these men and women shared a more elemental arena of communication: sound and silence. These two aspects of communication were part of informants' daily lives, present in their most ordinary routines. I begin this chapter by examining sound and silence—two properties that might be considered commonsense and second nature. Yet informants' narratives reveal that even these supposed universals are subject to cultural interpretation. Because informants incorporate the cultural systems of both the Hearing and the Deaf, their understandings of sound and of silence reflect this dual and often conflicting heritage. I will also evaluate particular modes of language—speech, writing, signs, gestures, facial expressions, and body movements—within a cultural context. In particular, I see talking as a culturally defined method of communication that not only determines how informants express themselves to others but shapes preferences for how others communicate with them. In the remainder of the chapter I examine informants' relationship to the languages of English and American Sign Language, and the implications of being bilingual between two languages that emerge from such fundamentally opposing extremes of sound and silence.

Language

Language has been hailed as a distinctly human mode of communication—often considered to be *the* primary attribute of our species. In both arts and sciences, language has provided a mirror for the broader culture as well as for the individual soul. Writers have debated at great length the relationship between language and self. Sapir and Whorf described the interrelatedness of language and thought, while others have proposed their arbitrariness. The particular language that is learned and the uses of language within a child's early environment are universally recognized as significant influences on psychosocial development.[1] Studies have examined language shift and language maintenance, the relationship between language and gender, language and personality. Despite this vast and sometimes conflicting array of language theories, researchers and writers share a nearly universal bias.

The studies and the expressions of language all presume one element, one that has implicitly been incorporated within the domain of "language" for both researcher and layperson. It is a quality simple in its recognition and profound by its absence: sound.

Hockett (1960) identified thirteen design features that set language apart from other forms of communication. According to Hockett, the first criterion of language is that it is a vocal-auditory channel of communication: produced through the mouth and/or nose, heard through the ears. This fixation with sound extends to writing as well. "True writing," Henderson observes, "is more commonly considered a surrogate for language—a system of graphic signs which conveys the equivalent of spoken communication" (1976, p. 409). Cole (1982) defines language as comprising "a set of symbols and a set of rules (a grammar) used in a meaningful way that permits communication. The symbols are expressed orally by sounds, or they can be communicated in a written form" (p. 3).

Equating language with sound is not merely the province of theoreticians and researchers. Common terms and synonyms associated with language indicate the pervasiveness of this association: "speaker," "listener," "talk," "speech." Grosjean (1982) finds that the United States is generally more tolerant of linguistic minorities, but he also observes:

> Although the official policy toward linguistic minorities has been neither one of encouragement nor one of repression but more a policy of toleration, the general attitude of the nation (as compared to its laws) and of the Anglo-American majority has been that members of linguistic minorities should integrate themselves into the English-speaking society as quickly as possible (p. 62).

The expected assimilation is not merely toward a particular language, but a *spoken* language. In contemporary American culture, the belief in sound as the basis for language and for communication has achieved unquestioned supremacy. This belief appears to be shared by many other cultures as well.[2]

Within the past two decades American Sign Language has begun to challenge traditional assumptions about the fundamental elements of language (Woodward 1972; Klima and Bellugi 1979; Padden and Humphries 1988). ASL has emerged from intriguing curiosity to recognition as a complete and separate language.³ No longer considered a stepchild of English, ASL has developed a sizable research following; many of these studies are oriented toward linguistic analyses and classifications. Ironically, linguistic recognition of ASL was precipitated largely on the basis of its inherent structural and morphological characteristics—qualities that are considered fundamental to more traditional sound-oriented languages. Although the growing acceptance and recognition of ASL represent an important milestone of Deaf history, its identification and classification as a bona fide language have glossed over a more fundamental feature of ASL. Whatever its similarities to other languages might be, ASL is not a *spoken* language. It is not based on *sound*.

Silence

As a reminder of the dangers of inaction, gay activists have introduced a slogan that captures the horrors of the Holocaust: "Silence = Death." Those of us who do not speak out are lost. Promotional ads for the movie *Alien* warned: "In space, no one can hear you scream." Cloaked in passivity and darkness, silence has come to mean the opposite of sound, of communication, of life. Paradoxically, silence also brings respite from a hectic and overstimulating life: a moment of silence; silence is golden. Unless we are given clues to the character of silence—"chilling," "peaceful," "ominous"—how are we to know what it means? Both ambiguous and paradoxical, silence embodies a void without shape and without meaning. All these versions of silence reflect a world of hearing people, a world of sound.

Silence has also become synonymous with deaf people. Explicit titles on the Deaf such as *They Grow in Silence, Growing Old in Silence, The Other Side of Silence,* and *In Silence* or implicit ones such as *Outsiders in a Hearing World* and *When the Mind Hears* draw from this association. For most people, the pairing of deafness and silence is automatic. Like many informants, Roger recalled a typical response when someone found out his parents were deaf: "Oh, it must have been so quiet around your house." As we shall see later in this chapter, deaf households, in fact, were often *not* quiet: sound is quite familiar in the everyday lives of deaf people and their children. The discussion here, however, focuses on this presumed realm of the Deaf: silence. Given the often paradoxical and ambivalent meanings attached to silence by those who hear, what place does silence have in the lives of these informants—men and women who stand within the crossroads of Hearing and Deaf cultures?

The Deaf community has often embraced the association with silence—in national newsletters such as "Silent News," "Silent Worker," "Silent Advocate"—or in the names of Deaf organizations like "The Silent Club." The sign for silence is among the most fluid and beautiful of signs: both hands are held prayer-like over the mouth, then slowly and steadily spread apart and downward; a related sign is "peace." When describing their parents' attitudes about silence, informants frequently invoked a state of serenity without any sense of doom or lack of communication. While recognizing the advantages of certain environmental sounds such as a siren or loudspeaker, many informants explained that their parents equated sound with noise—bothersome, obtrusive, and sometimes morally corrupt. Donna explained:

> My Mom always told me she was glad she couldn't hear all that noise. All those bad ugly things people say all the time. She was glad she didn't have to deal with it.

Many men and women echoed their parents' positive associations with silence. Sidransky (1990) describes silence as "peaceful, almost musical, a lilting harmony that gives me rest and ease" (p. 282). Many other informants were similarly comforted and transported by silence.

Silence also characterized interactions between informants' deaf families and hearing people. Instead of tranquillity, silence here represented an uneasy and awkward stillness. This version of silence came from both hearing and deaf people; hearing people who were unsure how to talk with deaf people; deaf people who became unusually guarded about any attempts at sound. Carl explained:

> Oh, I don't know, it just feels too quiet. It's not the same as when Mom and Dad are talking. I mean, they don't use their voices, but it's not that quiet. It's like they're being careful not to sound funny or make any wrong noises.

Padden and Humphries (1988) note that ordinarily "the lives of Deaf people are far from silent but very loudly click, buzz, swish, pop, roar and whir" (p. 109). Tanya described the lack of communication between her parents and her hearing relatives:

> Everybody's standing around but nobody's talking. And I get this urge, I feel this pull to break the silence. It's funny, even though I get mad about being the interpreter, it's almost better than facing the silence.

Several informants similarly mentioned a pressure to fill this void of silence. Lorraine recalled that she was always made anxious by her ex-husband's silence:

> I kept thinking that something was wrong. God! He was too quiet. But I kept nagging him to say something. It used to drive me up the wall. And then this one time he had the nerve to say, "Well, you mean with your deaf parents and all that you aren't used to this by now?"

When informants used silence to characterize social interactions, it often expressed not the self-possessed environment of the Deaf but a level of social discomfort—and one that often signaled them into action.

An even darker side of silence emerged among some informants' narratives. In contrast to visions of silence as either peaceful or discomforting, for some informants silence was desolate and terrifying. Some of the most difficult and poignant moments during these interviews concerned informants' very personal memories of silence. John remembered falling when he was a young child, unable to call out for his mother:

> I wanted to call out, but I wasn't able to. I just had to cry until the pain was over. I never got to call out.

After an hour of being guardedly positive about her family experiences, Celine risked sharing her most secret childhood fear. She spoke to me as she would have to her deaf parents, in a voice that was both woman and child, deaf and hearing:

> Why can't you hear me? Why you deaf? I scream, you don't come. Why can't you hear me? Why you deaf?

Feelings of hurt, of fear, of isolation. Although they did not represent the majority view, these versions of silence push at the limits of cultural relativity. How does one reconcile these disturbing images of silence with those that picture a rhapsodic serenity? Is there a fundamental human need for sound?

Anthropologists have been concerned not only with the real, the tangible, but with the perceived. Among hearing children of deaf parents, it is what each woman and man brings to the realm of silence that gives it form and meaning. In *Illness as Metaphor* Susan Sontag (1977) criticized the metaphorical use of illness for a host of negative images ranging from war to decay.[4] Yet disease and silence *are* metaphors because they express feelings that Sontag and others disdain: the lyrical, the magical, the amorphous. It is precisely these properties that reflect the complexity and the contradictions of the human condition.

Whether their parents used signing or lipreading, all informants recognized that silence does not preclude communication. The question, however, is how effective is that communication? For these informants, communication has come to mean more than auditory production and reception. The fundamental basis of communication is not sound, but connection—not only whether one is able to express, but also whether one is heard. For Douglas, both aspects were essential:

> For me, when someone's lying next to me in the dark, I want to be able to talk to them, I want to know that they can hear me. I want to know that they're there. I don't want to be alone, just surrounded by the darkness.[5]

Varying modes of communication—spoken or signed, written or drawn—are evaluated according to differing cultural standards. But they are also experienced by individual people. Metaphors like silence do not merely demonstrate cognitive associations; they express actual experiences and preferences. Being "heard" is not only metaphorical for being understood. For the message to be heard, it must be given in a particular mode of communication—whether by preference or by necessity. For most of us, the range of communication depends on cultural sanction, familiarity, and skill. In both the Hearing and the Deaf worlds, strong adherents exist—those who elevate clarity of voice, those who ennoble the expressions of hand and body. And for some, no mode of communication is sufficient.

Metaphors of silence reflect two cultural standards: a Hearing culture that reveres sound as the basis for communication, and a Deaf culture that sees sound as an inessential and often unnecessary ingredient of communication. Informants' metaphors and experiences of silence draw from this dual heritage. For many, silence represents a realm of comfort without alienation, a familiar place of refuge. For some, silence is a reminder of the anxiety and fear of not being heard—regardless of the mode of communication. Among all these women and men, silence was a familiar presence. Informants were regularly reminded of silence by their own heightened awareness of sound as well as by outsiders who pitied and marveled at their family of silence. As metaphor and as lived experience, silence draws from the most ordinary routines and the most profound depths of these informants' experiences. Revered or reviled, silence is a prominent and enduring feature within the childhood and adult landscapes of hearing children of deaf parents.

Sound

Padden and Humphries (1988) describe two ways to think about sound: as an acoustic event, and as various meanings associated with that event. To paraphrase their example, a cough can mean a variety of things depending on the context: clearing the windpipe, disapproval, or a signal.[6] Padden and Humphries point out that the Deaf are no strangers to the world of sound, but "Deaf people know that sound belongs to hearing people except in the few situations they are allowed to use it" (p. 103). Deaf people must carefully learn the complex and varying meanings of sounds. This is possible through control: self-control and being controlled by others.

In navigating the confusing and potentially self-incriminating world of sound, many deaf parents relied on their hearing children. Hearing children provided their deaf parents with glimpses of sounds that were both subtle and routine. How do the songs of the canary and the mockingbird compare? What causes a floor to creak? Sidransky (1990) remembered her mother wondering if a yellow tulip had a sound of its own. Dorothy told me:

> I think I first realized how profound my mother's deafness was when [signs, *"Mother asked me, 'That sound, sound of a drop of water in the sink, Why? What from? When does it make that noise? When it first comes out of the faucet? Or when the drop hits the sink?'"*]

Monitoring the sounds of and around their parents in public was a common occurrence for most informants. In public settings, sound was often experienced negatively—as cause for either embarrassment or alarm: Your voice is too loud. The car's making a funny noise. Your shoes squeak. There was a loud crash over there. As Leonard pointed out, the origins of these responsibilities were often unclear. Were these efforts on behalf of the deaf parent or the hearing child?

> I got so used to telling my father to hush, you know, when he got too loud. I'd always [signs, *"Too loud, noisy, quiet!"*]. But one day I noticed that he seemed hurt when I told him. And I thought, Well, who am I doing this for?

Regardless of whom sounds were regulated for in public, they invariably became tinged with a sense of caution and control.

At home, some of the rules of sound changed. While screening for urgency or danger continued, informants could now be less concerned with stigma than with interest, amusement, or danger. All those noises inside and outside the family home: a burbling toilet, a creaking mattress, ticking clocks, dogs barking. Which one is worth noting, which one signifies important information? Evaluating sounds often tied informants to their family even when they were not home. Don remembered:

> When the [tornado] sirens went off I had to run home and tell my parents. After a while the neighbors would tell them, and you just kind of know that your neighbors will. But there's always that scary part, Well, what if the neighbors aren't home?

Screening home sounds continued to be a part of many informants' adult obligations as well. Such responsibilities could be mundane and even comical:

> I went to visit them [parents] one time and the minute I walked in I asked my Dad, What on earth is that noise? It turned out the alarm on their clock had been stuck for who knows how long. My Dad smiled and said, "Well, it doesn't bother us."

Sounds could also be life-saving:

> When I heard on the news that there were these flash flood warnings, I called my parents [in another state]. At first I couldn't get through and I panicked and thought, Oh God, what if something already happened. They would never even have known.

The home environment also released the usually hidden voices of the deaf. High-pitched, gruff, unmodulated, these deaf voices were unbridled by propriety or custom and became pure expressions of unrestrained anger or laughter. Deaf voices clearly illustrate the contrast between public and private domains. As children, many informants remembered cringing when their parents' voices were heard in public.[7] Informants expressed embarrassment or anger when others mocked their parents' voices. This contrasts with informants' descriptions of voices within the home. Here, deaf voices were familiar and often comforting. Evelyn remembered her mother's lullaby fondly:

> I still remember the way my mother would tuck me in at night. I was just a little girl, and my mother would come in and sit on the edge of my bed and begin to sing to me. [Evelyn started to imitate her mother's voice but she began to choke up.] Her voice was so beautiful. [As she started to cry, Evelyn suddenly stopped and looked at me.] How dare they make fun of our parents' voices! How dare they!

Technology introduced the outside world of sound into the home—through radios, telephones, and televisions. The presence of these telecommunication and media devices in the informants' family homes varied, depending on historical and economic factors. Some older informants remembered none of these devices in their childhood home; all three were routine among most younger informants. Although each piece of equipment differs in its specific use and in its accessibility to the deaf, all three have to do with the family's response to sound and to communication. A number of informants mentioned that their parents bought radios and televisions specifically for them as young children. Whether these devices actually helped these hearing children to talk touches upon a fundamental disagreement within linguistic theory: whether language is essentially innate, or whether interaction and human modeling are essential for language development. The psycholinguist George Miller (1992) takes aim at the attempt to resolve the debate: "The trouble with language acquisition is that the nativists have proved that it's a mystery and the environmentalists have proved that it's impossible" (p. 51). The few informants who remembered no radios, telephones, televisions, or persons who used spoken English within their early childhood homes *still* developed spoken English skills. In all these cases, however, the children had initially developed sign language skills. Since these children did not exist in a language-deprived environment, the apparently spontaneous development of spoken language is more reasonably seen as an indication of transferable language skills from sign language to spoken English rather than an indication of innate language ability.

The question of spoken language development aside, these auditory devices were sources of information for the entire family. Sound-based technologies also acknowledged the hearing child's separate heritage while reinforcing the culturally sanctioned modes of speaking and hearing. For some parents and their children, these devices were unwelcome intrusions, continual reminders of the differences between being hearing and being deaf. Wanda said that she would turn the radio off whenever her parents came to visit: "I guess I just felt too guilty." Some informants described these devices as increasing their interpreting responsibilities or further exasperating their attempts to explain sound:

> It's one thing to try to sign a song with words, but what are you gonna do when it's just music? I mean, there's only so many ways you can go—loud, soft, fast, slow. After a while, you've kinda covered it.

In their portrayals of their parents' inquisitiveness about or responses to sound, informants rarely revealed feelings of loss or longing. However, informants themselves were saddened and occasionally frustrated by how cut off their parents were from sound. Martha told me, "I just keep thinking, my father will never hear my voice. Never know that part of me." A number of informants described how their parents encouraged them to explore sound through music and speech. Dennis reasoned that it was as if "they could hear through me."

Control over the volume and selection of programs on radio and to some degree television placed the hearing child in a unique position of power—although some informants reported that their parents were quite adept at regulating their children's activities:

> I used to keep the radio on after I was supposed to be asleep. My father came in and saw the little red light was on so he made me turn it off. A few nights later, I kept the radio on but this time, I hid it under my blanket. When my father came in, I turned it off. But my father reached down and felt the radio. He could feel it was still warm, so he knew I had been using it. Every night he took the radio away and gave it back to me the next morning.

Surprisingly, however, many women and men supervised themselves:

> The first thing other kids would say is, Oh, boy, you can turn up the radio at your house as loud as you want. But I never did, me or my brother.

Some informants admitted they turned the radio on as loud as they wanted—but rarely when other hearing people were around. Many informants saw self-monitoring as an extremely moral responsibility— not wanting to cheat their parents, who were often perceived as deceived by the Hearing world. These actions also reflected the family's overall response to sounds: they are to be monitored and controlled.

Talking

One of the most frequent reactions when people found out that informants' parents were deaf was "How did you learn to talk?" Along with the term "deaf and dumb," few remarks provoked as much anger and sense of insult among informants. Although I, too, had often brushed off this remark, as a researcher I now pondered the apparent reasonableness of this inquiry. How, in fact, did hearing children of deaf parents learn to talk? And why was this question so offensive?

"Let's talk" is one of the cornerstone phrases of modern life—whether over lunch, around the conference table, or lying in bed with your partner. Learning to talk is a major milestone in a child's development; DeVos (1973) suggests that American mothers emphasize verbal communication as a means of instilling independence in their infants. From talk therapy to talk shows, talking is a significant aspect of information, individual expression, and social connection. The previous sections on silence and sound described how these two features vary in cultural meanings and social use.[8] Although they are valuable forms of communication, neither sound nor silence can be considered a language. Talking is identified as a special form of communication: a language shared among human beings. The major bias of Hearing culture has been to limit "talking" to producing an audible language. This prescribes not only how things are expressed but how they are received.

Informants' overall experiences of talking included a wide range of auditory and sign language systems. Is there a difference in how these differing modes of communication were used? What expectations and interpretations did informants bring to each situation? What does "talking" mean?

When I first tried to develop a matrix of communication modes for informants and their family members, I was overwhelmed with an endlessly complex and confusing layout. Initially, family communication options were broadly characterized: speaking, sign language, or lipreading. These categories expanded to include one-handed or two-handed fingerspelling, American Sign Language, various English-based sign language systems (SEE, Signed English, SimCom), home signs, pantomiming, lipreading with and without voice, as well as spoken and written English. The choice of communication mode often varied between the informant and each parent, between parents, among siblings and parents, and over time.[9] Particular situations often determined the technique chosen. Todd's job as a church interpreter illustrates this diversity of communication:

I'd shift back and forth, sometimes ASL, sometimes mouth the words, sometimes use fingerspelling. You know, a little bit of this, a little bit of that. ["So, how many different kinds of sign would you use?"] Gosh, I don't know, five, six, you know, probably as many different kinds as there were deaf people.

The multiplicity of options and uses occurred not only when one family was compared with another, but often within a single family. In abandoning my attempts to develop a reasonable communication matrix, I realized that the diversity of styles and modes of talking was itself a significant feature among this population.

The assorted ways of talking among hearing children and their deaf parents suggested resourcefulness and flexibility, but they also confounded communication. While recognizing the apparent diversity of sign languages, the editor of *American Annals of the Deaf* (1990) hypothesized that all sign language systems fall into two basic categories: "whether they were based on written or spoken English or whether they had developed outside of the educational setting independent of English" (p. 201). Present data from informants, however, indicate that this is a gross oversimplification. Although many informants were proficient in more than one communication mode, this was not true among all family members, relatives, and family friends. In this broader group, each system was different enough to be unintelligible to those not familiar with it. Communication modes were frequently dyadic, and these separate systems often precluded a holistic interaction—even within individual families. This confusion is pointedly illustrated by one woman's description:

> My father used mostly ASL, but my mother could use ASL or sometimes fingerspelling. My brother didn't know ASL but he could fingerspell. . . . He and I talked, but when he talked to my father he would use, I guess, home signs.

A number of informants evaluated their own or their siblings' abilities to communicate with their parents as insufficient and inadequate. What contributed to this communication quagmire, and how did it affect deaf parents and their families?

In *Life with Two Languages,* Grosjean (1982) describes how the dominant language opposes secondary languages. Although Grosjean generally confines his study to spoken languages, this opposition seems to place sign language consistently at the bottom of the language totem pole—regardless of cultural setting or the particular dominant language. In the United States, sign language has had a long history of educational opposition and denigration. Over the years, educational tactics toward sign language have shifted from acceptance to annihilation to forced assimilation.[10] This history is reflected in informants' descriptions of their family communication systems. Informants in their sixties and seventies reported that ASL had been an acceptable form of talking—among their parents as schoolchildren as well as within their childhood families.[11] This contrasts with the reports of middle-aged and younger informants, who remember their parents' vivid stories of the antagonism toward and oppression of sign language.

Critics have faulted sign language for having a limited vocabulary—particularly with regard to emotions and abstractions. At face value, this assessment reflects a highly ethnocentric bias which judges a language according to how well it matches an idealized hierarchy of language traits (most often one's own). Much of this criticism of ASL is also based on English approximations by non-native speakers unable to grasp the complexity or nuances of the language. Several informants described how they too had dismissed the form of talking used at home:

> I just thought my mother wasn't as smart because she couldn't speak or use English very well. I used to correct her English all the time. It wasn't until I went to an interpreter training program last year that I learned about sign language. I never gave my mother credit for knowing a foreign language, and she passed away two years ago and I never told her [breaks down crying] . . . I just wish I could tell her how beautiful it was.

The attempts to abolish or reform sign language not only promoted secretive and guarded attitudes toward this form of talking, but contributed to the proliferation of diverse and often incompatible com-munication systems—between generations and between family mem-bers.

Despite this long history of linguistic oppression, nearly half of all informants described American Sign Language as their first or primary childhood language.[12] This was true of informants of all ages. While the number of informants who talked in sign is a tribute to the resilience and perseverance of deaf people and sign language, there remains a more problematic picture. Twenty-one informants reported that although their parents' principal language was sign language, they themselves did not know or use sign language as children.[13] Another fifty-six informants reported that although they used sign language, one or more of their siblings did not know or were not fluent in sign language—again, despite sign language being the principal language used by their parents. Two informants offered contrasting explanations for why hearing children of deaf parents did not learn sign language:

> A lot of hearing children of deaf parents that I know don't sign—even though their parents stand around and try to communicate with them. A lot of the kids are like [signs and mouths exaggeratedly, *"I don't want to learn."*] And they're embarrassed and they're angry. They're very angry they have deaf parents. The whole business. And the parents could teach them until they're blue in the face. And the kid is like, "I'm not going to learn."

> I don't believe it when I hear that they [hearing kids] refused to learn sign. I believe that parents teach you from the day you are born. I feel like my Mom did . . . We're talking about communicating—from the day you're born. A child that's only a few months old doesn't decide whether or not he wants to learn sign language. It comes from the parents. And if there's negative feelings about sign language, then maybe we should ask where it's coming from.

Despite their alternate hypotheses, both of these explanations ex-press the insidious stigmatization of certain forms of talking that pervaded the lives of many hearing children and their deaf parents.[14] Fragmented family communication not only affected some informants' ability to talk with their parents, it also strained sibling relationships by creating communication imbalances among them. These family situations parallel those seen in other minority language groups. Ervin-Tripp (1973, 1977), Grosjean (1982), and others emphasize that cultural attitudes, the particular setting, and individual attitudes cause individuals to choose one language over another, rather than the inherent properties of the language itself. True diglossia—which Grosjean (1982) defines as "a situation in which two languages . . . have very precise and distinct functions, so the bilingual speaker has little leeway in deciding which to use"—is felt to be "extremely rare" (p. 130). In the family experiences of many informants, speaking and signing represent just such unalterable choices.

Among informants, "talking" encompassed a diverse and complex system of communication. In response to the question of how they learned to talk, most informants cited various hearing relatives or neighbors or playmates. Only fourteen informants reported needing speech therapy or special classes because of language problems, and many of these felt that their spoken language development could have been resolved without remedial attention:

> Boy, they could see me coming. That deaf and dumb couple's kid. The minute he says one thing wrong, yank him and put him in speech therapy.

Studies by Chomsky (1968), Shore (1989), and others propose an innate schema for language learning. Whether this extends to spoken language is uncertain, and is not answerable within the confines of this study.

Even among the majority of informants who experienced no spoken language problems, the question of how they learned to "talk" was often felt to have negative implications. Some resented the insinuation that they came from an abnormal family:

> Everybody always asks, "How did you learn to talk?" And I would say, Well, I learned to *sign* when I was a few months old. When did you learn to sign?

Another informant was more explicit: "They might as well ask, 'Well, when did you become normal?'" For many men and women, "talking"

was inextricably identified with using spoken English, and this association was often a reminder of a linguistic tyranny that had very
personal family consequences. Albert explained his parents' dilemma:

> I know they thought they were doing it for me. Not teaching me sign
> so I would fit in, so I could talk. But it created a wall between us. It
> pisses me off. How could you do this to your son?

For many of the informants, the question of learning to talk was
ultimately unanswerable: "You know, I really don't know. I know it
happened. But I haven't got a clue how." For most of us who identify
talking as speaking, our recollections reflect a culturally acceptable
schema, a generic process so seemingly natural that few question how
it happened. Ambron (1975) suggests that no one can actually answer
the question of how he or she learned to talk: "None of us has the
faintest recollection of how he learned to speak—perhaps for the very
reason that memories cannot persist in the absence of linguistic tags"
(p. 135). For many of the women and men interviewed, the question
of "talking" was neither obvious nor straightforward. This simple
question often recalled sensitive memories of linguistic oppression,
miscommunication, and insinuations of difference. The inquiry also
reveals a bias that most people are unaware of: Which kind of talking
do you mean?

Bilingual Options

The legacy of stigmatization and repression of sign language clouds a
fundamental issue of talking: What is the difference between speaking
and signing?[15] Grosjean (1982) proposes that because most deaf people never master spoken English, it is only their hearing children who
may be considered truly bilingual. Recent studies of adult hearing
children of deaf parents have examined the linguistic phenomenon of
code-switching[16] in order to determine which language is used in
which situations. Many of these studies have relied primarily on adults
who are professional interpreters—that is, those who are reasonably
fluent in sign language. However, following Ervin-Tripp, Grosjean, and
others, I use bilingualism here to describe the functional *use* of two

languages rather than fluency in two languages. Previous definitions have also excluded those who may have primarily receptive bilingualism, a characteristic common to many children of immigrant parents. Seventeen informants described themselves as having little or no expressive sign language as children, but as able to understand some signing. A functional definition of bilingualism encompasses a broader population of informants who used speaking and some form of signing—regardless of their fluency in either language. As such, at least 122 of the 150 informants could be considered functionally bilingual: using or understanding more than one language within their families.

In the following discussion I do not focus on specific situations of code-switching among informants but instead adopt a symbolic stance: What meanings and feelings does each form of talking invoke in informants? How does this affect the way informants express themselves and hear others? Rodriguez (1982) criticized bilinguals who attributed associations to a language rather than to family ties. Like Sontag, Rodriguez attempts to refute the metaphorical realm. Yet research has repeatedly demonstrated that many bilinguals (as well as second-language learners) associate different emotional characteristics and a different sense of identity with each language—regardless of actual fluency or performance.[17] Differing associations can even occur within a single language. Studies such as those by Tannen (1990) illustrate how men and women bring different expectations to spoken English, and these expectations often determine modes of expression as well as reception.

Among these informants, signing and speaking were often used differently and frequently evoked highly contrasting emotional associations.[18] John characterized his sense of speaking as goal-oriented:

> When I talk, it's like, I've got to get to the point. You know, hurry up, get it out. Get on with it.

This compared to the more processual signing:

> I have a hard time explaining [Deaf] joke-telling to hearing people. In sign language, it's in the telling, like you want to hear the whole story, no matter how long it takes. It doesn't boil down to a punch line.

The contrasts between sign language and spoken English also extended to writing. Stuart described his exasperation with talking to his
mother on the TTY (which is primarily a written form of English
communication):

> And then my mother backspaces every time she wants to correct her
> word and I feel like saying, Okay, I know that's not the word you want
> to use, it doesn't matter! It reminds me of an old comedy skit on a Slow
> Talkers Conference. My mother will take forever to type: Dad . . . is . . .
> And I want to say, Okay, Dad is not feeling well. Hurry up and finish
> the sentence!

Separate usages and settings enhanced the contrasts between the two
languages: speaking was used in public, often for a specific purpose
or to fit in; signing was used conversationally at home and among
friends. Many informants identified speaking as useful for information
gathering, protection, and negotiation. Several informants mentioned
how strange their voice sounded to them. Speech was often characterized as "limiting," "distancing," "formal," and "tight." In contrast,
informants described themselves as using sign informally, for "just
talking." Two signs for "talking" illustrate this difference: to talk as a
hearing person, the right hand moves quickly back and forth from the
mouth; to talk as a deaf person, the arms are relaxed downward while
both hands move—often at a slower pace. Although the particular
style of signing varied among these men and women,[19] when they
signed informants frequently described themselves as feeling more
"intimate," "natural," "expressive," and "comfortable." Even those
informants who did not sign or knew only rudimentary signs attributed
many of the same contrasting associations to signing and to speaking.

During the interviews, the majority of informants spontaneously
signed particular words or phrases—although rarely simultaneously.[20]
These usages generally conformed to informants' historical and emotional associations with each language. The use of signs during the
interview fell into four distinct situations: when informants felt that a
sign expressed the concept better; when they were momentarily unable
to think of the English word; when they were paraphrasing deaf
people; or when they became emotionally unable to speak. Although

additional instances of sign language occurred sporadically during some interviews, my analysis does not indicate identifiable pattern(s) to their uses. Two informants requested that the entire interview be conducted in sign, both initially explaining that they no longer had any opportunities to sign with anyone. One of these, Antonio, told me: *"Through signing, I remember a long time ago. I can feel the memories in my hands."* This sense of signing—as not only an option of expression but one that kinesthetically accessed a realm of nostalgia and memories—permeated many other informants' associations with signing.

The few studies of bilingual hearing children of deaf parents have concentrated on their two languages: spoken English and American Sign Language. Yet sign language is not merely a language of the hands; it involves the entire face and body. Gestures, body postures, and facial expressions can have specific cultural meanings and associations. Restricting the focus to language alone also ignores the previously discussed realms of sound and silence. Although he was not fluent in sign language as a child, Alex's description of talking illustrates the range of options:

> One thing that I notice is that when I communicate with deaf people, which I don't do very often, I'm using my body a lot, my whole body, using my face, using a different voice and I can feel body reactions, I can feel it . . . but in the Hearing world, it's more mental, more verbal, more confined. Not so much physical . . . There's not a lot of affect, no aggression—totally the opposite of the way I've been trained. It's like [here he used his hands to create a box around his mouth]. When I speak, it's like this.

During the interviews, several women and men remarked that they knew I was listening to them because I used appropriate facial and body expressions.

These differing modes of expression and associations with them often affected informants' adult communication as well—both expressively and receptively. Many mentioned feeling somewhat disconnected from the expressiveness that sign language would normally bring when trying to communicate in the Hearing world: "I find it very hard to focus all your information in this space" (pointing to the mouth). Several women and men expressed frustration at communicating in spoken and written English—in the classroom, in work situations, with spouses, or even during their interview: "I don't think you want to interview me, I have such a terrible time talking like that." A number of informants felt that, even as adults, signing remained a better option of expression; through signing, they revealed more of themselves:

> To me, I think it's [signing] the greatest gift. It's not just a talent, it's a gift that I'm fortunate to have deaf parents because I've learned a language that's so expressive. If any person really wanted to know what I was saying and not hear it but see it, this is the language to go to. That's how you get to know me.

Five informants who were or had been in therapy described feeling blocked because they could not express themselves to therapists who knew no sign language. A few younger men and women stated that they had taken some exams in sign language and that this had improved their grades.

Informants provided numerous examples of how their communication with hearing people was misinterpreted because of the wrong cultural cues. Many informants mentioned that prolonged eye contact—crucial in Deaf culture—often made hearing people feel uncomfortable, and several had learned not to use it as much. These men and women similarly reported not feeling heard when other people did not give them "good eye":

> Barbara [his wife] was always talking to me from the other room. And every time, I would go into the room and say, I can't understand a thing you're saying. And she said, "Well, I'll just talk louder." And I said, "No, you don't understand, I need to see you in order to understand what you're saying."

Dorothy explained that one college professor gave her a lower mark during an oral exam because she gestured when she spoke—which he felt indicated that she was uncertain of what she wanted to say. Gwen remembered the time her husband became angry when she asked "Did you see my key?" because he felt she was accusing him. Later she realized she routinely asked questions using the standard ASL question format—arched, furrowed eyebrows—an expression her husband misinterpreted as accusatory and angry. Informants also described how they often perceived another person's emotional state by reading visual cues, facial expressions, and body language. Yet such perceptions risked resentment or misinterpretation.

Alex weighed the advantages and disadvantages of his bilingual upbringing:

> You do have an advantage by being able to read another hearing person's body language . . . and they can feel it, almost like I'm raping them. The world doesn't communicate in the way deaf people do, so if you want to be accepted in the world, you try to be and do like they are—speak like this, don't show too much . . . if you have deaf parents, you often will give more away about you and that's the hard part because it gives others more information and awareness about you. They can see you when you don't want to be seen so obviously. When you've had deaf parents, it's hard, not all environments are safe and you may not want to be seen everywhere you go.

Robert's explanation of the difficulty he had trying to speak and sign at the same time reveals a strong moral commitment as well:

> The big challenge was, for me, to sign and talk at the same time. I could not do it. So help me God, I could not do it. I didn't know how to do it. I decided that if I was going to do that, that I would have to let my mouth run my hands. So that became the primary goal—and *that* was very uncomfortable for me.

Stella explained that she had learned "how to do it," how to alternate between the two languages and cultures:

> Oh, it took me a while, but I finally figured out how to do it. ["Do what?"] Oh, you know, that English and sign are different. I just learned to use them at different times.

Not all these men and women disavowed the spoken word. Almost one-third of all informants expressed a definite preference for spoken language as adults—even though many continued to feel a fondness for sign language. A number of these men and women felt that, whether or not they had used sign as children, spoken English was their natural language as adults. Brian said matter-of-factly:

> Sure I sign. But I'm hearing. I have a hearing wife, hearing kids, hearing friends. I live in a Hearing world.

When groups or cultures with different languages remain in contact, the maintenance or abandonment of a particular language is highly dependent on the status and power of one group compared to the other. Not surprisingly, "language shift has been the prevailing strategy among most immigrant groups in the United States" (Eastman 1990, p. 155). Like most bilinguals, hearing children of deaf parents appear to follow a more transitional pattern of bilingualism in the United States: the gradual adoption of the dominant language.

Bilingual studies have demonstrated that linguistic maintenance depends on functional needs; when these psychosocial factors disappear, children and adults usually revert to monolingualism. This pattern was particularly evident among older informants whose parents were deceased or who had no professional or social contact with deaf people. Most informants, however, continued to use sign language—with their parents, in their professions, or in their social contacts with other deaf people. Informants shared additional reasons for their continued use of sign language. For some, signing and gesturing acknowledged their Deaf heritage and represented the positive side of being "different."

> It's weird, sometimes I'll be talking and all the hearing people are all taken by what I am doing with my hands or my body. ["So, how does that make you feel?"] Oh, I like it. I like the attention. It makes up for all those stares when I was a kid.

Some informants questioned whether sign language could ever be sufficient for those who can hear. Alice told me she never heard her parents say they loved her, and when I asked whether she meant in sign or in voice she responded: "Oh, I knew they loved me, but I never heard the words. I needed to hear the words." Sharon described the effects of her childhood with a sense of humor: "After all that, I want a husband with giant ears so I know I'll be listened to."

Trying to decipher metaphorical or actual meanings with regard to communication processes becomes confounded by the enormous oppression of sign language. These contrasting and competing interpretations of the two languages also reflect the biases of Hearing and Deaf cultures—each of which remains sharply divided on the value of speaking and signing.

Cultures differ in what is affectively arousing. Among many deaf people, American Sign Language remains a central and cherished symbol of their cultural identity. Among their hearing children, however, the use and maintenance of ASL vary greatly. In examining the relationship between culture and language, Pi-Sunyer (1980) asks whether one can truly be Catalan without speaking the language: "If the answer is in the affirmative, what does it mean to be Catalan once language takes a secondary position as a symbol of identity?" (p. 114). To rephrase this question for the informants in this study, What is the relationship between sign language and culture, and how does it affect cultural identity and affiliation?

The lives of these informants suggest three responses to the issue of language and cultural identity. First, the focus on language often ignores nonlinguistic forms of communication. Informants' family experiences included not just specific forms of sign language, but the realms of silence, sound, face, and body. Each of these features not only became a means of communication but also developed into powerful symbols of cultural experience. Second, parity between language and cultural identity presumes homogeneous use and fluency among all members of a cultural group. Not only their hearing children but culturally Deaf people as well vary in their fluency and use of sign language. Yet, whatever their personal history of sign language, the overwhelming majority of informants—even those from oral backgrounds—expressed strong loyalty and support for sign language. Finally, both deaf parents and their hearing children have experienced attitudes of repression toward and even annihilation of sign language. This shared history suggests that although sign language is an important symbol of Deaf culture, it is not the only measure of cultural membership. Oppression, too, contributes an important dimension to cultural solidarity.

Grosjean (1982) describes four types of bilinguals: those who align with one side, with the other, with both, or with neither. Each of these characterizations fit at least some of the men and women interviewed. From language use to cultural affiliation, each represents a certain facet of the experience of being a hearing child of deaf parents. Those who identify themselves as more deaf than hearing:

> If any person really wanted to know what I was saying and not hear it but see it, this is the language to go to. That's how you get to know me.

Those who stress that they are hearing:

> Sure I sign. But I'm hearing. I have a hearing wife, hearing kids, hearing friends. I live in a hearing world.

Those who straddle both worlds:

> Oh, it took me a while, but I finally figured out how to do it. ["Do what?"] Oh, you know, that English and sign are different. I just learned to use them at different times.

And those who feel lost between these two worlds:

> It's like me telling you about a song you never heard before. I can try all sorts of ways, but until you hear it, you can never really know what it's like. Not really. [Shakes his head and signs *"can't"*].

Although each of these four informants reveals a different aspect of bilingualism, it would be a mistake to presume that these categories are exclusive or permanent. Conflicting characterizations appear within the narratives of many individual informants. This fluidity underscores an important heritage among these women and men. Signing, speaking, sound, and silence—whether evaluated positively or negatively—have each contributed to the development of a sense of self, of conscience, and of cultural affiliation.

EIGHT

EICHI

Inside Out or Upside Down

["Do you feel your family life was any different from other people?"] I don't know. [Shakes head.] It's like we were all inside out or upside down from everybody else. [Laughs.] Or maybe we were the ones right side up and they were all topsy-turvy.

For most of us in contemporary Western cultures, the question of identity is invariably linked to our childhood and our families of origin. Yet the conviction that each of us is the creation of a mother, a father, and early family experiences mingles biological and sociological beliefs with particular cultural assumptions. We evaluate ourselves and others against two elusive and culturally dependent yardsticks: the normal family and optimal childhood experiences. Certain roles and interactions are prescribed for both parent and child. Those who deviate from these expectations risk social alienation and psychic dysfunction. In the previous chapter I considered how the informants' family experience of communication—both practically and symbolically—fundamentally differed from the dominant views of the Hearing world. How did these distinctions affect the day-to-day workings of their families? What changes in childhood roles resulted from having deaf parents? And how have these modifications affected informants' adult identities?

The family has been studied as the primary arena of socialization—particularly for children but also for their parents. The family is seen as responsible for the development of the self in the social world. McLain and Weigert (1979) describe the family as both "a deeply subjective personal experience and a powerfully objectivated social emergent" (p. 167). This chapter has three overall goals: (1) to examine distinct features of deaf-parented families; (2) to explore the relationship between certain childhood roles and adult identity; and (3) to consider how the roles of children and of parents differ between Hearing and Deaf cultures.

I begin by examining two related activities that recur throughout most informants' descriptions of their childhood: interpreting and being responsible. In most cases, the scope of these activities intermingled and broadened to include decision making, mediation, advocacy, and generally "taking care of things." The degree and nature of informants' obligations varied from family to family and were often mitigated by the parents' education and income, as well as community support and resources. Yet, despite variation in individual circumstances, almost all informants acknowledged that these activities were typical—if not within their own families, among most other hearing children of deaf parents.

In the remainder of the chapter I examine three recurrent features in the informants' narratives about their families: dependence, boundaries, and reciprocity. Each of these family characteristics often suggests positive or negative outcomes: independence or co-dependence; individualism or enmeshment; validation or lack of recognition. It is difficult to raise these issues without adopting a similarly value-laden framework. Although all of these features have considerable psychological implications for the individual, it is my intention to explore them here not along a continuum from pathological to healthy but within the context of different cultural norms and perspectives.

Interpreting

Whether in a department store or during a church service, it is a sight most people take note of: a small child interpreting for her deaf parent. Interpreting is perhaps the one feature most associated with hearing children of deaf parents. As has been described, actual interpreting responsibilities vary greatly among hearing children of deaf parents.

Yet the focus on who interprets and with what frequency overlooks a more fundamental conceptual issue. Questions such as "Did you interpret for your parents?" or "How often did you interpret?" presume a uniform understanding of the term "interpreting"—one that is defined only as translating from one language to another. Informants' narratives, however, reveal a much broader range of activities that are subsumed under the rubric of "interpreting." What does "interpreting" mean?

Interpreting entails conceptually organizing what is being said as well as putting oneself in the place of the speaker and the listener. G. Herbert Mead (1934) emphasized the dual importance of children's play in learning social roles: the acquisition of specific roles themselves, and the acquisition of the skill to shift roles. Like Mead, Adorno (1950) also focused on taking the role of the other, which he hypothesized was absent in persons fixated at the earlier projective level. Hastorf and Bender (1952) distinguished ethnocentrics as "projectors" and egalitarians as "emphathizers." Adorno found ethnocentric persons deficient in insight (a consistent self-evaluation with an outside criterion). These findings reflect the informants' consistent self-evaluation, which stressed that their family experiences developed and encouraged their ability to empathize with others.

Methods and styles of interpreting evolved within the context of informants' families. In the previous chapter we saw the myriad methods of communication that existed in informants' families: various forms of sign language, speech, lipreading, and pantomime, as well as combinations of these methods. This diversity demonstrates that even on a pragmatic level, the actual languages used in interpreting varied from home to home. Interpreting contexts varied as well. Several informants reported they interpreted only in certain situations: business rather than social, or emergencies rather than casual interactions. Styles of interpreting also varied—from one that is more simultaneous (translating at the same time as someone is speaking or signing) to one that has been humorously labeled "stand-and-pray."[1] Languages, methods, contexts, and styles each color the experience of "interpreting."

When informants were asked to describe their interpreting activities, a number of inconsistencies emerged. Several informants wavered when I asked them whether or not they had interpreted at home. A few felt that interpreting was reserved for those who were fluent in American Sign Language. Informants did not always recognize their use of other forms of communicating (such as lipreading or home signs) as "interpreting." Roberta expressed this disparity:

> Are you kidding? Oh, I couldn't be an interpreter. I never learned all the things, you know, that you have to go through . . . I just did it at home, for my Mom and Dad.

More common than the few informants who underestimated their interpreting experiences were the vast majority of informants for whom interpreting represented a much more diverse range of endeavors than merely translating from one language into another. Most informants readily acknowledged the subjective nature of interpreting. The sign for "vague" is often applied to conversations that are ambiguous and deliberately evasive; this sign was used by several informants to describe how they altered interpreting situations that were embarrassing, confrontational, problematic, or awkward. Whether out of exasperation or clarification, these changes occurred both in sign language and in speech.

Telephone interpreting offered the greatest latitude in manipulating conversations by placing the conversation completely in the hands of the hearing child. Deaf parents often had little experience with the routines and customs of using this distinctly Hearing mechanism— from the dial tone to the particular style of spoken interchange. Without visual cues from either side, both the deaf parent and the hearing person relied on the informant to relay the conversation. Agnes explained that she always made sure to find out everything her parents wanted to say before making any phone calls:

> I didn't want them to think my parents were stupid. One time this [hearing] guy asked me what was taking them so long. He said, "Well, don't they understand what you're saying?"

George remembered how his father wanted him to call up all the garage mechanics in the Yellow Pages in order to compare prices:

> I tried to tell him that there were just too many, but he insisted. So, I sat there and pretended to be talking to someone when it was just the dial tone.

Interpreting opened the door for informants to interject their own opinions:

> These hearing parents with a deaf child came to our house one day. They wanted to find out what my parents thought would be best for their kid, what kind of school they should choose. So, of course, Mom and Dad both said, "Send him to a residential school." And I interpreted the whole thing. But later, I pulled these people aside and said, "You know, it would be a lot better if you sent your kid to an oral school."

How does the interpreting arrangement affect the availability of roles for the parents as well as their children? Are deaf parents able to participate in a broader spectrum of social interaction, or do their children preclude greater participation by assuming certain roles for them?

The professionalization of sign language interpreters dramatizes these issues. A sharp division has occurred between those who argue for a more mechanistic model of interpreting (translating only the literal information) and those who advocate making appropriate cultural adjustments and clarifying when necessary. A more mechanistic approach is thought to provide deaf people with unfiltered interactions with the Hearing world; any attempt at clarification merely sustains the barriers between the Deaf and the Hearing. Most informants who were professional interpreters, however, cited their family experiences as favoring a less rigid and mechanistic approach to interpreting. Informants—whether professional interpreters or not—repeatedly pointed out that many deaf persons lack the English verbal proficiency and Hearing cultural sophistication necessary to participate on a peer level with hearing persons. For most of these informants, years of societal isolation and stigma could not be ignored:

No, of course you shouldn't go in there and take over the whole thing.
That's what they're [professional interpreters] always afraid of. But you
can't always just give the words. Sometimes you've got to explain—to
the hearing people or the deaf people. You can't just assume that if you
say the words or do the signs that everybody understands. Deaf people
and hearing people aren't operating from the same set of experiences.

Like many foreign language interpreters, informants were aware of
the cultural issues as well as the problems of translation. These men
and women became "culture brokers" between the Deaf and the
Hearing. Grosjean (1982) points out this issue among children of
immigrant parents:

Like many children of immigrant parents, BS found herself in the
situation of liaison between her minority language environment and the
majority language community. Her parents and uncle's family turned to
her not only for translations but also for explanations concerning the
language and the culture. She tried to explain why things were the way
they were. (p. 200)

"*Explanation* concerning the language and the culture" is another
indication that language fluency alone is not a sufficient determinant
of cultural boundaries.

Although many informants were secure in their sense of interpreting
as a form of cultural mediation, two aspects of interpreting remained
problematic: the loss of identity (discussed in Chapter 6) and inappropriate situations. Almost all the informants had an interpreting "horror
story"—from their own experiences or from someone they knew.
These episodes ranged from accompanying parents to the doctor's
office to interpreting parents' divorce proceedings to interpreting a
family member's funeral. Informants' examples generally fell into two
(not mutually exclusive) types of inappropriate situations. Sometimes
the informant was too young:

So, there I was. I don't know, I was probably five or six. And the doctor
is saying, "Tell your mother she needs a mastectomy." I didn't know how
to spell it. [Starts to cry.] And I didn't even know what it meant. And
my mother is looking at me like, "What? What did he say?"

At other times, the hearing child was emotionally involved:

> When I found out that they wanted this teenager to interpret for her parents' divorce, I went through the roof. I marched down [to the lawyer's office] and slammed the door open and started screaming, "Are you crazy? Do you have any idea what you are asking that girl to do?" I thought that kind of crap stopped long ago. It's still going on!

These two types of interpreting situations stress different aspects of informants' family experiences. Informants were more likely to assess situations as age-inappropriate in retrospect. Only as adults did most informants learn that their experiences contradicted culturally acceptable standards of childhood. In this regard, hearing children were dependent on others to determine which situations were appropriate:

> Sometimes I think my parents should have known, that they should have looked out for me because I was just a kid—what did I know? But I'm not sure they really could have, I mean who was really looking out for them in their families when they were growing up?

In contrast, informants were acutely aware of circumstances in which they had a personal investment at the time it was happening:

> I didn't want to do it [interpret at her father's funeral], but I had to. For Mamma. There wasn't anybody else. I just kept sobbing and signing, all mixed up, all at the same time. [signs, *"Never again."*] I never want to do anything like that again.

Telling these "horror stories" serves several purposes: admonishing others that these circumstances not be repeated; searching for other solutions; illustrating a person's unique life experiences; and expressing feelings that had been suppressed at the time. Although several informants dismissed these problematic situations as "past history," many continued to use these stories didactically. Indeed, many of these stories surfaced as informants discussed the advice they would give deaf parents. Most informants felt that there was nothing intrinsically wrong with using a child as an interpreter, yet they also conceded that the parent (or other adult) needed to evaluate each situation. Interpreting stories also served to dramatize the unique experience of being a hearing child of deaf parents. Whether the interpretation involved holiday meals or a mother's hysterectomy, these stories are highly specific to hearing children of deaf parents. Informants described how they often resolved interpreting in personally charged situations by suppressing their emotions at the time. Several men and women also commented that their interpreting efforts had not been appreciated at the time. Retelling these stories was emotionally cathartic as well as personally validating for many informants.

Despite their reluctance to interpret in these emotionally charged situations, most informants met their family obligations because they conceded that there were usually no other options. Professional interpreting services were not available during most informants' childhoods. Most hearing neighbors, friends, and professionals did not have sufficiently reliable and detailed language skills to ensure an adequate exchange of information. Family emergencies or crises often accentuated parents' desire for family members rather than outsiders to be involved. Even today, many informants reported that their deaf parents continued to use them rather than professional interpreters in some situations—whether out of habit, concerns with privacy, or simply because the son or daughter was more familiar with the often idiosyncratic communication system used by deaf family members.

Family Responsibilities

During our interview, Diane brought out a drawing she had done in college. The assignment had been to depict herself and her family, and Diane's picture showed a man and a woman in the center of the paper surrounded by a circular wall. All around the outside of the wall were television sets, telephones, musical notes, and a multitude of faceless figures. I presumed the central figures were her parents, and that the wall represented her parents' deafness—but, finding no obvious trace of Diane, I asked her where she was. She pointed to the wall:

> That's supposed to be me—not a solid wall, but like a screen. Keeping things in, keeping things out. That was me. That was my responsibility.

Responsibility. Few themes recurred as prominently in the narratives of these informants:

I learned one thing, that's for sure. I learned to be responsible.

Well, I know I had to be responsible from day one. I'm more responsible than anybody I know.

What were most informants actually responsible for? One obvious responsibility was the realm of sound—ranging from vigilance about environmental noises to interpreting conversations. As has been shown, interpreting did not mean just translating but often included a much broader range of activities such as cultural information, mediation, intervention, and decision making. In Chapter 3 we saw that some informants assumed a role of protection and advocacy on behalf of their parents, including responsibilities of impression management and disavowal of deviance. Many informants gave examples of being responsible by describing how they had to monitor themselves. Playing the stereo or radio was a frequent example. Although the specific limits varied, there was almost always some point beyond which informants did not go. As Regina explained, "It wouldn't have been fair to my parents."

One of my most memorable interviews was with Beth. Beth described how she had gotten pregnant at age 16 and run off with her boyfriend. Within a year after she left home, Beth's parents lost their family home and car as a result of financial mismanagement, and the stress pushed a difficult marriage toward divorce. Beth returned home with baby in tow, filed legal papers to reclaim her parents' possessions, tempered her parents' marital struggles, and held two jobs in order to reverse her family's fortunes. She had just turned 18. I was genuinely overwhelmed and asked her, "Isn't it too much?" Beth looked somewhat surprised. Without a trace of stoicism or bitterness, she smiled. "You just do it."

The imposing nature of informants' family responsibilities can also be seen in counterexamples. A number of informants criticized themselves or their siblings as having been *irresponsible*. Several siblings explained how they avoided the excessive responsibilities that their brothers or sisters accepted or had thrust upon them. Others, like Bill, recognized different times in his life when he felt overwhelmed by his family responsibilities:

> As soon as I turned 18, I moved to [another state] just to get away. Because I didn't know what I wanted to do. Especially all that pressure. After I moved out, every time I went home, they were still asking me questions like, "What do you think about this?" or "Can you do or call for this and that?" So I went and lived away for two years. And then I decided that it wasn't so bad.

And a few removed themselves altogether from their families in order to avoid the burdens of family responsibility:

> I had to move away. I just couldn't take it . . . Yeah, sure, I feel guilty about it. But it was just too much. I couldn't do it. My sister is still there. If it wasn't for her, maybe I would have to do it. God! Sometimes I just don't even want to think about it.

Between those who took on extraordinary family obligations and those who avoided them altogether were the majority of informants who accepted varying degrees of family obligations. Assessing these childhood responsibilities was an emotional and divisive issue for many individual informants as well as among this population as a whole. During the interviews, the mention of childhood responsibilities often provoked an outburst of resentment or immediate disclaimers:

> I hated it! They never should have made me do all those things! I was only a kid.

While another informant observed:

> I had to do a few things for my parents, but so what? It was never any kind of burden.

Several informants heatedly accused other adult hearing children of deaf parents of betraying their parents and blaming their parents' deafness for their own shortcomings. Others told me they felt that some adult hearing children were "in complete denial"—unwilling to acknowledge family difficulties because of their propensity to defend their parents. As informants discussed their childhood responsibilities, two different but highly interrelated contexts emerged: what it means to be a child, and evaluating how certain childhood experiences affected adult life. Both of these situations incorporate a significant struggle for informants: trying to determine the elusive line between cultural relativity and psychic damage.

Carl was explaining why his family responsibilities were of a different magnitude from those of other children. He said there was a difference between a child who had to mow the lawn and a child who was involved in the financing of a house:

> If the lawn doesn't get mowed, well, you just get tall grass. If *I* make a mistake, we lose the house.

Carl conceded that, although burdensome, many of these childhood responsibilities were unavoidable:

> You have to wait until the child is old enough to push the mower, but many times the communication needs force the situation. It forces the young child into premature duties and responsibilities.

The family obligations of these informants contradict prevailing cultural beliefs about the expected roles of children and parents. Their childhood responsibilities appear unmistakably inverted from those within a "normal" family. In the vernacular of current self-help literature, these children appear to have "become the parents." Like Carl, more than half of all informants used popular psychological terms to describe their family obligations: "premature duties," "parentified child," "overly responsible," "a little adult," "a lost childhood."

While all informants acknowledged that there were some responsibilities that should not be given to a child, a number of women and men argued that their own childhood roles were primarily adaptive within a different kind of family. Edward saw the factor of deafness as "creating certain types of situations that wouldn't be there otherwise," rather than the idea that "deafness caused this or caused that." He saw deafness as changing the family dynamics. John said:

> Sure, I had to do things that other kids didn't have to do. It was part of my role. But you do what you have to do in the situation. I don't have any hard feelings about it.

John and Edward endorse a version of their childhood responsibilities as culturally dictated—that is, to be understood within a specific cultural context. A number of informants explained that whatever sense they had as children of being burdened was not that different from the situation of any other child or adolescent. Hannah explained the difference this way:

> Oh sure, you look at what I did and you think, She had to do all that? God, how awful! And, yeah, I guess I felt like that sometimes, but what kid doesn't? But I think the real difference is that the kind of things I had to do weren't normal. Weren't considered normal. No kid goes around talking for their parents. If kids weren't supposed to take out the garbage, then any kid who took out the garbage would be abnormal. They'd have a special support group for kids who took out the garbage.

Informants' families were doubly star-crossed: struggling to live ordinary lives within a dominant culture that not only holds hearing and speaking to be normal but extends its dictates to the shape and functioning of the family. The myth of the normal family is fashioned from beliefs about what children are for, and about the role of parents in creating and socializing their children according to culturally acceptable norms. The child is to be protected, taken care of, nurtured. This is not to suggest that children do not need this support, but rather that the experience and understanding of these activities vary culturally. Practitioners and researchers alike have adhered to a model of the family that is linear, unidirectional, and absolute.[2] Contemporary Western definitions of childhood contrast with cross-cultural studies that reveal widely differing attitudes and beliefs on childhood. One fundamental difference with regard to socialization theories is that childhood is *not* universally regarded as the most significant period of an individual's formation (Takanishi 1978; Korbin 1981; Wagner 1983). A second major difference is the contemporary Western emphasis on individual achievement—a cultural norm that stands in stark contrast to many other family systems.

Culturally defined roles of children complement culturally defined roles of parents. Informants often pointed out their parents' struggle with roles that were defined within a Hearing context. One woman pointed out how difficult it must have been for any deaf parent to ask his child for assistance:

> So, after a whole lifetime of not having their own parents be there for them, sending them off, not able to talk with them. Imagine what it must feel like. Instead of turning everything around and doing everything you can to make up for what your own parents didn't do for you, you end up having to get your own children do things for you. Look at it from their point of view. They must feel really uncomfortable or ashamed to have to ask their child to do some of those things.

Others reiterated that their parents were well aware of their socially disparaged status, and often put the presumption of adult-identified roles into perspective. Ellen explained:

> One time when I was a teenager I started telling my parents something. They turned to me and said [signs, *"Do you think just because we're deaf that you're going to take control and run our lives? No way! Yes, you can hear, yes you help interpret, but remember: You're our child, we're your parents!"*]

Although functional within a culturally different family, these family roles also reflect the hegemony of the dominant culture. Deaf people are devalued and given a particular status: if you cannot speak or hear, you must be helped by those who can. Hearing children inevitably assumed roles denied to their parents. Outsiders to the family frequently reinforced the hearing child's sense of responsibility and implicitly superior status. Eileen resented the fact that her hearing uncle constantly checked up on her family to make sure her parents were raising their children properly. Greg gave an example of how blatant the presumption was that to be a parent, you must be hearing:

> I got a traffic ticket and had to go to court. One of my parents had to go with me. So my mother was going to go this first time. We got to court, and when I got into court, my name came up on the docket, the judge starts talking, I start [signs *"interpreting"*]. The judge says, "What are you doing?" "I'm interpreting for my mother." "Why?" "She's deaf." "Oh." He thinks for a minute, says, "No." At first I thought he was going to say No, I couldn't interpret. But he says, "No, we can't accept your mother as a legal guardian. She's deaf."

LeVine (1989) suggests that research assumptions about socialization and child development parallel earlier evolutionist thinking. He criticizes not only those models that are based on dominant cultural groups, but models that implicitly represent "an ideal, an optimum development as a species: parental involvement, nutrition, health care, cognitive stimulation, domestic facilities, and an overall sense of emotional and social stability" (p. 51). Such perspectives on socialization may interpret deviations from these patterns as necessarily negative and inadequate deprivations—promoting an insidious form of ethnocentricity.

Informants' adult evaluations of their childhood responsibilities— whether positive or negative—often contrasted with their childhood sense of ordinariness about their families. A number of informants described a shift from perceptions of their childhoods as normal to unavoidable recognition that, in fact, their experiences were not normal. Thelma explained this change:

> It took me a long time to realize my parents were abnormal, I mean we hearing people were normal. Deaf people were abnormal. Took me a long time to realize that. ["How did that happen?"] I guess when I started going to school. Because the people that—we lived across the street from this woman whose daughter was my mother's best friend. She was deaf also. Everybody in their family could sign, okay. And their [signs *"mother"* and *"father"*] their friends signed. So it was just normal. But once I got into school and started meeting girlfriends, going over to their house, I'm like, everybody talks here! I didn't need to sign to them. So, it was like, out of the norm.

Although incidents of cultural conflict occurred throughout childhood, they were particularly salient as the informants grew toward adulthood. As they grew older, informants embraced a growing contradiction: they were hearing people within a Deaf culture. Which values should they embrace? To whom did they owe their allegiance?

Function or Dysfunction

Learning to be responsible and having broader life experiences were two of the most frequent responses given when informants were asked how their childhoods affected them as adults. Many informants saw these outcomes as demonstrating that deaf parents can raise children as well if not better than most parents:

["So, how does all this affect you now?"] Getting exposed to so much more of life than most kids. I learned things. Banking, life insurance, hospitals, all sorts of stuff.

Others argued that, even if traditional childhood roles were compromised, these responsibilities better prepared them for adulthood:

Sure it was different! But I didn't have a choice. Nobody asked me if I wanted deaf parents. Nobody asked them if they wanted to be deaf, either. That's just what our lives were like. We just did what we had to do . . . So maybe I did miss out on some things as a kid. But I got a head start on being an adult.

Several men and women, however, felt they had been crushed by their family responsibilities and by a family system that dissipated their childhoods:

When you are a child—six or seven years old—you can't talk to them like an adult, tell them that what they are asking for is too much or is frustrating. You don't have the sensibility or maybe the vocabulary to express it. It's always: You have to do it . . . When things would go wrong sometimes, I had a little fantasy. I wanted to crawl into my mother's lap and have her take care of me. But that never happened. Never.

Differing assessments of the eventual outcomes of their childhood responsibilities became more contentious as informants considered the long-term effects of their family system as a whole. A number of informants' narratives encompassed a prevailing family ethos of interdependence, uncertain boundaries, and unmet needs. Such family dynamics appear to conform to patterns and characteristics described in countless popular treatises on dysfunctional families. The majority of informants were well aware of the potential for branding their families and their childhoods as "dysfunctional." Informants' responses to the question of family function or dysfunction often exploded in a highly combative struggle—a fiercely moral determination of one's upbringing. Douglas (1970) emphasizes that in contemporary

Western society, moral categories are polarized and interdependent: good is defined by *not* evil, moral by immoral. I will explore some of the roots of this dichotomization in Chapter 10.

Have some of these informants fallen prey to a dominant culture that interprets any difference from child-centered nuclear families as deviant? Or are others are so embedded and invested in their family context that they are unable to perceive its inherent dangers? Although either of these perspectives is possible for individual informants, these are ultimately unanswerable questions. It is impossible to strip the actual childhood experiences of these informants from sociocultural interpretations—whether from the Hearing culture or from the Deaf culture. What is possible, however, is to reiterate how these interpretations often reflect cultural, not empirical, stances. Without an understanding of the comparative values and meanings of Hearing and Deaf cultures, it is impossible to recognize how these values conflict and how they affect the personal life of each informant.

Independence, Dependence, and Interdependence

Few ideas are as central to or as emblematic of American life as independence. From studies of earliest childhood to essays on our national character, we consider how independence is engendered in infants and whether we still have it as adults. As we age and weather the calamities of life, a critical measure of our self-worth is whether or not we remain "independent." It is no surprise, then, that terms like "dependence" and "co-dependence" run contrary to normative American values. Issues of independence and dependence are encountered throughout many of these narratives. Ella nodded as she told me that issues of dependence were a trademark of children of parents with disabilities:

> It's a dependency thing. Absolutely! The reality is that one feels more attached or needed. It's one of the things that being the child of handicapped parents is. I remember seeing this two-year-old child who was telling her [deaf] mother that something was going on. She was so tuned in. She was so alert. Most two-year-olds aren't that alert. I've taught early childhood and I never saw that. What a great thing! I mean, we are all

of us more aware, more seeing, more conscious in ways that lots of children are not. I looked down and I thought, God, there I am. I'm only two, I can't possibly know everything that's going on, but they depend on me, and I do what I can.

Many informants told me they had dealt with being co-dependent or were currently "working on my co-dependence." For several informants, co-dependence was limited to their relationship with their parents; others extended it to their spouses and friends as well. Although the majority of these men and women stressed how independent their parents were, nearly one-third of all informants concluded that their upbringing resulted in their being "co-dependent." How can these contradictory family outcomes be explained?

Informants evaluated their own independence and that of their deaf parents against different cultural standards—those of the Hearing and those of the Deaf. Although independence is valued among the Deaf, it takes on a different shape in the context of the Hearing world. Independence becomes equated with a lack of external assistance and "core American values [of] competitiveness, individualism, and social mobility" (Becker 1980, p. 37). Deaf peddlers are generally scorned within the Deaf community precisely because they perpetuate the sense of deaf people as "helpless and broken"—not so much among deaf people but, more important, among hearing people.[3] Informants frequently asserted their mothers' and fathers' independence—even though their parents may have used interpreters or compensated in other ways. Informants often saw their parents' dependence as encouraged by the Hearing world; many informants distinguished between those situations in which assistance was genuinely needed and those situations which, as Robert put it, his parents "did just out of habit." Determining "independence" often corresponded to a culturally determined hierarchy of behaviors. Certain behaviors are judged to be more independent than others: to use a crutch is more independent than to use a person to lean on; to use a white cane more independent than to ask a person to help you across the street. These examples also indicate that independence is frequently synonymous with *non-human* assistance.

Deaf people reflect the particularly paradoxical attitude toward independence among the American disabled community. The individual and collective histories of many persons with disabilities range from being viewed as helpless dependents to repeatedly affirming their independence (Zola 1982). Many of these people have had to reassess the autonomous American version of independence and question its applicability to their lives. How much help is too much? Does it matter whether the assistive device is a pair of eyeglasses or a motorized wheelchair? If I employ an attendant, am I dependent on my attendant or is he dependent on me? The disabled civil rights movement has reframed the parameters of independence from excluding all signs of external support to a sense of control over one's destiny.

In addition to qualifying the measures of independence, informants' narratives take the issue of independence a step further—by proposing that interdependence is at least as valuable as independence. Tom explained that being dependent on someone was not necessarily bad, but it was a matter of extremes:

> Oh, you know, there are people who don't want to depend on anyone to save their life. And then there are people who depend on somebody whether they need to or not.

A dominant cultural emphasis on individual autonomy and achievement may lead to feelings of loneliness and alienation, a dynamic often countered by group identification with other adults with similar backgrounds. Within the peer-based Deaf community, which relies on its own members for information as well as normative standards, interdependence is a vital and socially important behavior. Their emphasis on the group rather than on the individual underscores a critical difference in how independence and dependence are perceived. Interdependence is seen not as a negation of independence but as a means of achieving it. The contrast in standards can be seen in Ray's description of his parents:

> My wife always gets on me about my parents. You know, she says I should just let them take care of things themselves. She says, "You're just keeping them dependent on you." But they only ask me when they need my help. They're both proud. They're both real independent.

Although the discussion thus far proposes differing cultural perspectives on independence and interdependence, there remains the issue of co-dependence. As used by these informants, co-dependence referred to a pattern of behavior that stressed two aspects: being depended upon by others and lack of volition. Rhonda was quick to assume this label:

> Definitely! I am definitely co-dependent. With my husband, my kids. It's my whole way of life. I learned it since I was a kid. It's how I am. I don't know if I can ever change it.

Although some forms of co-dependence have profoundly crippling implications, I focus here on its symbolic and existential dimensions: What do informants mean when they use this term to describe their lives? Why were so many women and men willing to accept this particular negative outcome despite their generally loyal and protective attitudes toward their parents? And does this concept—popularized within Hearing culture—apply equally within Deaf culture?

Most informants were reluctant to criticize their parents "because, after all, they didn't choose to be deaf." Yet the terminology and conceptual framework of "co-dependence" provided a socially recognizable way of talking about the dynamics of their families, which had often been outside most hearing people's experiences:

> And Bob [a friend] and I were both talking about our families and being co-dependent. And he said he felt like he finally understood what it was like for me.

Other informants told me how frequently outsiders labeled their family system as co-dependent:

> One time I was telling this friend about having to interpret for my parents, she said, "Oh, you're co-dependent!"

The risk of stigmatizing their parents was countered by a sense of social inclusion. A number of informants recounted how parallel their own family situations were to others from co-dependent families. Maria gave this description of a support group for co-dependents:

And after I finished explaining about myself and my family and stuff, everybody understood . . . They all said it was just like their family. That it didn't matter that my folks were deaf. We were all co-dependent.

Many informants who acknowledged issues of co-dependence felt that it was only human nature, often qualifying the extent of their co-dependence:

Oh, I know, nobody's supposed to depend on anybody because we're All-American. Well, that's bullshit.

Robert jokingly said that he thought all parent-child relationships were co-dependent, and by this measure "everyone is in a co-dependent relationship because everybody has parents."

Talking about co-dependence also gave informants an opportunity to advocate ways of changing these family systems. Although many informants dismissed co-dependent traits within their own families, most men and women felt it was a term that fit some deaf parent/hearing child families. Many informants underscored that deaf people were encouraged to be dependent—by their families of origin, by the schools, by society. Gary said:

Yeah, it was a perfect fit. They were taught to be dependent, and I was the one they depended on.

The lack of volition was a salient feature of co-dependence because it suggested the need for options as well as the inevitable recognition that often there were no better options.

For several informants, being co-dependent was the unwaveringly negative outcome of their childhood experiences, one that was not mitigated by cultural relativism or opportunities for social discourse or advocacy. These informants used co-dependence to describe a childhood of deprivation and a lifetime of caregiving. Other informants were less concerned about co-dependence in their childhood than about its continued presence in their adult life. They felt that their co-dependent adult relationships were a direct outcome of their relationship with their parents. Tanya's sense of exasperation at having to take care of others is commingled with her longing for others to take care of her:

Yes, I mean, nobody has taken care of me all my life. I mean, now my husband has a physical disability and obviously he has to be taken care of.

The question of co-dependence is not only a matter of different cultural definitions and attitudes toward dependence. Co-dependence is also based on a particular construction of socialization. Kessen (1979) responds to the presumption that a child is "a free-standing isolable being who moves through development as a self-contained and complete individual." He suggests that in preferring the model of individualism, "we have never taken fully seriously the notion that development is, in large measure, a social construction, the child a modulated and modulating component in a shifting network of influences" (p. 819). Cultural attitudes that envision socialization as a direct result of individual (usually parental) responsibility may also contribute to a need to assign blame in those cases which are felt to be unsuccessful.

Boundaries

A second aspect of informants' family systems has to do with boundaries. Establishing boundaries is considered a crucial part of the developmental process of separation and individuation that every child must go through in order to form his own distinct identity (Bowlby 1969; Mahler 1975; Stern 1985). A lack of boundaries implies a lack of identity. The narratives of many informants are replete with situations in which family relationships appear fluid and often without boundaries. Several informants described feelings of invasiveness, others a lack of privacy. A few openly admitted: "I have no boundaries."

Some of these boundary issues relate to the mismatch between Deaf and Hearing cultural roles. When informants assumed family responsibilities that contradicted culturally accepted roles for children, boundary lines indeed became confused. This sense of diffusion was compounded by many informants' interpreting responsibilities, which broadened from merely translating to include much more diverse forms of cultural mediation:

> The problem, I think, that lots of us have is that we play so many different roles. That when we finally get to adulthood we don't know which one we're supposed to take on, which one is supposed to be real.

Although some informants recognized this paradigm shift only in retrospect, in many cases the disjunction between Deaf and Hearing cultural norms was understood precisely because informants were cultural mediators and aware of the different cultural standards. Very often, however, the norms were decided in favor of the dominant Hearing culture:

> Yeah, all the time, I used to think, well, we do it this way in my family, but everybody else does it different. So, we must be doing it wrong. We've got to do it their way.

Regarding fixed boundaries as a goal of identity also reflects a cultural bias of individualism and autonomy and runs contrary to many Deaf ideals of interdependence and community. Although individual distinction is important in the Deaf community, it occurs within the community—not apart from it.

Apparent boundary transgressions can also be understood as intrinsic features of Deaf culture. Particular behaviors reflect the importance of visual information and contact as well as the frequent lack of other options. These narratives are full of examples that suggest different rules of privacy and intimacy:

> Every time I had to go to the bathroom, I had to let everyone know. Otherwise my Mom or Dad'd be yelling for me and what was I supposed to do? Jump off the toilet and run down the stairs?

Another informant:

> One time this friend in high school came over and she asked me why I didn't close my [bedroom] door. I told her it didn't do any good to close the door because my parents would have to open it anyway in order to ask me if they could come in. And she said, "Well, why don't they just knock, and then you can answer the door?" And I said, "Yeah, and if I don't answer does that mean I don't want them to come in or that I'm dead?"

A different sense of boundaries is also created by a visually-oriented communication system—whether sign language or lipreading—in which speakers are spatially closer. Gerald told me that one friend found his family interactions "too intense, like you're on top of each other all the time." The contrast can also be seen in many informants' sense of auditory communication as distancing:

> I told my husband, I can't hear you when you're not in front of me. I have to see you.

Finally, most members of local Deaf communities are known to one another. There is often little sense of anonymity or separateness. One woman mentioned how much the experience of deafness was informed by a home community in which everyone knew her parents. When she moved to another city, "none of those deaf people knew my parents, no one knew me."

Reciprocity

A third dimension of these childhood responsibilities concerns reciprocity. Here, informants weighed their family responsibilities against some sense of recognition or appreciation for their efforts:

> It's kind of what we felt as kids, it's part of our job to take care of things, to do things. And I think people kind of take it for granted and that appreciation is never given. It was just part of our job. If you can hear, it's your responsibility. I mean, after all, your parents are *deaf!*

Other informants remembered their parents' continual efforts to demonstrate their appreciation. Laura compared her father with her mother:

> My Dad! He is always so polite when he asks me to make a phone call. I don't mind doing it at all, but every time [signs: *"If you're not busy, would you please make a phone call?"*] But my mother, she just barges in and starts handing me stuff and telling me what she needs. I think maybe she's thanked me once.

Situations of responsibility provided a paradoxical status of both importance and burden. Although Louise resented her responsibilities, her narrative shows that these duties also provided her with a certain distinction:

> Yeah, I always felt like, just a babysitter, go clean the house, take care of the kids . . . I'd go and interpret once in a while and make a lot of damned phone calls. I just hated it. Never even had a phone until we were fourteen. Knocking on the neighbors' doors, using the school's phone . . . I don't know, I think at the time I really didn't mind it. That attention was kind of nice. Oh, I get to go to the neighbors and use the phone. I liked that attention, sort of, but then it's like, God, after getting to be a teenager, this is getting old! I really hate this!

For other informants, the burdens of interpreting were countered by having a greater degree of visibility and control when assuming this pivotal family role.

Informants not only talked about appreciation for specific childhood and adult duties; a number of informants expressed anger or sadness that their overall situation was not acknowledged—by hearing people and sometimes by their own parents. As Ruth explained, it was particularly difficult when her own father was unaware of her situation:

> Dad and I watched *Love Is Never Silent*[4] . . . There were so many things in that movie that were so true. I cried several times in that movie. But later on all my Dad could say was, "It really wasn't like that when you were growing up. We gave you a good home, bought you things, not like what that girl had. And we didn't live in the city." He was only looking at all the physical and material things in the movie. He didn't get it.

Al felt that his parents' unfamiliarity with the Hearing world made it impossible for them to appreciate fully all that was involved when he did something. Other informants pointed out that their parents assumed that "because you can hear, it's just easier," and several informants referred to a standard phrase among many deaf people: "Hearing people know everything." Donna remembered confronting her family about their apparent lack of awareness:

I was back home with my family [deaf parents and deaf siblings]. And I finally said [signs and talks: *"You know, not easy me one hearing! Not easy life!"*] And they all just looked at me and they said, "We know." That just blew me away that I couldn't say anything more. Why didn't I say, You know! What! You know it's been hard on me all my life! And here I was thinking, You don't know this, and you know! And I didn't know for such a long time. I didn't know. Why didn't they tell me?

The reaction of Donna's family was repeated in a number of other informants' narratives, suggesting that apparent hardships and life struggles may be viewed more routinely within Deaf culture. These differing perspectives are reminiscent of the way many deaf parents and hearing grandparents differed in their views on the origins of deafness: as incidental or as a calamity. The sense of struggle and resilience could also be shared by both deaf parents and their hearing children. Tom remembered one time when he was angry with his mother for asking him to interpret and she responded:

[Signs: *"I know, hard on you. Hard on me too. Hard on both of us. Not like hearing people. They have an easier life."*]

Sharing their parents' perspectives, history, and language was often given as a positive outcome of informants' family experiences. More than half of all these women and men mentioned that they felt as if their parents gave them "the gift of Deaf culture" in exchange for their childhood efforts.

In exploring the family roles and responsibilities of these informants as children, as well as the kinds of bonds within informants' families that were often recreated as adults, we have seen a fluctuating mosaic of perspectives—from children who are now adults, from Deaf who are now Hearing. Their conflict and disjunction reveal some of the differing sociocultural beliefs about children and about adult identities: A Hearing culture whose nuclear, child-centered families rely on defined roles, a hierarchical structure, and, at times, an obsession with individualism. A Deaf culture in which the family reflects a community that is peer-based and interdependent, and whose goals are to provide support and communication to other Deaf people while countering the oppression of those who speak and hear. Two cultures whose communication methods appear to distance or to enmesh.

Ogbu (1981) describes the Western model of optimal human development as having three fundamental assumptions: (1) the origins of human competence lie in early childhood and intrafamilial relationships; (2) the nature of human competencies can be studied through a micro-analysis of the child's early experiences; and (3) a child's successful socialization will lead to success in school and as an adult. Pointing out the failure of increasingly earlier intervention programs, Ogbu rejects this white middle-class model as insensitive to cross-cultural diversity and as one which presumes that only particular competencies are in fact worthwhile: "In general it can be said that researchers have not yet reached the point of clearly delineating the unique competencies of minority groups and how such competencies are acquired" (p. 417).

The sense of different competencies or standards does not negate the pain and struggle that a number of informants have shared with me. I do not dismiss their accounts or interpretations of pathology— whether these originated within the Hearing culture, the Deaf culture, or the conflict between them. My intention in this chapter has been to suggest cultural interpretations for some of these central life experiences—not only from my own perspective but from that of this broad range of informants as reflected in their narratives. Often separated from other adults like themselves, these informants struggled to make sense of family experiences that frequently bore the brunt of economic oppression and social stigmatization. Their struggle is epitomized by the repeated question: "What was the deafness, and what wasn't?"

Most of these informants searched for suitable explanations of their family experiences. Both "culture" and "dysfunction" have escaped the confines of the professionals and become part of the vernacular. Freed from the domains of anthropologists and psychologists, these terms have also taken on symbolic meaning. As a group, informants alternately used "culture" and "dysfunction" to express their childhood experiences—whether to vindicate or to vilify, but most important, to explain. Their explanations shifted according to differing cultural paradigms as well as their particular family experiences. Each informant's words provide not only views of two different worlds, but a glimpse into the heart and soul of that individual. The danger of cultural generalizations is that they ignore the exceptional experience of the individual, who is both a part of and apart from that broad schema called culture. The locus of each informant's perspectives can lie anywhere between these two dynamic cultural paradigms, creating an extraordinary but frustrating vision. I can still picture Alan as he described his struggles to make himself heard among the Hearing and the Deaf:

> Wrong word! You're using the wrong word! [signs, *"Wrong, that's not the right sign."*] That's all I heard from people. Well, maybe I was using the wrong word, but when will they ever hear what I want to say?

The Heritage of Difference

You know, none of us are nothing but the same underneath. I know it. I know it 'cause of my folks. It just takes some people longer to figure it out.

Sameness and difference are continuously negotiated. Cultural groups evaluate certain characteristics positively or negatively—whether skin color or religious beliefs or ethnic origins. Rosaldo (1988) observes: "Culture . . . is defined by difference. Difference both makes culture visible to observers and makes it relatively easy to separate nature from nurture. Cultural similarities could be biologically based, but differences require cultural explanation" (p. 78). In American culture there is an emphasis on conformity, but also a need for distinction. This pull between homogeneity and individualism creates a major cultural tension. What place and function does difference have in American society? Can difference be disencumbered from feelings of stigma and inferiority? Or does difference ultimately provide a necessary psychological, social, and cultural dynamic?

Almost all of the men and women interviewed spontaneously brought up the subject of feeling different—many as children, others as teenagers. Several informants felt different even as adults. From whom were they different? "Other kids." "My parents." "My family." "Hearing people." "Deaf people." "Everyone." Only a handful of men and women said they never felt different—or at least "no different than all kids feel at some time or another." As was typical of most informants, Arlene's sense of being different was often negative and ostracizing:

Oh yeah, I felt different. I felt like, it's awful to say this but, Why me Lord? I felt at times like I was some kind of creep or something because I had deaf parents. There's nothing wrong with having deaf parents, but it's just that they were different from everybody else's parents. My mother couldn't be a homeroom mother. She couldn't talk with the other mothers or call them up and say, Oh, what are we going to do about this or that. She couldn't do that. Little things like that. Then, when there were these parent-teacher conferences, even in the first or second grade I had to go into the conference room with my parents. The other kids all had to stay out of the room when their parents talked with the teacher, but I had to go in there and interpret my own progress and stuff. I felt real uncomfortable about that.

Arlene's narrative touches on three recurrent aspects of difference within informants' lives: (1) deafness itself; (2) roles within the family; and (3) the feelings and consequences of being different. As explored in Chapter 7, the major distinction of deafness is its effect on communication. The informants' families represent a continuum of parental hearing losses and communication systems. In addition to whatever differences deafness contributed to each parent's personal, educational, and social development, it also created distinctions between deaf parent and hearing child. Chapter 8 focused on a second source of difference: roles within the family. The typical deaf parent/hearing child family challenges traditional assumptions about family members' roles and how "normal" families function.

What are the consequences of being different in American culture? Whatever its physical, moral, or tribal origins, how does a sense of difference affect an individual's development and sense of self? This chapter is a collection of perspectives on difference: how it is constructed, experienced, and responded to. As adults, how do these informants—those whose lives are so familiar with a difference that centers on deafness—respond to other types of difference?

Shame and Stigma

Much of this chapter concerns the negative aspects of being different. This bias is perhaps common sense to most people. Feelings of embarrassment, shame, and stigma would appear to be routine among hearing children of deaf parents.[1] Indeed, informants remembered many experiences of difference as negative and volunteered incidents ranging from the sounds their parents made, the use of signs, and just having parents who were overtly different from other parents. It is important to recognize, however, that positive responses and outcomes of being different were also expressed by these men and women. Informants and their parents often found ways not only to counter culturally stigmatized differences but to develop pride in themselves and their Deaf culture. Nevertheless, these adaptive and transcendent responses were frequently overshadowed by the predominantly negative experience of difference—not as intrinsic personal failures but as evidence of broader social and cultural constructs.

In his seminal work on stigma, Goffman (1963) defined stigma not by a particular external or internal mark but by the negative attribution made within a social context.[2] He emphasized that although the potential for stigma is universal, the perceptions and specifics of stigma are very much culturally determined. Goffman's theoretical framework has given rise to numerous studies which have examined specific types of stigmatized conditions, including the construction and management of stigma as well as interactions with those who are not similarly stigmatized. Goffman attempted to underscore the relative and quixotic nature of stigma by asserting that all of us have the capacity to play the role of the normal or the stigmatized; it is only social situations that determine which role is more easily played out.[3] Yet Goffman's presumption that "the stigmatized and the normal have the same mental make-up" slights those with lifelong conditions. A congenital disability or condition is often an integral and shaping variable in an individual's life. This life course is even more notable among Deaf people. Differences are readily observable when comparing someone who is a lifelong deaf person with someone who becomes deafened as an adult. Deafened adults share the language and culture of the Hearing majority, and rarely become active participants in the Deaf community.

Hearing children of deaf parents present a unique paradigm with regard to stigma: the parents belong to a stigmatizable group while the children themselves appear "normal." Unlike children of ethnic or racial minorities, hearing children do not overtly share their parents' condition. Barbarin (1986) proposes a model for examining the family experience of those with a stigmatized family member:

> The challenge in understanding family dynamics in relation to stigma arises from the need to account for the numerous individual, group, and system factors that make for diversity in family functioning . . . Families are embedded within a particular social and historical context, are shaped in response to a particular set of cultural norms and demands, and are heavily influenced by the unique personalities of their members. (p. 164)

Although he did not mention hearing children of deaf parents, Goffman described two dimensions of stigma that are useful in discussing these informants' experiences: socialization in an alien environment and "courtesy stigma."

An Alien Environment

Goffman proposed four different learning patterns of those who are stigmatized.[4] These patterns depend upon the sequence and interplay of learning the standards of being normal and learning the consequences of being stigmatized. Hearing children of deaf parents illustrate Goffman's least discussed socialization path: "those who are initially socialized in an alien community . . . and who then must learn a second way of being that is felt by those around them to be the real and valid one" (1963, p. 35).

Stigma is an interactive, dialectical process. It depends not only on particular cultural values but also on interaction and evaluation. It is within the public arena that certain marks and behaviors are identified as different and evaluated as negative. For example, informants routinely cited the first day of school as a time of realization. Bob remembered this scene:

> My first day of school my mother came with me. I don't remember really thinking about my parents being different before then. When I got to the schoolyard I just remember seeing all these mothers who were making these strange movements with their mouths [mimics exaggerated mouth movements.] And when my mother signed to me, everyone stared

at her. And then at me. I didn't understand what I was doing there. These people aren't like us. I don't belong here!

In Bob's story, it is the hearing mothers who are strange. Yet, because he and his mother are unique in this community, it is they who are different. In contrast, those few informants who grew up in communities with a visible Deaf population generally reported less overt public stigma.

Jean's description was typical of many childhood memories of being watched and stared at:

> I remember being with my family at McDonald's. We were all just [pantomimes signing and talking]. We'd be sitting at this table and there would be a row of tables all around us—all empty. All the other tables were full. And everyone was looking at this one table. Our table. Everybody is staring at us like we're putting on some kind of show. I felt like we were in a fishbowl!

Jean's perceptions raise the question of why outsider curiosity was necessarily perceived as negative. Langer and colleagues (1976) suggest that it is the novel that promotes outsider interest rather than an intent to stigmatize. Yet informants often contradicted this benign interpretation. Strangers' interest in their parents' deafness often *was* paternalistic and stigmatizing:

> People would stare at us or come up to us on the street and ask me, "What's wrong with your Mamma and Daddy? Why are you moving your hands like that?" Total strangers would come up and ask, "How did your Mommy and Daddy become deaf and dumb?" And when I told them, then they always shook their heads. "Oh, that's too bad."

Strangers' choice of words, such as "deaf and dumb," as well as their reactions of pity or sadness promoted a negative association with outsider interest. This perception was reinforced when informants overheard comments that were overtly hostile or cruel:

> How many times were we sitting with our families and everybody thinks we're deaf. And we can hear what the hearing people are saying. All those laughs they're making. They're saying deaf people're dumb or creepy or they're thieves. They think you're deaf too, but you can hear this. So, what are you supposed to do?

Informants recalled trying to sustain their intrinsic sense of normalcy against those views imposed by others. Linda and Tom both remembered their struggles to sort out family and societal versions of normalcy:

[Linda:] Growing up, I was teased a lot. Kids made fun of how Mom talked. They made fun of her expressions. And, you know, it was hard to separate it out. But in my home, that's my Mom. That's her way. That's what we do. They use all these expressions, they make these noises which is their very own voice.

[Tom:] Sometimes I was ashamed. When I was in a restaurant with my family, hearing people would stare at us. People would stare at us. I turned around and looked at them. "What the fuck you looking at? Stop looking at me, mother-fuckers!" Sometimes they just hit my chord. My mother and father were fine. What were those people looking at? I don't know those people. What do they want?

Overhearing conversations coupled with the ability to speak prompted many hearing children to respond.[5] Stigma management and disavowal on behalf of deaf family members or on behalf of oneself were often intertwined, as Ray's description suggests:

I can remember being on buses where I wouldn't talk. I would be sitting there with my sister and her friends and they'd be all animated and signing. I would hear the people on the bus going, "Isn't that sad, it's so sad. They really shouldn't be out in public." So as we were getting off the bus I would say, "Yeah, it's really sad that you're out in public too!" People would just drop their eye teeth. I wouldn't say anything until I walked by them. Then I let 'em have it.

Informants' reactions and responses varied according to a constellation of individual, family, and community factors. Ralph grew up in a town in which the state school for the deaf was located; there the Deaf community was large and visible:

I never really overheard people making fun of my parents. I never felt that my parents were ever ridiculed. Never. I never felt defensive. They could defend themselves very well. I never had to deal with that . . . It was never really an issue. The kids, my friends knew my parents were deaf. There were a lot of deaf people in our town. People had no problem with it. Occasionally, some stranger would refer to my parents as being "deaf and dumb." That will always drive me up the wall. It still drives me crazy.

Donna pointed out that assuming the role of protector frequently occurred without her parents' knowledge:

No, of course I didn't tell them. It would just have hurt them. What for? They've been hurt enough.

Many other men and women described how their parents had long since developed their own responses to stigma, typically one of resignation or indifference:

I asked my father, "Doesn't it make you mad? How can you not be mad?" And he just looked at me and said, "It's not worth it. Just ignore them. They don't know any better."

In retrospect, many informants acknowledged that some of their sensitivity to public scrutiny may have been partially a factor of their developmental age:

As I got older and knew better, it didn't bother me. I knew it was just a fact of life. That you had to accept it. You weren't ashamed, it was just the fact that they were just people who were different. I never for a moment—once I grew up—never was ashamed of my parents. People say I was, but I never was ashamed.

Others suggested that hearing people's choice of words or responses were probably unintentionally negative; many excused these strangers as uninformed or unaware. Yet, whether because of their own sensitivity or strangers' insensitivity, these childhood responses did not have the benefit of adult hindsight and became part of an enduring emotional heritage of childhood difference:

People don't realize that deaf parents have feelings, that we have feelings. Our feelings just have been ignored. So when people called our parents dummies, we had to deal with our feelings at an early age.

Wariness of public scrutiny did not only come from hearing outsiders; it came from deaf parents as well. As we have seen in previous chapters, many deaf parents were exposed to lifelong prejudice and stigma: their own families frequently rejected or minimized them; educational systems separated them out as different and denied them alternate forms of communication; restrictive employment opportunities limited their economic power. Although informants repeatedly pointed out their parents' valiant efforts to rise above lifelong oppression, internalized stigma and devalued status often took their toll over generations.

Grosjean (1982) suggests that language status frequently correlates with the socioeconomic status of the linguistic group. Until recently, sign language was both an economic liability and a social stigma. One of the most evident battlegrounds of stigmatization among the Deaf is signing, which, as Higgins notes, "makes deaf people visible." Self-consciousness about signing came from the hearing child as well as the deaf parent. Signing was an easy target for mockery by childhood peers:

> God, when I went to the store, the other kids would be there, and they would all make these weird gestures and wag their tongues. "Here comes the dummies' kid! Here comes the dummies' kid!"

Many informants described the disparity between their parents' unrestricted signing within the home and "signing small" or not at all in public:

> It's kind of funny. I would tell my mother or father not to speak too loud and they would tell me not to sign too big. We all had to be careful.

As children, many informants were socialized in this "alien community" in contrasting ways: understanding the experience of deafness as normal, and feeling the reactions to deafness as stigmatizing. These contradictory perspectives reinforced the boundary between the Deaf and the Hearing worlds.

Courtesy Stigma

Goffman proposes two groups of people who are sympathetic to those with stigma: the Own and the Wise. Hearing children of deaf parents fall into both categories. The Own are those who share the same stigma; in the company of their families, hearing children were sometimes presumed to be deaf as well. The Wise are those who are normal but intimately familiar with and sympathetic to those who are stigmatized. Jack had been discussing the more recent social acceptance of sign language. While expressing gratitude for this change, Jack also pointed out lingering childhood memories and associations:

> I think a lot of us have that experience . . . maybe not now because of all the attention to sign language, but growing up—to use sign or to be associated with sign was an incredibly negative experience. I can remember at sixteen making a decision that if I could get out I would get away as far as I could.

Jack's description suggests a second aspect of stigma for those who are Wise: courtesy stigma. Goffman used this term to describe the tendency for stigma to spread from the stigmatized individual to family and friends—that is, stigma by association. Research on courtesy stigma within the family has generally been restricted to parents and siblings of disabled children. However, for these informants, it was their parent who was primarily stigmatized. How does courtesy stigma differ from stigma?

Goffman suggested two differences that characterize those with courtesy stigma: the possibility of avoiding or terminating the relationship with the stigmatized person, or, for those who maintained an ongoing relationship, sharing the discredit but not the defense of self-elevation. Self-elevation refers to the ability to reject disparaging remarks made by those not similarly stigmatized—in this case, by *hearing* people. Roger had been describing how his schoolmates made fun of him and his parents, adding "That's just how *hearing* people act." When it existed, the desire to avoid association with their parents because of stigma was usually a childhood phenomenon:

> Oh, God, I never wanted my parents to come with me [to school functions]. When I had to take the invitation home from school, I always managed to lose it. [Laughs.] But when they started mailing them out, I was stuck!

As adults, those few informants who discontinued their relationship with their parents cited not stigma but rather concerns with over-responsibility or "just wanting to be with hearing people."

The second difference between courtesy stigma and stigma—sharing the stigma but not the self-elevation—was true among informants in two different senses. First, there was a more concrete application: although both parents and children may have shared strangers' stares, the informants, unlike their parents, could overhear stigmatizing remarks. Hearing children were less able to ignore or dismiss this additional auditory input. Second, because of the growing militancy and self-advocacy among Deaf people, hearing children were increasingly less secure regarding their full membership in the Deaf community. A few informants felt that the common heritage of difference they had shared with the Deaf was now left suspended.

The additional input of both seeing and hearing stigmatizing responses suggests a third aspect of courtesy stigma for hearing children of deaf parents. Many informants not only experienced the normalcy of deafness, but perceived its loss more acutely than their parents. Sometimes this perspective was generated by their hearing relatives, sometimes by hearing strangers. Yet many informants themselves assessed their parents' deafness within the context of their own hearing lives:

> Sometimes I would just love to be able to have my parents hear music. I just can't imagine what it is like not to have that in your life.

In this regard, those with courtesy stigma may be more aware of the perceived deprivation and deficiencies than those directly stigmatized. Joe's declaration that he was "more deaf than deaf people because most of them grew up in a hearing family" is both an affirmation of cultural membership and the suggestion of a more fully realized experience. Is it possible to understand fully what it is like to be deaf without knowing what it is like to be hearing?

Passing as Adults

Given an identity and an association that are potentially stigmatizing, hearing children of deaf parents have the potential either to accept their difference or to disconnect from it. Two informants corroborated these options:

Sometimes I would just let them think I was deaf. One time this guy yelled right in my ear, but I didn't bat an eye.

I remember this time I was with some friends and we saw these deaf people. I didn't look them [deaf people] in the eye. I was afraid it would show. ["What would show?"] Oh, that I was connected to them somehow. I wasn't ready for it.

Because of their childhood responsibilities and family ties, informants as children had limited opportunities to distance themselves from their parents. Most of these women and men shrugged off the issue of disclosure—"Well, everybody knew"—or looked at it as inevitable: "Well, they found out when they came over to the house and walked in the front door." However, as adults in a complex, heterogeneous, and mobile society, informants found that their past and present biographies could be contradictory. Their history of difference need be known only to themselves. Page (1984) observes:

It should be remembered that we are all likely to limit the amount of information we disclose about our private lives during brief discussions with comparative strangers. Indeed, we would be surprised if brief acquaintances violated the rules of social etiquette by divulging intimate details of private lives. (p. 97)

Yet embracing one's family heritage—however stigmatized—also provides a sense of belonging within an otherwise faceless and disconnected society. DeVos (1977) suggests:

American society promises mobility. It is a society that assumes ideally that no one needs to be stigmatized . . . The simple ideal, however, goes counter to psychological truth. Our emotional lives cannot be uprooted from past pain in the promised pursuit of happiness. Social mobility has its own price. How is one to measure the costs of bearing the heavy burden of a socially shameful minority or low-status inheritance on the one hand, versus the loss one suffers by casting off our intimate heritage, good or bad? (p. 227)

Informants' disclosure of their parents' deafness—as children but particularly as adults—was very much dependent on context. For a few informants, only intimates knew of their family history. Most

informants, however, found it to be the source of ongoing adult identity:

> Oh, I don't know, I tell whoever. I mean, I don't wear a sign around my
> neck but I tell people. It's a part of who I am.

DeVos (1977) feels that maintaining and acknowledging the connection to stigmatized parents is an affirmation of the relationship:

> An ethnic self derives from a sense of integrity that comes from the
> knowledge that we are true to those who have given us birth and life.
> Such integrity draws on some continuity with a community of peers who
> have tempered our childhood experiences. This sense of integrity is
> strengthened when one or both parents are members of a depreciated
> ethnic minority. Thus, an ethnic identity may be maintained out of a
> sense of responsibility felt toward stigmatized parents . . . We accept and
> assume the stigmas of the past as marks of acceptance and love. To
> assume stigma is to accept parents. (p. 227)

In addition to accepting their parents, acknowledging their potentially
stigmatizing history had two additional dimensions for these informants: a dual heritage of difference which was not only stigmatizing but
distinctive in a positive sense, and the opportunity for ongoing stigma
disavowal on behalf of their deaf families.

In a culture that alternately values homogeneity and heterogeneity,
individual traits can be potential detractions or attributes. Despite
responses that stigmatized their difference, most informants also recalled beneficial aspects of being different. Even though they were
more likely to be sensitive to the negative aspects of difference as
children, informants remembered situations in which having deaf parents gave them positive attention from the Hearing world:

> It was like clockwork. Sooner or later every teacher I had would have
> me come up to the front of the room and tell the class: What was it like
> to have deaf parents. Show us some signs. ["So, how did you feel about
> it?"] Oh, sometimes I was embarrassed, but a lot of times I liked it. I
> got to be the center of attention.

Other men and women talked about how their uniqueness was positively recognized in the Deaf community as well:

> [In the Deaf club] my Dad was always telling me to come over so he could brag about how I interpreted this or did that for him.

Informants' narratives indicate that their difference was more often perceived positively when they, not their parents, were the focus of attention.

As adults, most women and men were less concerned about difference as stigmatizing and offered several examples of how their family background distinguished them from others:

> I remember this time I was filling out all those college applications. You know, where you're supposed to say something about yourself that will make people think, Oh, I want this guy. Well, I talked about my parents and all that. I don't know for sure, but it was probably something that made them remember me.

Emphasizing one's differentness also depended on the situation. Several men and women working as interpreters often minimized their family connections. These informants explained that they did this not because of a sense of stigma, but because they wanted to downplay whatever advantages their family background might have given them:

> I want to be known in my own right. I don't want them to think, Oh, that's all she can do, or Well, if my parents were deaf, I could sign just as well as she can.

A focus on themselves rather than their parents caused a sense of ambivalence among some informants. As Martha put it, "I felt like I was using my parents' deafness to my own advantage." Yet, more often, informants felt as if they were affirming their family heritage. Page (1984) proposes that "the extent to which individuals engage in passing is likely to depend on whether they accept or reject that a particular attribute is evidence of inferiority" (p. 22). For most adult informants, being deaf was decidedly *not* a mark of inferiority.

Acknowledging their family history also gave informants a potential forum to de-stigmatize deafness. Researchers have described encounters between those who are stigmatized and those who are not. Initial encounters are typically cumbersome, strained, and inhibited. Interaction and prolonged contact have generally been found to reduce prejudice and stigmatization. But Goode (1978) qualifies these findings by noting that exchanges which are "stylized, socially distant and unequal" will sustain rather than diminish stereotypes (p. 90). Goode's qualification can be taken a step further by recognizing not only the importance of how these interactions take place, but whether they can occur at all. Access to interaction is often precluded by class differences and social isolation. The condition of deafness alters the expected patterns of communication. Higgins (1980) suggests that "unlike many other outsiders' 'failings,' deafness *does* inhibit interaction with the larger social world, regardless of whether the deaf are stigmatized or not" (p. 143; emphasis added). Hearing children of deaf parents could provide a means of de-stigmatization through direct facilitation of encounters between the Deaf and the Hearing. By acknowledging their Deaf heritage as adults, informants could also continue this advocacy by forging new inroads into a world often impenetrable to their deaf parents.

Advocacy also tempered how informants responded to the question of difference. Several informants like Brian told me: "No, we weren't different at all." Brian went on to explain that he and his family did all the usual things that families do:

> We watched TV, had dinner, went to movies . . . sometimes we'd fight, sometimes we'd tell jokes. Just because I had deaf parents didn't make my life different.

Brian understood difference as a synonym for abnormality. Cheryl and Gene adopted similarly negative interpretations in describing the outcomes of difference in their parents' lives:

> [Cheryl:] My father wasn't treated any differently . . . and I think that's why he didn't feel inferior because he was deaf.

> [Gene:] Mom was always treated differently from the rest of her family. She always felt inferior, like she couldn't do anything.

Yet difference cannot be reified into a singular state. Gene later talked about how his grandparents "refused to see my Dad was different" and this caused a lifelong pattern of denial: "They just didn't want to admit they had a deaf son." Difference was a blessing and a curse.

Almost all informants felt that their childhoods had given them compassion and empathy for others who were different—even though they themselves often had conflicting feelings about their own heritage of difference.

Having a Deaf Child

Thus far, I have been considering differences centered on having deaf parents. Yet all the informants—as children and as adults—were touched by other kinds of differences as well. Some of these differences mirror distinctions within the larger Hearing society, such as being a racial minority or being gay. Other informants represented minorities within their communities by their religious affiliation or economic status. Some differences were intrinsic to a deaf family, such as being the one family member who did not sign or being the only hearing child among deaf parents and siblings. Although any one of these differences usually characterized only a handful of men and women, they were an integral part of that individual's childhood and adult experiences, augmenting and compounding the experience of difference.

Here I consider a context of difference that was more widespread among informants: having a deaf child. Concerns about having a deaf child shadowed almost all informants—even though the probability of this occurring was usually no greater than among the general population. The anticipated stigma of having a deaf child broadens the parameters of difference, shifting from backward glances at childhood to a possible future of difference as well.

At least half of all profound hearing losses in childhood occur as a result of genetic causes (Fraser 1976). Although genetic research has proliferated within the past few years, hereditary causes of deafness are extremely heterogeneous and remain difficult to isolate. Most are not distinguishable by clinical features. Perhaps because of these uncertainties, only one-tenth of all informants mentioned genetic causes of their parents' deafness. Several informants reported that although they suspected a genetic basis for deafness, they had been given other explanations:

My grandparents insisted that my mother wasn't born deaf. She got sick somehow. So then out of nowhere this deaf cousin turns up. And then another one.

Unlike deafness related to illness or accidents, genetic origins of deafness are less explicit. The detection of deafness was often not apparent to informants' grandparents, and expectations of a hearing child often lasted well beyond the first few months after birth:[6]

They said it wasn't till she [mother] was about three years old that they finally realized something was wrong with her hearing. And when they found out she was born deaf, they couldn't understand how they could have missed it. It wasn't like she was their first child. But . . . well, they just never even noticed it.

Although it was highly improbable that most informants would have a deaf child, the question of hereditary deafness frequently persisted in the lives of these men and women:

How many parents of my dates have asked me if the deafness is genetic. And, I'm like, if they think their son is interested in me, I want to say, Screw you! It makes me so mad.

Another informant said:

My mother-in-law kept grilling me about how my parents became deaf. She wanted to be sure that it wouldn't happen to any of her grandchildren. As if *she* gave birth to all perfect children.

As indicated by these two remarks, informants were frequently sarcastic and angered about such interrogations and the negative implications of having a deaf child. Such reactions from outsiders represented an insult to their parents and to themselves as well.

Informants were generally nonplussed at the possibility of having a deaf child; several welcomed it. Mary Ann responded quickly to the question:

I would love to have a deaf child. I think I would be a great parent for a deaf kid. Who better? I know it would be hard, it would be difficult. See, I really don't think deaf people have a disadvantage. I just think it's different for them . . . I think a lot of deaf people think, including my mother, and my Dad probably does too, that if I could hear I'd have a better life. And that's not necessarily true. It's what you make of your life that makes it better, your quality of life has a lot to do with how you feel about yourself.

Yet a few informants—particularly those who felt they had a serious chance of having a deaf child—were ambivalent and shared their private concerns about having children:

> I wouldn't say this to most people, but I know how different it can be. Before I had children, I had to make sure. I wanted to know exactly what the chances were.

A few men and women acknowledged that the stress of raising a child who was different might have been too great on their marriages; others felt they had "done enough for one lifetime." Several informants agonized over whether or not to risk having a deaf child and, in a few cases, made a decision not to have children. Yvonne explained how going for genetic counseling became a family and a cultural issue:

> If you don't know the origin of your parents' deafness, then it is an unknown. It becomes a big concern. I knew I could cope with it, but I didn't want that child to go through life and have such a rough go of it. I was concerned about how my husband would react. Would he learn sign language? How would it affect our marriage? When my mother found out I was going for genetic counseling, she asked me, "Why? Nothing wrong with having a deaf child. I hope my grandchild *is* deaf." She felt rejected. I felt guilty and embarrassed. She was coming from a Deaf perspective. I was coming from a Hearing perspective. I never brought it up again. I just kept my worries and my fears to myself.

John had been talking about how different he felt as a child because of his parents' deafness and how this pivotal issue had been resurrected by having a deaf child:

> I thought when my parents were dead then I would be out of the Deaf world, but now that I have a deaf daughter I see I'm going to be in it for the rest of my life.

Although all five informants who actually had a deaf child felt that their family background was a major asset in understanding and raising their child, these women and men also acknowledged that having a deaf child was not the same as having a deaf parent. Several described how they struggled with balancing difference: recognizing it yet not making too much of it. Two informants described how they "gave in" to their spouses, who preferred that their deaf child not be sent off to a residential school or taught sign language. When I asked these informants why they went counter to their own beliefs, Roy described his own lingering doubts about a life of difference:

> I hate to say it, but I guess somehow I still wanted her to be normal. Even after all that my parents had to go through, you know, trying to make them talk when they couldn't. Yet I ended up letting them try to do the same thing with my daughter. My wife thought our daughter could be just like anybody else, not like my parents. And I guess there was a part of me that wanted to believe it was possible . . . It was such a mistake.

Most informants told me they could see themselves having a deaf child but not a deaf spouse. What was the difference? Informants themselves offered varying explanations. Rita described how having a deaf child was accepting fate; but a deaf spouse was a choice:

> Deafness happens. So, if I have a deaf kid, it happens. But I'm not going to go out and choose a deaf person to marry.

Informants also stressed different expectations for being a parent as opposed to a life partner. Many informants felt that their family experiences and roles had prepared them to raise a deaf child:

> If I had a deaf child, I feel like I'd have a chance to get them on their feet, help them realize they can do almost anything. I wouldn't burden my kid with all those negative things that hearing people put on deaf people.

When I asked Scott how a deaf child raised by him would be any different from other deaf children, he replied:

> For one thing, my child wouldn't feel left out, not talked to, not knowing what was going on. He wouldn't feel different.

In contrast to the possibility of parenting a deaf child, most informants did not want to continue this type of intimate relationship with another adult. Informant after informant stressed wanting to have a partner who was the same as themselves. Informants also felt it was just as important for a deaf person to have a deaf spouse. Although many men and women thought an equal relationship with a deaf partner was possible, most conceded it was unlikely:

> Oh, it'd be hard for him [a possible deaf husband] and hard for me. We'd both probably fall right back into the same old patterns [signs: *"I need you to interpret for me. Please."*] and me going right along and doing it.

A deaf child offered the possibility of rectifying the past, and providing the communication and family support that many parents and other deaf adults had struggled to find.

Having either a deaf partner or a deaf child could be viewed as a way informants could continue their Deaf heritage. But, for most informants, only one of these alternatives seemed plausible. This suggests a recapitulation of the relationship of hearing children of deaf parents to Deaf culture. Margaret Mead (1953) had proposed that "any member of a group, provided that his position within that group is properly specified, is a perfect sample of the group-wide pattern on which he is acting as an informant" (p. 648). Hearing children of deaf parents shift Mead's emphasis on a phantom cultural center: their position is a crucial part of their cultural experience. These men and women experienced Deaf culture as the hearing children of deaf parents. Because they could hear, the informants could function in a Hearing world in ways their parents could not. Their difference alternated between being deaf and being hearing, between sharing the stigmatizing aspects of difference with their parents and partaking of the distinction of difference as their hearing children. Informants paradoxically rejected the negative difference that outsiders made of their parents' deafness while acknowledging that being deaf *was* different from being hearing. All these cultural paradoxes were familiar in the context of parent and child, but less so or not at all between peers or spouses.

Considerations of having a deaf child or spouse are largely hypothetical. Most hearing children of deaf parents neither marry a deaf person nor have a deaf child. Yet most informants maintained their relationship with the Deaf world in other ways. Almost half of these women and men worked in careers involving the Deaf; a number of them continued to socialize with deaf people as well as participate in Deaf social events. These situations provided informants with opportunities to reclaim their own unique identity of difference: minimizing the negative implications of difference to hearing people, and remembering the normalcy of difference when among the Deaf.

. . . .

In the lyrical and poignant stories of *The Man Who Mistook His Wife for a Hat,* Oliver Sacks suggests that masking or altering a person's condition risks losing the creativity and the spark that made the person unique. The condition of deafness provided deaf people entry into a different world while they continued to tangle with the Hearing world in unique and special ways. In the struggle, some were victorious, some became victims—changed, inspired, or defeated by the physical mark that has such profound social consequences. The informants in this study wear a badge of difference that is invisible to most, one that represents their parents' history and their own struggle with difference. It evokes memories of both stigma and distinction. Bretherton (1985) writes that "it is not a person's internal working model of attachment figures . . . per se but how the person construes these internal models in adulthood that appears to be involved in intergenerational transmission" (p. 55). The paradox of being different is that it becomes apparent only in comparison; for many informants, this occurred only when they stepped away from their family of difference.

As adults, most informants had increasing opportunities to minimize or disclaim their heritage. Yet few did. Goffman (1963) suggests:

> It is often assumed, and with evidence, that the passer will feel torn between two attachments. He will feel some alienation from his new group, for he is unlikely to be able to identify fully with their attitude to what he knows he can be shown to be. (p. 87)

For most of these men and women, the fear is not that they will be shown to be deaf or even that they have deaf parents. The fear is that they may be shown to be just hearing—and to be hearing is to be identified with the group that has stigmatized and oppressed. DeVos (1987) emphasizes the difference between those cultural members who grow up in isolation and those who are minorities in a larger social context:

> A number of [studies] do not distinguish sufficiently between growing up in an ethnic minority situation and growing up in a traditional culture . . . These patterns have a different meaning in situations of cultural isolation than they do in situations in which the individual is being socialized in a traditional pattern (as part of a minority subculture). (p. 24)

As members of an interactive, complex society, hearing children of deaf parents participated in the dialectical process of the stigmatized and the stigmatizing. Higgins (1980) reiterates that "Deaf people can only be understood in relationship to their position in a hearing world. To view them outside that context is fundamentally to distort their experiences" (p. 175). These informants have a unique position with regard to perspectives on difference—difference not only about deafness, but about being hearing as well. Difference is not a monolithic badge, but an amalgam of experiences and feelings. It can vary not only in its origins and reference groups, but also in its moral outcome and evaluation.

Hyphenated Lives

When I turned eighteen, my father took me aside. He pointed out the window and said [signs, *"The time is coming. Soon you must go. That's your world out there. The Hearing world. You belong there"*]. For eighteen years I had grown up Deaf, and now all of a sudden I'm supposed to be Hearing? I looked at him and said [signs, *"What do I know about the Hearing world? I hear, yes. I speak, yes. But I thought I was Deaf"*]. My father smiled and said [signs, *"True, you're Deaf, but you're Hearing too"*]. I grew up Deaf. I guess now I'm Hearing. But some part of me still feels Deaf.

This informant's dilemma captures the sense of liminality[1] and paradox frequently expressed among many adult hearing children of deaf parents interviewed for this study. Marks of difference frequently polarize human communities into two groups, each clinging to separate practical and symbolic histories: male/female; black/white; gay/straight. Often these dichotomies seem natural. Hermaphrodites, people of mixed races, and bisexuals mystify us and make us anxious. Sapir (1924) suggests that "we disagree on the value of things and the relations of things, but often enough we agree on the particular value of a label . . . It is only when the question arises of just where to put the label, that the trouble begins" (p. 308).

In this chapter I explore the construction of polarized categories of Deaf and Hearing and consider the enigmatic identity of these informants. The concern here is not the shifting and sometimes contradictory membership within each category, but what each category represents. Such categories not only depict a polarized history between two groups; they also provide informants with a way to talk about themselves and their relationship to others.

Membership in one category is invariably related to and determined by the other. Douglas (1986) observes:

> Defilement is never an isolated event. It cannot occur except in view of a systematic ordering of ideas . . . the only way in which pollution ideas make sense is in reference to a total structure of thought whose keystone, boundaries, margins and internal lines are held in relation by rituals of separation. (p. 309)

Those who are on each side of the equation contribute definitions, boundaries, and meanings for themselves and their counterparts. Both perspectives provide not only an understanding of each experience, but an exploration of more broadly based social and cultural factors which are shared as well as those which maintain the polarization. Between apparently mutually exclusive categories, there are frequent overlaps—resulting in ambiguities, paradoxes, and realignments. The previous chapter focused on difference. This chapter asks, How can different be the same?

Categorization

What explains this tendency to categorize, to separate one group of people from another—and, often, to assign negative or positive attributes to one group against the other? Are separating and labeling an inherent part of the human condition? Lévi-Strauss and others endorse an innate rather than a cultural basis for thinking in binary, opposed categories. Recent child development research examines the possibility that the act of separating out those different from oneself is indeed an inherent developmental process, possibly arising from early childhood projection and individuation (Ainlay, Becker, and Coleman 1986). In *The Need to Have Enemies and Allies,* Volkan (1988) proposes such a psychological need in early child development. Volkan explores the development of a cohesive sense of self and of others within which the concept of the enemy is interwoven; he suggests that this individual psychological drive to develop a schema of ally or enemy becomes the precursor for shared enemies and allies based upon culturally constructed notions of similarities and differences such as ethnicity, race, or religion.

Other writers have examined the cultural construction and implications of dichotomies. Hsu, DuBois, and others described the American predilection for oppositional categories. In his classic study of American national character, Hsu (1972) observed "pictures of contradictions with little or no attempt to reconcile the opposing elements" (p. 378). DuBois (1955) notes that "oppositional propositions are a consistent aspect of Western European culture" (p. 1232). Despite the appearance of a flourishing multi-ethnic and multi-racial population in the United States, recent national events such as the 1991 Supreme Court confirmation hearings of Clarence Thomas or the 1992 Los Angeles riots demonstrate the staggering polarity that continues to exist between genders and between races.

Researchers add their own distortions to the construction or embellishment of dichotomizations. For example, they may infer artificial memberships within a group or relationships between such members. Turner (1967) warns that "one of the main characteristics of ideological interpretations is that they tend to stress the harmonious and cohesive aspect of social relationships" (p. 33). Dichotomous comparisons may accentuate greater internal homogeneity within each category or greater cross-category heterogeneity than in fact exists. Fitzgerald (1977) suggests cultural and personal reasons for such researcher bias: "In our culture we often expect 'either/or' types (stereotypes). Anthropologists are not immune to this weakness, especially when it concerns an area about which they are emotionally uneasy" (p. 390).

My selection of informants—hearing children of deaf parents—may overemphasize dichotomy. I did not, for example, look at deaf parent/deaf child families. Yet the dichotomization between Deaf and Hearing is supported by numerous studies of deaf people (Higgins 1980; Becker 1980; Padden and Humphries 1988; Foster 1989; Wilcox 1989; Evans 1991). In Chapter 3 I described the lack of gradations among those identified as deaf despite actual physiological variations. Social, educational, economic, and individual differences were all subsumed by the critical delineation: Are you deaf or are you hearing?[2]

Being the Same

As young children, few informants remembered feeling that their parents' deafness was remarkable, or that they were somehow different from their parents. This follows expected developmental patterns in which young children remain strongly identified with their parents. Because most informants' parents socialized exclusively with other deaf people, their early home life provided a homogeneous environment with little opportunity for comparisons between being hearing and being deaf:

> We were a family. My Mom, my Dad, and me. There was nothing strange about it.

Although many women and men felt their parents were not partial to having either a deaf or a hearing child, more than half of all informants indicated that their parents had definite preferences—usually for a hearing child. Anna said her mother got angry at deaf people who wanted deaf children:

> My mother yells at deaf people who say they want to have deaf children—she scolds them: "You're wrong! It's a mean thing to do! You're terrible!"

A few informants said their parents would have preferred a deaf child. Ted felt his mother's choice made sense:

> One time I asked my mother. And she was quiet for a while and then she looked at me. [Signs, *"It would have been easier if we were the same, deaf–deaf."*] And she's probably right.

Several informants commented on what appeared to be a growing number of younger deaf parents who wanted *deaf* children. The stigma of having a "defective" child was increasingly displaced by wanting to have a child who was like themselves and who shared the same standard of normalcy. Ablon (1984) has noted a similar trend among those dwarfs who have developed a more positive self-image and are less conflicted about having a child like themselves.

Most of the informants were known to be hearing at birth. In a few instances, however, informants were initially assumed to be deaf. This was especially true if there were several generations of deaf people within the family. Two informants recalled that it was not until school age that they were discovered to be hearing. Ruth explained that it was not that she could not hear; the act of hearing simply had little significance:

> Sure, I remember hearing things. I guess I always heard things. But I didn't know that I was supposed to let anybody know. I mean, why should I? We could see what was going on around us. If I heard it too, well, I guess that was just extra . . . Or maybe it just wasn't important.

Sahlins (1976) suggests that even the physical world is shaped and interpreted by cultural context. Situations like the ones described by these informants underscore the fact that hearing or deafness—as criterion for membership in one of two worlds—needs a context in which these conditions are evaluated and become socially meaningful.

Learning the Difference

One source that emphasized the distinction between being hearing or being deaf was pragmatic. As children, most informants' hearing and speaking abilities provided an obvious resource for the family's communication system, and generally distinguished them from their deaf parents. Yet identification as hearing was not straightforward. Informants' family responsibilities frequently set them apart from hearing children who had hearing parents. Although the degree of interaction with these hearing peers varied among informants, almost all informants felt some degree of difference from these other hearing children. Informants repeatedly described themselves as "special," "burdened," "more responsible than," "more mature than," "different from" their childhood peers.

Both family and outsiders contributed to the construction of a polarized world. Hearing and deafness—each expanded from a strictly functional condition into one of considerable social importance. Walter's description exemplifies how categories were constructed by deaf parents:

> In my family, every day there was a debate or a refinement or a comment about the implications of deafness. Everybody was identified either as deaf or hearing. Every issue, every piece of communication was, Deaf do this. Hearing do that. Deaf way, Hearing way. Deaf world, Hearing world.

Informants reported that their parents attributed a number of characteristics to hearing people. Although all such attributions were not consistent, the two characteristics most frequently mentioned were "Hearing people can't always be trusted" and "Hearing people know everything."

> My father always distrusted hearing people. Still does. He would say to me, "Oh, that guy's going to raise the price because we're deaf, he thinks we're dumb—he's going to take advantage of us."

Derek, who had a deaf mother and a hearing father, remembered his mother telling him that he was very smart but stubborn—just like his hearing father. Derek said his mother could not understand why they were both so stubborn when they could hear. Parents' generalizations, stereotypes, and assumptions about hearing people contrasted with their depictions of deaf people, which—whether positive or negative— generally included many more detailed physical, behavioral, and personal characteristics.

Complementing the family's evaluation of hearing people were public reactions to deaf people that reinforced feelings of separateness and difference. Prevailing moral evaluations of deafness and responses to deaf people augmented the desire of informants not to identify with those who stigmatize and oppress. Lorraine was unforgiving in her condemnation of hearing people:

> My parents have gotten ripped off by hearing people. And have gotten shit on by hearing people and treated like shit. My Dad's lost jobs, you know. I can't believe the cruelty from hearing people, you know, people

he works with. And they laugh at him, and they don't even do it behind his back.

Although many other informants pointed out positive interactions between their parents and hearing people, they rarely identified themselves as Hearing. When I asked Ron whether he considered himself Hearing or Deaf, he qualified his answer:

> Well, I can hear. Of course! But, well, I don't know that I'd say that I'm a quote "hearing" person. That's different.

Ron's remarks reiterate that functional condition and cultural affiliation are not equivalent within the Deaf community.

Affiliation issues extended into the larger Deaf community as well. Hearing children of deaf parents have been described as the only full-fledged hearing members of the Deaf community (Higgins 1980; Sacks 1989). Yet here too, membership is problematic. Padden and Humphries (1988) provide a telling example of how the Deaf community vacillates about this issue. A local Deaf club attempted to allow a hearing son of deaf parents to play in an exclusively deaf basketball tournament by labeling him hard-of-hearing. This ploy eventually failed when he was asked to take an audiological examination by tournament officials, who were also deaf. However, as the authors note, "The club probably would not have tried to violate the rules if the hearing player had not had Deaf parents" (p. 49). Many informants described how they would sometimes confuse other deaf people by their sign language fluency:

> This deaf man asked me if I was deaf or hearing. And when I told him, we just kept on talking about stuff. But it's like he needed a basis upon which to interact with me or judge me.

Among these informants, two important exceptions to the typical profile for members of the Deaf community surfaced. One or both of the features of being Deaf that have such historical and emotional salience for the Deaf—their language and their peer association—were absent among most of these men and women. As described in Chapter 7, nearly one-fifth of the informants did not consider themselves fluent in or did not use American Sign Language as children—even if this was the principal communication system used by their parents:

> My parents signed to each other, but my mother insisted that I not sign to her. I had to speak to her. First of all, she didn't want me to become dependent on signs to communicate. Secondly, she didn't want me to lose out, as best as I can understand what her motives were, she was afraid that it might be a handicap to my oral development. She didn't want that to happen. So, I was not allowed to sign in the house . . . unless I was going to say something that she just couldn't get. In which case, I was to spell it out. I learned signs, but only to talk with her friends.

Second, almost four-fifths of these informants reported little contact with deaf peers while they were growing up. Even the presence of hearing children in the Deaf community set them apart: deaf children were usually absent—either because they were attending residential schools for the deaf or because they were kept away by their hearing parents who perceived the Deaf community as socially deviant.

Sorting It Out

Amid conflicting interpretations by the Hearing world and the Deaf world, informants discussed sorting out their own affiliation and identity. Vance remembered this scene when he was about 12 years old:

> My mother was going on and on about how she could never trust hearing people. And I looked at her and said, "Well what about me? I'm hearing." And she looked at me and said, "No, I didn't mean you. You're different."

As children, many informants were thought to be deaf when they really wanted to be seen as hearing; others were hearing when they wanted to be deaf. Gender research indicates that children typically react against being typecast (as masculine or feminine) until they can assert where in the spectrum they feel they fit (Basow 1986). In the tension between being deaf and being hearing, informants reflected a similar resistance. Lorraine described countering her parents' attempt to categorize her:

My parents kept telling me, "You should know, you're hearing." How come I'm supposed to know everything? Just because I'm hearing, they think I know everything. I *don't* know.

Lorraine's rejection of equating functional status with a particular attribute was mirrored by Barry:

This one time this friend said, "Why do you go to those deaf meetings with all those deaf people? You're not deaf." And I said, "Huh, a lot you know!"

For many informants, the paradox of their ambiguous identity continued into adulthood. Despite appearing to matriculate within the Hearing world, a number of informants admitted that they were not always comfortable with hearing people, nor did they necessarily identify themselves as a hearing person. Public perceptions of informants were also problematic because their deaf heritage was largely invisible; their familial link to a separate culture and identity was not readily apparent. Most informants identified themselves as variously Deaf and Hearing:

["Would you say you're Hearing or Deaf?"] Oh, I don't know, part Deaf, part Hearing. ["50–50?"] [Laughs.] Some days. Other times it's like 90–10 or 10–90. But there's always some part of me that's Deaf and some part of me that's Hearing.

A number of informants described how the Hearing and Deaf parts were "all mixed up," and many felt it was important to separate out what was Hearing and what was Deaf. Several used the concept of code-switching to explain how they alternated between the Deaf and Hearing worlds:

I quickly learned that there was a Hearing world and a Deaf world and you did one thing in one place and another thing in another place. The hard thing for me is that when I am in the Hearing world I find it hard to stop talking about the deaf, to go to a party and not talk about deafness, not meet another deaf person—I just want to be hearing . . . but when I am in the Deaf world, I want to be deaf. I know that sounds half and half, but I feel half and half.

The categories of Deaf and Hearing represented not only issues of membership, but a symbolic pairing. Many informants used these categories to talk about themselves: "the Deaf part of me . . . the Hearing part of me"; "in the Deaf world . . . in the Hearing world"; "Deaf values . . . Hearing values." Often, concerns and issues were directed at one pole or the other: "I never learned how to be Hearing" or "Only now am I beginning to understand the Deaf part of me." Lakoff and Johnson (1980) suggest that metaphors rather than categories themselves are the basis for behavior: a metaphor "connects our memories of our past . . . experiences and serves as a possible guide for future ones" (p. 140).

Although almost all informants acknowledged a polarity between the Deaf and Hearing worlds, at least one-third of these men and women did not place this dichotomy within themselves. Two circumstances seemed to mitigate these feelings: the degree to which this polarity was experienced within their families, and the informant's family position and role. Unlike most informants, Cheryl had parents who moved in both Hearing and Deaf social circles. She felt this decreased her sense of dichotomy. Although his parents socialized exclusively with other deaf people, Ken did not remember his parents attributing values or behaviors to deaf or hearing people per se: "They just treated people as they came—didn't matter if they were deaf or hearing."

A sense of internalized polarity was more pronounced among those informants who were the interpreters and cultural mediators within their families. As we have seen, this role often fell to the oldest child or the oldest daughter. Other siblings also reported feeling both Deaf and Hearing, but appeared less conflicted about it. Yvonne's family illustrates different emphases of the Deaf/Hearing dichotomy among three hearing siblings. Yvonne herself was the main family interpreter, and saw herself as "very much in the middle, in-between." She described herself by saying, "I feel like I'm on both sides of the fence at the same time." One brother was "very Deaf culture, I mean he's married to a deaf woman, works in a place that employs deaf workers, and has mostly deaf friends." She described her other sibling as having nothing to do with deaf people and as being the one who had the fewest mediating responsibilities as a child.

Informants frequently described a sense of duality which separated them from hearing people as well as from deaf people. Although public identification as deaf or hearing could often be adapted to fit differing circumstances, informants' internalized sense of themselves was not always dependent on external cues. For more than half of these women and men, hearing *and* deaf—both sides of the equation— have been internalized, as well as the invisible chasm that connects and yet separates the two:

> I always felt like I didn't belong either place. I didn't belong with the Deaf 100 per cent and I didn't belong with the Hearing. I didn't feel comfortable with Hearing. I felt more comfortable with Deaf, but I knew I wasn't deaf. I feel like I'm somewhere in-between.

Emily evoked a sense of disorientation, of separateness from both the Hearing and the Deaf:

> When I was a little girl, I remember walking into the room and seeing my father signing into the air. He was talking to God. I couldn't un- derstand what was going on, so I asked my mother what he was doing, who he was signing to. My mother looked at me and [fingerspells *"h-e-a-r-i-n-g"* across her forehead. "You're hearing, you don't under- stand"]. I had always felt different from other kids because of my parents. Now I realized I was even different from them.

Acknowledging their particular sense of liminality, however, poten- tially intensified the separation between informants and their Deaf heritage. Several women and men questioned how to assert their own identity without further stigmatizing or alienating their parents:

> Who am I gonna tell this to? Nobody's gonna understand, or they'll get the wrong idea.

Family allegiance was not the only concern. For hearing children within the Deaf community, identity and membership—as with all other deaf people—do not just depend on self-identification. Status is contingent on the Deaf community's sense of them as culturally familiar. Because hearing children already occupy a paradoxical position within this culture, the risks of alienation are all the more perilous. Lucy treasured her connection to the Deaf world:

> It's not my parents I worry about. They're both gone now. But it's the connection to other deaf people. That's still important to me . . . It's like what I felt right after Mom died. There were all these deaf people at the funeral. And they were telling me stories about my Mom. And then this woman I didn't know asked me if I was deaf [signs, "*You're deaf, aren't you?*"]. These are my people, they know me, they know my Deaf part. To risk losing that would be to risk losing myself.

Adult Identity within the Deaf Community

Within their families, hearing children often provided a crucial link between the Deaf world and the Hearing world. As adults, however, their role and their identity shifted into realms of greater uncertainty. The ensconced role of hearing children of deaf parents as members of the Deaf community has become increasingly problematic in the context of recent social changes and in terms of their own adult development. First, paralleling many other minority groups, deaf people have become adamant in their demands for self-recognition and autonomy: Deaf for deaf. The recent Deaf rights movement realigns the messenger with the message: to speak for the deaf, you must *be* deaf. Power struggles, exemplified by the rejection of a hearing person named as president of Gallaudet University (the world's only university for the deaf) and the eventual installation of a deaf president, dramatize this concern. Although overt confrontation was rare, informants frequently described a sense of personal conflict. Mario worked in a community agency that provided services for deaf people, and I asked him if he ever felt that a deaf person should have his job:

> If it's between me and a deaf person for a job, then it should go to the deaf person. But, you know, I feel like I know every bit as much about the Deaf world as they do. A lot of deaf people grew up in the Hearing

world, they think Hearing, they act Hearing. I'm more Deaf than a lot of them are!

Second, the extraordinarily popular fascination with "adult children of" groups, introspection, and childhood reassessment has resurrected unsettled issues of identity. As adults, many informants described searching for appropriate analogies and interpretations of their family experiences. These adult self-explorations reflected a continued sense of conflicted identity and oppositional categories:

> I was a problem. I kept trying to solve the problem that I never understood. I kept trying and trying, but I never could solve it. So one day I asked my mother, "Was I really a problem?" My mother sat for a while and she said, "You know what the problem was?" I said, "No." And she said, "The problem was you could hear."

Whether in one-on-one interviews or in regional meetings of adult hearing children, informants' preoccupation with their deaf parents underscores their mutual cultural heritage—a heritage emphatically linked through their parents. Although many of the issues and struggles of hearing children of deaf parents parallel those of children of other ethnic and racial groups, there is one important difference. Within the Deaf community, the critical measure of cultural identity is neither degree of language proficiency nor shade of skin color nor knowledge of customs. It ultimately depends on neither declarations of allegiance nor degree of interaction. Above all, to be deaf is to *not* be hearing.[3] This paradigm underscores why the emphasis on parental linkage is so crucial. Because hearing children share neither their parents' functional hearing loss nor, in many cases, their parents' language, the primary source of cultural identity and community entrée is their connection with their parents. Only by association do these informants have access to this exclusive identity and community: mother father deaf.

. . . .

We are conditioned to think in categories, to make distinctions and to interpret them according to culturally specific standards of meaning and behavior—even if they are "preponderantly spurious" (DuBois 1955, p. 1232). Although splitting is a normal developmental process, in many cases we develop the capacity and the tolerance for ambivalence. Yet those issues which remain individually or culturally charged continue to be polarized.

There is tension around any variation from the norm. In the Deaf world, the idealized center of that world reflects the long history of polarity with the Hearing world: non-speaking, signing, often those who are from multiple-generation deaf families: those who are clearly *not* hearing. Despite their oppositional status, the Deaf and Hearing cultures reflect a common ideology: In order to be normal, I must be the same as you.[4] The women and men in this study represent exceptions to this rigid dichotomization, a rift in the boundaries of two cultures. How do these opposing cultures resolve this disruption? Like their deaf parents, many informants have been stigmatized by those who hear. Yet the Deaf world does not necessarily offer safe haven: to speak for the Deaf, you must be deaf. From Hearing and from Deaf, the response is the same: the risk of anomaly is to be disenfranchised.

The informants' hyphenated lives provide a functional link between the Deaf and Hearing worlds. A few years ago I spoke with an anthropologist who had been studying Malay humoral systems. She explained that, in Malay, most things are classified as either hot or cold. I asked her if there was anything that was neither hot nor cold. She said, "Yes, rice (cederhana) is neither hot nor cold; it is neutral. It is a mainstay." These informants' own neutral metaphors of identity—"in-between," "fence-sitting," [sign: *"half-and-half"*]—also represent the ballast between two polarized worlds. Symbolically, if not practically, hearing children of deaf parents provide a means of linkage. Yet this connection is paradoxical. Hyphens connect, but they also keep apart. Could the Deaf and the Hearing meet without bridges, without these mediators? Goffman (1963) had proposed an unalterable dichotomy for those with courtesy stigma: either become members of a stigmatized group or disavow such membership. Such continued polarization ignores the real-life possibilities of synthesis and transcendence. DeVos (1977) comments on the limitations of conceptual dichotomies:

Ethnic background, while present and part of the self, is not the essential constituent of the individual as a human being. Transcendence of narrow ethnicity is desirable if we are to live together in some degree of harmony with others different from ourselves. Such transcendence is to be distinguished from passing. (p. 241)

These informants provide a vision of cultural conflict, but also of cultural resolution.

The men and women in this study are a dialectic between two competing world views. Among characteristics and values frequently dichotomized as either Deaf or Hearing, these informants have inherited dual, often polarized interpretations of the meaning of deafness and the meaning of hearing. These conflicting perspectives demonstrate a central tenet of anthropology: the responses to and the meanings of human conditions are ultimately dependent on their social context. From hearing people, these informants understood deafness as brokenness, as stigma, as disability. From their parents, they experienced deafness as viable, as normal, as a cultural community. They learned that to be hearing is to be powerful but capable of oppression. They learned that they themselves are the exception to those who hear and those who are deaf. And this liminality itself was often more distressing than being at one pole or the other.

Adler (1977) proposed a questionable outcome for those who live with two languages and two cultures:

Often [bilinguals] have split minds . . . all the particularities which language conveys, historical, geographical, cultural, are re-embodied in the bilingual twice: he is neither here nor there; he is a marginal man. (p. 38)

In the final chapter I will examine the question of marginality between two cultures—as experienced both symbolically and practically by men and women who were both Deaf *and* Hearing.

A Distant World Called Home

Identity on the Margins of Culture

At the close of *The Scarlet Letter,* Nathaniel Hawthorne turns his attention to Pearl, Hester Prynne's daughter. What happened to that elfin child whose first earthly sight was that infamous scarlet mark on her mother's chest? It was Pearl who shared her mother's stigma and her mother's triumph, and whose childhood encompassed the practical and symbolic conflicts between her family and the larger social world. Yet, within the confines of Hawthorne's novel, Pearl's adult life remains forever mysterious:

> But where was little Pearl? If still alive, she must now have been in the flush and bloom of early womanhood. None knew—nor ever learned, with the fullness of perfect certainty . . . But there was a more real life for Hester Prynne, here, in New England, than in that unknown region where Pearl had found a home.

This book has been a voyage to an unknown region—unknown to most hearing people and deaf people alike. This land of enigma and paradox is often difficult to appreciate or explain because of the tremendous chasm that separates the two cultures of the Deaf and the Hearing. In addition to differences in language and custom, the shadow of stigma often keeps this territory concealed from view. Although these inhabitants bear no visible mark, their dual heritage is an indelible part of who they are. These distant shores are frequently clouded by the temporal gulf that separates parent from child—whether deaf or hearing. Research, too, has enhanced this disjunction by limiting its focus to defined periods of life—most often that of childhood. As with Pearl, we are left to wonder about the fate of children now adults whose lives have continued well beyond the gaze of parent and researcher alike.

The previous chapters have touched upon family histories and childhood experiences that inform the present-day lives of one hundred and fifty men and women. Amid frequently oppositional worlds and within a uniquely defined template of individual, family, and community variables, each informant has developed a narrative of self. Yet, apart from the distinct fabric of a Deaf family, informants have drawn from beliefs and values that prevail within the larger American culture: in particular, that our identities are inextricably linked to our families of origin. In locating ourselves within a universe of meaning and chaos, we inevitably come to consider the significance of that place we called home. The relationship between self and family lies at the heart of this final chapter.

Parts of the Whole

Identity is one of an array of interrelated concepts that we use to talk about ourselves. Mead (1934), Goffman (1955), Mauss (1967), and others have distinguished those concepts like identity which are public, interactive presentations (along with role, individual, person, Mead's "me") from those which are private and uniquely personal (self, ego, psyche, Mead's "I"). Cultural identity is considered a special form of identity: a subjective orientation to one's cultural group.[1] Although both Alba and Gans were investigating ethnic identity (rather than cultural identity), their comments regarding form versus content apply to cultural identity as well. Alba (1990) contends that ethnic identity is not merely a state of mind or self-presentation:

> As important, if not more so, are the behavioral and experiential expressions of identity, its crystallization into concrete patterns of action and relationship . . . If an ethnic identity has no *content,* no commitments in terms of action, then it represents a pure form of what Herbert Gans (1979) has called "symbolic ethnicity," a self-conscious attempt to "feel ethnic," to the exclusion of "being ethnic." (pp. 75–76)

By diminishing the internal dimension of identity, Alba attempts to readjust a perceived imbalance in favor of concrete expressions of identity. Yet, on the basis of the narratives of hearing children of deaf parents, I would turn Alba's dualism on its head. Public "patterns of action and relationship" are *not* separate from how we think and feel about ourselves. Sapir (1917), Hallowell (1955), and other interactionists emphasize that we act on the basis of how we conceive our context and our world. Nor, as these informants have continually shown, is cultural identity merely some sort of hat worn for public display. Cultural identity is an integral part of overall identity, which includes public expressions as well as private notions of self.

The lives of these informants have challenged the apparently innate and inviolate features of communication and family. I now turn to an exploration of theoretical and popular assumptions about the nature of identity. In exploring the essence of who we are, we must consider not only the relative nature of identity but why its very conceptualization has taken the particular form it has.

Leaving Home

Our occupations are one way we define who we are. Although I made concerted efforts to include as wide a range of informants as possible, one feature occurred repeatedly. At the time of this study, 65 out of the 150 informants (43.3 percent) worked primarily with deaf children or adults. These occupations included interpreters, teachers, psychological counselors, administrators, vocational counselors, speech therapists, ministers, and audiologists.[2] Twelve other informants, including lawyers, insurance agents, priests, travel agents, and physicians, routinely saw deaf people as part of their general clientele. One informant explained:

> I didn't plan on it. They just started coming in. Probably word of mouth. And once one came in, that was all it took.

In addition to the 77 informants mentioned, nine men and women had previously worked with the deaf. Another five currently did volunteer work with the deaf, such as interpreting, coaching a sports team, or serving as a phone relay operator. In total, nearly two-thirds of the informants in this study (91 out of 150) currently or previously worked in some capacity with deaf people.[3] I have not included occupations that are somewhat related to those previously described, such as a counselor for persons with physical disabilities, an interpreter in other languages, or a special education teacher.

In examining studies of other ethnic, racial, and cultural groups, I could find few other populations with such a high degree of correlation between childhood family life and adult careers.[4] Although sampling bias is possible, the informants themselves confirmed a similarly high incidence among other siblings, childhood acquaintances, and friends who were not interviewed for this study. What accounts for this tendency?

When I asked these men and women how they ended up working with the deaf, informant after informant gave testimony to an often serendipitous turn of events. More than half of those currently working with the deaf described how they had initially been solicited by someone who knew their parents were deaf:

> I remember picking up the phone and this guy says, "Your mother and father are deaf, aren't they? Well, how'd you like to earn some money." At first I didn't know what he was talking about. I thought he was some kind of pervert. [Laughs.]

Although a few informants like Keith told me they could "never imagine continuing doing this for a living," many informants felt that their careers were the inevitable result of their earlier childhood experiences, direct extensions of their family responsibilities. Several women and men mentioned starting off in other types of jobs only to find their sign language or knowledge of deaf people a more marketable skill:

> I don't know, it just happened. I didn't plan on it, but one thing led to the next and, well, I was making money for what I had done my whole life, so why not?

Career choices also recapitulated the separation between Deaf and Hearing cultures. Informants—those who currently worked with deaf people as well as those who never had—repeatedly used two phrases to describe their career options: "in deafness" or "not in deafness." During the interviews, several spoke of how they were currently reevaluating their career decision: some who worked with the deaf wanted to "get out of deafness," while others who did not work with the deaf felt it might be time to do so.

Another recurrent theme among informants' occupational choices was the continued sense of moral obligation. Denise explained: "It's the one thing I feel I can do that makes me feel worthwhile." Although there was still a sizable minority of informants who had never worked with deaf people, many of these men and women spoke of resisting external and internal pressures to pursue a career related to deaf people. The intensity and strength of this dynamic can also be seen in several informants' use of the term "abandon." One man told me, "I felt like I was abandoning deafness when I changed jobs," while another countered:

> When I hear someone say, "Oh, you abandoned deaf people," it makes me angry. I didn't abandon deafness. I chose to go into something else.

Apart from the explicit mention of their occupations, the stories of informants who worked with the deaf were generally distinguishable from those who did not. The narratives of those working with the deaf often reflected the particular vocabulary and conceptualizations of their professional backgrounds—whether in their linguistic explanations of sign language ("Sim-com," "code-switching," "Cued Speech versus SEE") or in their assessment and opinions of such topics as the Deaf power movement, trends in educational policies, and current state and federal legislation. Many men and women felt that their training and their careers offered them ways to talk about their family experiences. Richard told me:

> Until I started [a degree program], I didn't have much perspective or understandings about deaf people—or even my own life.

Yet a number of other informants questioned whether these interpretations clarified or pathologized their family experiences. This was particularly true among informants who were interpreters and teachers of the deaf. Inez recalled her interpreter training program:

> Oh, you go in thinking you have a lot of experience. And then they tell you, "That's not the way you're supposed to do it. You're doing it all

wrong." [Inez then demonstrated "correct" ways of interpreting.] And before long, you feel like, God, my family was really fucked up!

Yvonne explained how much a Deaf education program had altered her understanding of her own family:

> When I was growing up, our lives were comfortable. Normal. I wanted to date deaf guys, even thought I might marry a deaf man. Then I went to college. That was a real jolt for me. I learned more about hearing people and their ways, their customs. I went into deaf education and studied all about deafness. I learned all the negative things that deafness is. How it is isolating and cuts a person off from society. I learned about reading levels and achievement tests. I just kept absorbing all these negative ideas.

In explaining why he stopped being a teacher for the deaf, Phil wondered, "How come they can't accept that these kids are deaf and that there's nothing wrong with them?" Nevertheless, a number of informants confided that they discarded professionally endorsed methods and explanations, and frequently used their family experiences as their primary guide.

Hearing children's gravitation toward adult occupations related to deaf people suggests that earlier family adaptations often translate into life patterns. Rather than a more literal comparison with a parent's occupation, adult careers could be considered more broadly as a way of recreating and maintaining familiar childhood environments. Informants' occupations represented not merely the repetition of specific childhood tasks but a larger sense of belonging. Ella told me that "I get my strokes from deaf people—not from hearing people." Dwight explained that working with deaf people "was comfortable, like being home." Because most informants no longer lived in a deaf family nor appeared visibly Deaf, career choices were a practical resolution of how they as hearing adults could remain connected to their Deaf cultural heritage.

Another Family

These one hundred and fifty men and women were not just the children of deaf parents. They were often parents themselves—and wives, lovers, husbands, and grandparents. These second families were almost exclusively hearing. Most informants had neither deaf spouses nor deaf children. If these women and men learned the shape and meaning of family from their unique childhood experiences, how were their re-created families affected?

More than half of the informants spoke of having a greater sense of their distinct childhoods within the context of their new families. Many, like Ruby and Catherine, described a process of self-recognition:

> [Ruby:] I remember the first time my husband's family came to dinner. It wasn't like anything I had ever seen before. Not just the talking, I mean the way they acted, stiff, polite, and careful and all that. And, you know, [signs, *"vague."*] At first I thought it was just because it was the first time. But that was twenty years ago and they're still like that. Now I see that they're just acting like hearing people. [Laughs.]

> [Catherine:] When Sharon [her first child] was born, it was like, every little thing made me wonder. How did my mom and dad raise me? How did they know if I was crying in the next room? How did I learn to talk?

Other informants remembered being told by their spouses, their children, or their in-laws that there was something different about them. Stella recalled one time when her husband and daughter tried to explain it to her:

> My daughter started, "Mom, it's like you do things different, you react different, sometimes you're just weird." And I looked at my husband and he says, "Well, I guess I'm used to it, but I sure remember thinking when I first saw you with your parents that this really was pretty weird."

The previous discussions of communication styles and methods as well as family dynamics and patterns indicate that there might, indeed, be differences among those who grew up with deaf parents. And, as Stella's example indicates, these differences were often perceived as inferior or abnormal when compared to Hearing family norms.

Many women and men spoke of the extra burden of interpreting or explaining whenever their old and new families converged. As with family gatherings of deaf and hearing relatives during childhood, the cultural differences between their present families often created misunderstandings and misinterpretations. Art expressed the strain of trying to balance two families, two world views:

> My wife would say I was strange and different and she didn't understand me. I'll give an example. My father would be at the house and sometimes he'd get angry with my son [signs and pantomimes very angry deaf expressions]. And my dad isn't really that angry. I grew up with this. This is how he expresses his anger. It's cultural. But my wife, she sits there and says, "Your dad is being awfully upset. What's the matter with him?" And then she starts on me, "Everything's for your dad. Everything has to fit to your dad. And why can't he change? Why can't he modify to fit to our Hearing world?" And the next thing I'm into an argument trying to explain it. And all the while Dad doesn't understand what we're arguing about. He starts signing to me [signs, *"What the hell is wrong with her?"*]. And she's saying, "What the hell is wrong with him?" And I'm caught in the middle again.

Neither Art's hearing wife nor his hearing son could communicate with his deaf father. A few women and men felt fortunate that their spouses or children learned sign language or actively communicated with their parents. However, even among informants who were fluent in sign language, most spouses and children had difficulty communicating with informants' deaf parents. This pattern was not explained by a lack of contact between these family members: deaf parents were often a daily or weekly presence in the lives of adult informants. Many informants felt that their childhood role as interpreter had just continued into their adult lives as well. A few, like Deborah, had reached an impasse:

> I'd just had it. I was tired of having to sign everything for them. Back and forth, back and forth. I just left them [parents, husband, and four children] together for a whole weekend. And, I told them, if you want to talk to each other, then you do it. I've had it!

Although her absence promoted some direct communication between her deaf and hearing family members, Deborah confessed that the interactions were generally brief and superficial at best. Several informants felt that the social pressure to conform to spoken English had continued to its logical conclusion: the hearing grandchildren would show little or no trace of their deaf grandparents' language.

As informants discussed their childhood and adult families, one striking feature was how frequently they remained involved with their families of origin. Claire was adamantly outspoken about her feelings:

> Oh, I told him [husband] right off the bat! Don't you ever come between me and my parents. As long as we keep that straight, there won't be any problems!

Although less explicit, a similar perspective runs through many other informants' narratives as well:

> Evelyn [his wife] is really understanding about it all. She just understands that my parents need me to do some things, and that I have to go over there [parents' house] and take care of things . . . It's not like a competition or anything, it's just the way it is.

Such loyalty and interdependence runs counter to the dominant cultural pattern of separating from one's birth family. For several informants, this continued responsibility was accepted grudgingly:

> I show up at the door and they [parents] hand me a pile of letters and bills and ask me to deal with it . . . not even a hello first.

Yet most informants saw themselves as their parents' main resource in the Hearing world. Lola, an only child, described why she took her mother into her home rather than put her in a nursing home:

> Yes, of course it was hard. But there weren't any other options. When they wanted to put my mother in a nursing home, I couldn't let them do that. I couldn't. A deaf woman with no one to talk to, no one to understand her. You just have to do what you have to do . . . there's no one else.

Like many other ethnic groups, adult hearing children of deaf parents were part of an ongoing extended family, yet deaf family patterns were usually not recognized by the majority culture. Ralph commented on his public and private discrepancies:

> If I was Black or Italian or something, people might understand. They might say, Oh, your family is different because that's a different culture.

But, when they look at me, they just see this white guy who is too involved with his family. It doesn't compute.

This type of relationship also raised the issue of their parents' dependence, a stigmatizing image that most informants decidedly wanted to avoid.

Metaphors of Identity

Discussions and explanations of identity are threaded throughout these narratives. Higgins (1980) proposes: "In developing a sense of who we are, we compare ourselves to some people and contrast ourselves to others. We use both similarities and differences in establishing our identities" (p. 176). Previous chapters have shown how informants' views of themselves are reflected in their narratives about family members and childhood routines. The discussion now turns to a more immediate presentation of identity: How did these women and men see and describe themselves? Lakoff and Johnson (1980) propose that "human thought processes are largely metaphorical" (p. 6). Each culture provides metaphors which explain events, processes, and identities that otherwise may be confusing or contradictory. Thus, informants' narratives not only emphasized their unique personal histories, but expressed metaphors of identity which drew from both the Deaf and Hearing worlds.

The most prominent and most frequently discussed feature of identity was being Deaf or Hearing. As these women and men repeatedly demonstrated, these qualities were not limited to functional conditions but encompassed a much broader spectrum of values and behaviors. One informant explained:

When I'm sitting in a room or walking down the street, people look at me and they see this hearing person. That's all they see. But just beneath the surface, there's this deaf person. I'm not talking about hearing loss, I'm talking about a whole way of being. The real me is Deaf. If you want to know me, you've got to know that part of me.

Without an appreciation of the cultural dimensions of deafness, such paradoxical remarks would be nonsensical. For many informants, identifying oneself as "Deaf" or "Hearing" was akin to "coming out." Gorman (1980) describes coming out as achieving "an acceptance which is a new perception of one's self" (p. 6). For several informants, coming out meant seeing themselves as Hearing:

> A few years ago my [deaf] sister sat me down. She said, "You know, you're hearing." And I looked at her and shook my head. I said [signs, *"No, I'm the same as you, deaf"*]. She looked at me again and said, "You're hearing." And I guess that was the first time I really got it. I *was* hearing.

For many others, being Deaf was a reclamation of an important part of their history and identity:

> ["Do you feel that you're being pushed out of Deaf culture?"] Ten years ago I think that deaf people tried to push me out . . . But I got to the point where I started saying, Wait a minute! You can't get rid of your kids, and you can't get rid of people that are part of Deaf culture. We are as much a part of Deaf culture. We're not a hearing person coming in and telling you what to do. We're your kids! We grew up in the same household. You cannot deny me that.

Although being "Deaf" or "Hearing" suggests cultural allegiances and boundaries, these were also ways informants talked about themselves and differentiated themselves from one group or another. In this respect, the paradoxical identity of these informants—being deaf while being hearing—underscores the diversity and the contradictions possible among any group of individuals who are summarily viewed as a monolithic cultural whole.

A second metaphor of identity recalls a childhood of versatility and malleability. For Jim, this facet of his past expressed a present sense of unfocused identity:

> I'm constantly looking at my face in the mirror and [signs: *"I don't know. I don't know who that is"*]. It's one of the first questions everybody asks me, "What was it like being the child of deaf parents?" As a boy, I felt like a chameleon. I just adapted to every situation, I could be any role. And I was in that role—at least for a while. I was my mother when I had to interpret for her, I was my father when I had to interpret for him.

> I was the mechanic, the teacher, the car salesman. I assumed the personality of whoever was speaking at any given time. I *was* that person. I was whatever anybody thought I should be. You know, I fit into that mold just like a chameleon.

Using the identical image, Maureen's explanation took an entirely different turn:

> I was a chameleon. I learned it as a kid. Doing different things, being different things. I do it now. You can change your hair, you can change your clothes, you can go see what's going on. One night I could go into a French restaurant with somebody, then the next night I could go into a health food restaurant in another part of town, and then I could go to Chinatown. And I did. ["Did you ever feel like you didn't know who you were?"] Oh no. I'm not the kind of person that's easily affected and swayed by people. I've always had that inner strength where I know who I am. On the outside I changed so I could be invisible, but not my character. I kept my mouth shut because then I could get in and see what things were really like. I could physically go places where they wouldn't really know I was there. I was learning and watching.

These two different uses of the same metaphor illustrate an important point. In retelling who we are, we borrow from our past—but we explain from our present. Jim and Maureen's image of "chameleon" is rooted in similar childhood experiences, and it captures the sense of changing roles that many other informants have also described. Yet Jim and Maureen's explanations are different—not only because their actual experience may have been different, but because their present sense of themselves is different.

A third group of metaphors recalls informants' role of bridging the gap between deaf and hearing people. In describing themselves and their responsibilities, informants frequently used metaphors that evoked their special capacity to provide their parents and hearing people with glimpses of each other's world: "the conduit," "the link," "the medium," "the bridge," "the go-between." Such metaphors were routinely preceded by the definite article rather than the indefinite "a." This usage reiterates most informants' sense of their role as unique and crucial: "I was *the* bridge between my parents and the Hearing world." Narratives explaining this aspect of identity were often over-laid with a strong sense of moral obligation:

> If I didn't link them up, who would do it? ["Did you ever think about not doing it?"] Sure, sure I thought about it, but I couldn't. I had to do it. Who else would do it?

Many informants took pride in their ability to perform this service, and often suggested that these skills carried over to adult tasks such as conciliation and negotiation—in personal relationships as well as in the workplace.

Several men and women felt that the role of connecting the Deaf and Hearing worlds robbed them of a separate identity. Martha remembered one incident that dramatized this:

> I was asked to draw a picture of myself once, my body and how I saw myself. I started drawing my parents on one side, and then these hearing people on the other. But I didn't know what I looked like. I couldn't do it. I could draw anybody else in my family, but not me . . . [her voice fades].

The fourth metaphor of identity touches upon the previous three: a space between two worlds. For some, it expressed the limbo of being between the Deaf and Hearing worlds; for others, the constant shifting of interpreting and mediating roles:

> It's like you live in this mirror world, you reflect what they say, but where are you? Where am I? I live in the mirror, I'm only a reflection.

These metaphors of fused and amorphous identities are based on an ideal of separateness and distinctness. Yet this perspective reflects biases of the Hearing culture and contemporary American culture, both of which value individualism and regard identity as a separate and objectively defined phenomenon.[5] Such notions of identity conflict with cultures which value interdependence, and in which one's identity is part of an overall relationship to others. Hsu (1972) writes that "the Chinese and Japanese have stronger ties with their families and wider kin groups than do the Jews, and are, therefore, less self-reliant and less free but more protected from the uncertainty of identity" (p. 390).

The space between the Deaf and Hearing worlds becomes a particularly important metaphor for many informants, expressing the conflicting perspectives and values that contribute to feelings of cultural marginality. Feelings of ambiguity also suggest a compelling predisposition to seek out ways of resolving this marginalization.

Culture and Marginality

Sapir (1924) wrote that "the worlds in which different societies live are distinct worlds, not merely the same world with different labels attached" (p. 402). Whorf (1956) continued the argument that language is an indicator and shaper of thought. Although critics have downplayed the Sapir-Whorf hypothesis, their dismissal centers on what is presumed to be an overly deterministic relationship between language and thought. But Sapir and Whorf were concerned with habitual patterns that organize thought and influence behaviors—*not* invariable absolutes that constrain all thought. Looking beyond the implications of grammatical and semantic categorizations, language remains a powerful reflection of culture. It is, perhaps, among the Deaf that language and culture achieve an unparalleled relationship. In Deaf culture, language is *the* integral feature: both its soul and its demon, both the barrier to and the means of social interaction.

This paradoxical relationship with language is an important dynamic among deaf people. In reviewing some of the myths and stories in Deaf culture, Padden and Humphries (1988) observe:

> What we see in all these texts is the formulation and expression of ideas that Deaf people hold to be true and immutable. The ingredients for achieving the desirable world are the same: signed language and the shared knowledge of Deaf people, or what Veditz calls "their thoughts and souls, their feelings, desires, and needs." (p. 37)

Despite the centrality of sign language—as an expression of self and a means of interaction—this soul of Deaf culture has repeatedly been opposed and colonized by the Hearing world. Ironically, such oppression has enhanced Deaf culture. Blauner (1972) suggests that racism is the "single most important source of developing ethnic peoplehood"

(p. 140). As deaf people struggle to preserve their language and their world, they bring their index finger to their lips and point out their oppressor's idiosyncrasy: They use their mouths to communicate.[6] Deaf people have learned and adopted the fundamental dichotomy that initially set them apart from hearing people: If you cannot speak our language, you are different from us. The experience of deafness has come full circle. Now, to be hearing is to be shut out.

As the centers of the Deaf and Hearing worlds become more sharply defined, a paradox of identity emerges for these informants: those who are deaf remain on the periphery of the Hearing world; those who are hearing remain on the margins of the Deaf world. Caught between these conflicting worlds, these men and women appear to be people without culture.[7] Throughout history, groups of people have been separated off from the dominant culture by birthright, geographic boundaries, racial features, and occupational differences: untouchables (India), Cagots (France and Spain), Solubba (Arabia), potters (Africa), Kauwa (Hawaiian islands). These people remain on the periphery, unable to achieve the status, power, and visibility that ensure membership in the dominant culture. Park (1950) describes the marginal man:

> The stranger stays, but he is not settled. He is a potential wanderer. That means that he is not bound as others are by the local proprieties and conventions. (p. 351)

Bilinguals present a special case of marginality. Although they can often pass within one language group or another, bilinguals remain partially anchored outside the group. Grosjean (1982) emphasizes that the history of linguistic usage and interaction among bilinguals is a critical determinant of language choice; he cites children of immigrant families who continue speaking the minority language with their parents and grandparents despite knowing the majority language much better. The potentially expansive and harmonious aspects of bilingualism are often undermined by a history of conflict between the two language groups. These informants have lived this conflict, adeptly splitting their choice of expression between speaking and signing. Such splitting may account for why some researchers were unable to find significant differences between hearing children of deaf parents and the general population, since their studies were conducted using only the spoken word. McLaughlin (1978) thinks the character of the marginal man is overdrawn with respect to bilinguals. However, his assertion relies upon research which found that many bilinguals have formed their own community:

> Many people in contact with two cultures may at first seek to belong solely to one or the other, but with time they realize that they are most at ease with people who share their bicultural experience. (p. 28)

Although an organization like CODA offers members a bicultural respite, it is usually a temporary solution within a world largely defined as either Deaf or Hearing.

One phenomenon that arose toward the end of my research was "coda-talk,"[8] which refers to a highly creative combination of ASL and spoken English that is both voiced and signed.[9] Coda-talk was limited to a handful of informants and members of CODA, and was almost always used privately among hearing children of deaf parents. Rachel's father had been recently hospitalized in another state. As Rachel, using coda-talk, retold the story of her father's illness to a small group of other adult hearing children of deaf parents, the carefully crafted balance of shifting between two worlds crumbled under the strain of her father's illness and the different patterns of response from the Deaf and Hearing worlds:[10]

> What must tell you, me find bad news. Father very sick, hospital, heart. Deaf part of me think deaf way. But me live in Hearing world, have hearing roommates, have hearing friends. All act like hearing people. At my house, hearing house. Me sit by phone. Alone. What happen when me tell hearing roommates, they walk out of room. Me find out hearing people think, something happen, your private business. Not ask questions. Leave you alone. Think if you want talk, you talk they listen, but not ask questions. Me call hearing friends, please come over, need see you. One hearing friend say, busy, can't, but give phone support. Other hearing friend say, I have this block of time. Hearing time. This little block of time. Deaf way very different. Deaf come. In your face, ask ask ask. Want to know everything, A to Z. Important touch. We sit down. Discuss, group. Face to face . . .

I say what is this Hearing way? Stupid hearing people. I never hate hearing people so much in my whole life. That one week with Hearing. All hearing friends mine. They nice people, but something going on. Conflict. Hearing way, deaf way different. I was so mad. At who? God? Deaf? Hearing? It awful situation. I say I'm leaving tomorrow, go visit deaf friends. I'm out of this Hearing hell. I feel like I am in crazy world. Hearing way very different. I thought my goal to be hearing woman. Now, what? I have Hearing life. Me sick of this shit. Hearing friends not know sign language, not know parents, not know nothing!

Although coda-talk alternately follows the grammatical and syntactic rules of both languages, there appears to be a high degree of consistency among users. Coda-talk was seen by proponents as a way of expressing two conflicting linguistic heritages. Many other informants—even those who were active participants in CODA—were highly critical of coda-talk as "immature" or "a mockery of sign language." While conceding that coda-talk captured a certain sense of the mixture of signing and speaking, most informants felt that coda-talk was intensely private and personal; public usage was tantamount to a betrayal of a family and cultural trust. Although coda-talk is not fully explored here, it is one way that some hearing children of deaf parents expressed the duality and marginality variously described by most other informants. The informants' strong disagreements over coda-talk reverberated among other topics as well, such as ways of interpreting, educational methods, and, ultimately, the overall interpretation of their family experience. A few informants tried to steer me toward or away from certain other hearing children of deaf parents, depending on whether these others would corroborate or invalidate their own perspectives.

The cultural marginality of these informants was heightened by perspectives that were frequently circumscribed by their particular family histories. At various points along the border between these two worlds, hearing children and deaf parents provided each other with a distinct vision of that other world. Stigma and oppression also exacerbated the feeling of isolation and often prevented a more fully realized cultural experience. Yet, despite their disagreements over particulars, almost all informants described a sense of kinship among others like themselves.[11] Weber (1968) defines an ethnic group as one whose members

> entertain a subjective belief in their common descent because of similarities of physical type or of customs or both, or because of memories of colonization and migration . . . it does not matter whether or not an objective blood relationship exists. (p. 389)

As Dan walked down the sidewalk to meet me, he greeted me with an unmistakable affirmation of our common heritage, "I don't know you, but I know you."

The rift of language, of how we express ourselves, which parts of our bodies we can and cannot use—our mouths, eyes, ears, or hands—becomes a profound separation between worlds and between families. The more marginal, the more ambiguous, the more intangible one's position in the world is, the greater the need to attach to something—whether a belief system, an explanation, or a group. People need to have meaning and reasons for why things are the way they are. It is how people make sense of their world. Because there is so much ambiguity in deafness, the search for explanations and membership is part of the culture of Deafness. Separated from family and origins, deaf parents and their hearing children must ask: Where do I belong?

Explanations

When I phoned Ellen the night before her interview, she gave me directions to her home and asked me what time I was planning to get up the next morning. Knowing it would take several hours to drive there, I told her my alarm was set for 5:00 A.M. Ellen laughed and then said:

> I know you're a child of deaf parents because, you know, deaf people get up early.

In fact, my parents do get up early—but I had never considered this a cultural trait. Ellen later explained that her parents were raised in residential schools where they always had to get up early, and this lifelong pattern had shaped her own behavior. Ellen's observation came near the end of my fieldwork, so I was unable to test fully the accuracy of her generalization. (I did meet adult hearing children and deaf parents who did *not* get up early—despite having attended residential schools.) Although her generalization may have been flawed, what was striking about Ellen's remark was that, like most other informants, she regularly generated hypotheses about the personal impact of having deaf parents. Often, an informant broadened his or her hypotheses to include other hearing children of deaf parents as well.

During my months of fieldwork, these women and men offered me numerous explanations and hypotheses about their present adult lives, concerning certain behaviors, values, interests, ways of interacting—all the components of identity. Why were explanations made at all? Like most other informants, David felt, "It's got to mean something." When people are plagued by the need to have meaning and to have things make sense, Kleinman (1988) suggests that there is a comfort in explanatory models—even those that are negative. Explanations make people feel better. The heightened sense of marginality among many of these informants may accentuate the need to seek out explanations of their ambiguous and paradoxical experiences. Park (1950) suggests that marginal people are especially attracted to membership in ideological groups. Laura half-kiddingly confided:

> Sometimes I wish someone would just hand me a list that says, Here is what having deaf parents means. This, this, this. I'm tired of trying to figure it out.

Each of these men and women used particular terms, concepts, and analogies to explain their experiences—explanations that helped them tell their story. Thus I often felt after an interview that a particular informant's explanation made sense to me. However, an attempt to resolve ambiguity and paradox often results in a singular version of truth, an unconflicted world view that explains one's experiences. When I compared one informant's explanation with that of another, there were contradictions.

Although informants differed in many of the specifics of their family histories as well as the context of their present adult lives, three overall explanatory models emerged.[12]

1. The *medical model* centers on the biomedical causes and treatment of deafness. Medical explanations were sometimes pragmatic ("All I know is being deaf means you can't hear") and sometimes profoundly pathologizing ("Being deaf was like being sick your whole life").

2. The *psychological model* stresses psychological outcomes of deafness for deaf parents and their hearing children. Such explanations often reflected the popular literature on adult children of other types of parents. Among the informants, the two most frequently used analogies were children of alcoholics and adult children from dysfunctional families.

3. The *cultural model* proposes a cultural framework to explain differences in behaviors and world views. Informants using this approach often suggested comparisons with other minority groups and children of immigrants.

An individual informant's analogies and explanations usually did not conform to a single model. More typically, each informant fashioned an amalgam of explanations out of two or all three perspectives. Although I have endorsed a cultural view of Deaf people in this book, informants' cultural explanations are treated here as one possible model. There are a few points of clarification. First, not all informants were equally exposed to or part of Deaf culture, nor do I suggest that cultural explanations supersede all others. Second, the meaning of "culture" varied among informants, and this affected how cultural explanations were understood and used. Finally, because most informants did not have opportunities to test out their cultural hypotheses, some of them proposed cultural traits (for example, getting up early, eating left-handed, being fluent in sign language) that were not actually shared among the larger sample of informants.

The excuse . . . the opportunity . . . the challenge . . . the defect: Informants weighed all that happened and did not happen because of their parents' deafness. They considered both positive and negative outcomes. Whether their quest was lifelong or time-limited, informants were strongly opinionated about the meaning and outcomes of having deaf parents. In considering these three explanatory models, I am less concerned with critiquing each model than considering how informants used these models to describe their experiences. Generally, the medical model was acceptable only as a way to describe a functional condition: being deaf meant you could not hear. Most informants felt that attempts to correct deaf people—whether through such methods as speech therapy or cochlear implants—set a dangerous, near-genocidal precedent. Della explained her disdain for such explanations:

> It's this medical idea of deficit. That deaf people are broken, that we hearing children of deaf parents are broken. That somehow there is something broken, there is something deficient that needs to get fixed.

Among these men and women there was considerable dissension over the expected social and psychological outcomes of not being able to hear. Most informants felt that perceived handicaps were socially created:

> It's only because people think you have to talk that deaf people aren't normal. When everybody's standing around a jet engine, who can talk, who can hear?

Only a few felt that not being able to hear was intrinsically disabling. Yet most women and men acknowledged that in a less than ideal world, there were consequences of being deaf—for their parents and for themselves. Informants often proposed analogies to their experiences: children of alcoholics; children of immigrants; children of Holocaust survivors; minority groups, including non–English speaking people; women; gays. Psychological explanations vied with cultural interpretations—for individual informants as well as among the group as a whole. Although Richard and Hannah never met, they argued against each other's explanations. Richard felt that the "adult children" literature helped him understand his own family experiences:

> When I thought about being in a dysfunctional family, I tried to understand and to match up. I don't like the term but it helped me to understand my own family. In alcoholic families, the kids are the ones who have to cover up for their alcoholic parents, to keep everything

hidden away, not let the outside world see. They have to kind of take responsibility, adult responsibilities for their family's functioning. And it seems to me that's true for a lot of hearing kids with deaf parents. Not necessarily that we're covering up, but you were helping your deaf parents function in the Hearing world. And that's a terrible responsibility to put on kids. And as a result, we take on this responsibility to fix everything, to be the one who handles everything, and we take responsibility beyond our years.

Hannah felt the analogy with children of alcoholics was overdrawn:

I really resent being compared to the alcoholic. I think there are more differences than there are similarities. The symptom may be the same, but the cause is something different. In an alcoholic family a person is covering up an illness, covering up for whatever bad things happened in that family. They cover up for something that's really bad. Whereas with our kind we're fixing things, we're cultural mediators here. If we're covering over something or trying to help with something, it's like because they're cultural differences. And that's not something bad. But we're functioning the same way. We are given more responsibilities. So the symptoms may be the same, but just because you have a runny nose doesn't mean you have pneumonia.

As they considered various analogies and explanations, informants often commented on their own multiple perspectives. Phil felt that his dual heritage provided access to two world views:

We can see both sides because we're on both sides. A lot of issues can get very confusing. There are all these issues that get very intermingled . . . It's just a matter of continuing to sift and sift and sift and see which seem to apply.

Edith described herself as shifting perspectives according to her own life events:

I think my own perspective changes almost with the weather. Sometimes I feel as though some of the roots of my difficulties are pathological and sometimes I feel as though they are cultural. And when things are going smoothly and things are going well and I'm feeling a lot stronger and stable it becomes more "culturicized." And when I feel that I can't get to the root of the situation I tend to ask then what's wrong with this.

Then I flip over to the other side. I don't know that it's either-or, black or white.

Phil and Edith's descriptions echo the chameleon-like metaphors of identity described earlier in this chapter. Many informants' narratives indicate a relative comfort with dual or multiple perspectives. Al's remarks, however, evoke a faceless and unending limbo:

It seems to me that part of the problem we have is that we have too many different perspectives. Sometimes I feel blessed because I can see so many points of view. But sometimes I feel cursed because I never know my own.

In their search to find the right balance of explanations, informants borrowed analogies and terms more often from either medically oriented or psychologically oriented models than from cultural ones:

Those children that are involved with alcoholic situations in their homes are more or less a victim of the situation. And I don't think that we are victims of the situation. People with alcohol are a whole different thing because alcoholism is a disease and the family members are victims. Deafness is *not* a disease.

Yet explaining family phenomena through medical or psychological explanatory models reinforces an aberrant perspective of deafness. Even while using pathologically oriented models, informants frequently strained out pathological implications:

Somebody said I was being co-dependent, and I said "enabling." He said, "Well it's really the same thing." Well, it's *not* the same thing! You can call my family dysfunctional because we weren't like other families. But, that's not dysfunctional, that's just being different. We functioned better than most families.

Another informant said:

Well, the alcoholic thing doesn't play well for me and I think it doesn't play well for a lot of people. And some make comparisons with children of immigrants or Holocaust survivors. Maybe that's a more accurate parallel because we're dealing with children of people who have been oppressed and had to fight to survive no matter what kind of cultural background. And there are a lot of parallels that those children have that really mirror the type of things that we deal with.

Although almost all women and men acknowledged some sense of a Deaf culture, informants were generally more tentative and less precise when they used cultural explanations:

["So, what do you think Deaf culture is?"] Well, you tell me, you're the anthropologist! [Laughs.]

Another informant said:

Yes, I believe there *is* a Deaf culture. ["What is Deaf culture?"] [Long pause.] Well, I don't know. It's hard to explain. ["Can you give me an example?"] Well, it's like the way we did things. ["Like what?"] Oh, I don't know, everything!

Despite the fact that most informants felt a cultural model was less pathologizing and preferable, the use of noncultural explanations continued to dominate their narratives. This trend has significant implications for the individual and collective identities of these informants, reflecting a much broader cultural pattern of how we explain ourselves.

Joining a Culture

Almost all informants felt that having deaf parents was a major part of their history and, to varying degrees, their adult identity. As discussed, their interpretations often reflected the vernacular and analogies of psychological models. Why were some explanations more salient than others? What makes a "good" explanation? Is it the way it resolves contradictions, the way it fits within a particular scheme, the values it espouses? A number of informants told me that, over the years, they had changed their minds about the impact of having deaf parents. Harold's remarks were typical: "If you had asked me just a couple of years ago, I would have said, What? Deaf parents? No big deal." Like many other informants, Harold now felt that having deaf parents was indeed a "big deal."

What was the source of this change? Harold explained his own rethinking by saying, "Well, after a divorce, after 40, you start looking at things differently." As in Harold's case, one of the most common reasons given by informants was that some major life event—a birth, a death, beginning or ending a relationship, or other personal crisis— caused them to reexamine their premises of self. Although these changes may reflect intrinsic developmental stages of separation and individuation, such as those proposed by Erikson, the motivation to pursue self-exploration is also strongly endorsed in contemporary American culture. The search for and the explanations of self become a highly viable form of dialogue in adult life, and the overall shape of this quest is highly specific. Within a social context that values individual effort and objectivist definitions, the locus of explanations is sharply focused on the immediate environment of the family rather than larger social and cultural contexts. As the unquestioned source for our biological, social, and psychological origins, the family has become the ultimate arena for understanding ourselves and determining the origins of life's dilemmas.

For most informants, having deaf parents was part of this developmental and social process of identity. Nearly two-thirds of all individual informants' discussions about their identities and their parents fit an age-dependent pattern: younger informants were more matter-of-fact and less introspective; middle-aged informants tended to be more introspective and conflicted; older informants were generally more resolved about previous identity and family issues. There were, however, numerous exceptions to this pattern. Marjorie, a 71-year-old grandmother, told me:

> My whole life, mostly, people would ask me and I would tell them it didn't make any difference whatsoever. I wasn't lying. I just really felt that way. ["And now?"] Ha! Now I see it made all the difference in the world.

Jerry was a 19-year-old college sophomore:

> I don't understand how they [other adult hearing children of deaf parents] can think it was nothing. It's such a big part of my life! It's who I am.

More than one-fourth of these women and men were currently or had been in therapy, and most described having discovered that they had ignored or denied issues and feelings concerning having deaf parents.

Changes in perspective on oneself and family were not always a function of age or life crises. A number of men and women felt that increased public attention and the greater visibility of deaf people had led to their own interest in considering the impact of their Deaf heritage. Several informants reported that meeting with other hearing children of deaf parents, particularly those involved with CODA, had helped to redirect their focus:

> I thought I had dealt with a lot of it, but it wasn't until I was around other codas that something special happened. Because it is like deaf people who are isolated from each other, they end up pulling together. They have a different sense of who they are as a deaf person, and what deaf people can do. Somehow, for me, to be with other codas shifted and brought me in touch with things I never quite imagined were there.

Popular culture and the media also contributed to such reconsiderations; a number of men and women cited particular self-help books on "adult children" as well as John Bradshaw's television series on dysfunctional families.[13]

Although self-explorations were usually not initially centered on having deaf parents, this feature unfolded as a routine part of remembering and analyzing childhood and family experiences. During this process, having deaf parents often became *the* issue:

> Oh, boy, do I remember. After a year or so, my therapist sitting there and saying, "Well, so you're finally gonna deal with having deaf parents. Now we're getting to the heart of the problem."

Whether in therapists' offices or in conversations with friends, in matching themselves against the paradigm of the "normal family," these men and women often came up short. Cultural differences of the Deaf world became subsumed and reinterpreted according to the norms of the Hearing world. These men and women were still "enmeshed" with their families; there were issues of dependence; communication was undoubtedly a major problem. Whittaker (1992) suggests:

The knowledge of self has spawned a form of cultural negotiator, commonly called professionals, whose business it is to socialize, correct socialization, and resocialize persons into appropriate understandings and knowledge about oneself. (p. 196)

Some men and women felt that only within the security of being with others like themselves could they openly explore their heritage and their identities. A number of informants thought that CODA provided such a forum. Nick talked about attending a CODA conference:

I went to one [CODA] conference and there was this speaker who talked about how adolescents and parents sort things out. Even kids with hearing parents. And, see, I didn't know a lot of that stuff! I didn't know that! I thought it was the deafness. I blamed everything on the deafness. I didn't know that! My father would say, "You think just because I'm deaf that I'm nothing, that you're better than me?" But now I see hearing parents do the same thing, say, "Listen, you don't think your family is worth anything?" It's the same thing. It's just that this is how hearing parents say it, this is how deaf people say it. It was like, Oh, now I get it! Parents, apron strings, all that. It happens in all families!

Nick found CODA helpful in understanding how his deaf parents were fundamentally like hearing parents, and how they expressed themselves differently. Others, however, were skeptical about CODA, feeling that too often it mirrored groups that were more pathological in nature:

It seems like CODA has adopted a lot of ideas from Adult Children of Alcoholics. Maybe it's a first step, but I'm not sure it's the right step. Not that there aren't things in there that aren't helpful to us. But there are other alternatives that also can explain us. Like children of Holocaust survivors. Children of immigrants. And I think if you look hard at both of those populations we can see lots of parallels and maybe see different goals. And, it says something about how we see ourselves. We've had unique experiences, and maybe some of them *were* painful. But why were they painful? Is the source some cultural or social problem that we have in the world in terms of accepting differences?

Finding the right analogies and explanations was only part of the struggle for those within and outside of CODA. Identifying oneself as a member of a group with a shared history and values also involved conflicting cultural values: whether to be oriented toward the group or toward the individual. Most informants had experienced both perspectives: Deaf parents who often found security, understanding, and a strengthened identity within a community of others like themselves; a Hearing world that stressed individualism, autonomy, and the apparent loss of identity for those who are interdependent. Among those informants who participated in CODA, many used terms that recalled previous descriptions of the Deaf club: "I feel safe there." "I can be myself there." "I don't have to interpret for anyone." Others, like Pam, told me: "Oh, I don't really need CODA right now. I've figured it out on my own." Harry's dilemma expresses this conflict between group support and autonomy:

> Yes, CODA is helpful. I feel like these are people who really understand me. When I'm there, I don't feel judged because my parents are deaf. Everyone's parents are deaf . . . But, you know, it's an artificial world. They don't allow outsiders in, you know, deaf people or hearing people who don't have deaf parents. There might be too much misunderstanding. And, sure I understand, there probably would be misunderstandings. But CODA is this moment frozen in time, between worlds. There's a real world out there, with deaf people and hearing people. We can't keep ourselves shut off forever. We might feel like we would like to, but . . . ["But, what?"] But, at some point, I've got to figure it out for myself, in my own way.

The various ways of describing and explaining their lives posed a significant dilemma for these women and men. By espousing more broadly recognizable interpretations of family and self, they joined the mainstream culture whose norms often condemned their deaf family way of life. By aligning themselves with their deaf parents, they remained members of a marginalized culture in which their own status was ambiguous and paradoxical. In describing post-Hiroshima survivors, Lifton (1970) observes:

> I found that these survivors both felt themselves in need of special help, and resented whatever help was offered to them because they equated

it with weakness and inferiority . . . I found that this equation of nurturance with a threat to autonomy was a major theme of contemporary life. (p. 327)

For many informants, the uncertainties of membership in the Deaf world were often far preferable to a life of isolation and hollow individualism within the dominant Hearing culture. Bellah and colleagues (1985) suggest that the moral diffusion that stems from American individualism can be countered by collective memories such as ethnicity. Most informants continued to acknowledge and assert their cultural ties to the Deaf world. Helen's perspective corroborates this continued sense of connection:

Deafness is our lifeline. You know, when you're born, they cut the umbilical cord and you're a separate person. Well, with deafness you can never cut the umbilical cord. Those of us who were raised in it, we can never leave it behind.

. . . .

Our identities evolve from both similarities to and differences from others. Such distinctions emerge within historical, social, and cultural contexts which determine not only the significance of particular features but overall patterns of response: to assert our uniqueness or to emphasize our shared sense of purpose and being. Same, or different? Are you hearing, or are you deaf? Most of the men and women in this study faced a paradox of identity: wanting to be the same as their parents and wanting to be different from them. Wanting to be like hearing people and wanting to be like deaf people. Perin (1988) observes that "the stranger is the universal crosser of lines . . . the stranger is whomever we cannot place within our accustomed order" (p. 28). Without hesitation, Emily responded when I asked her:

Do I ever feel deaf? Yes. There is a deaf woman in me. And sometimes I'm very sad for her. I love it when she just gets to be, when she can be present without me being conscious of her. Like when I get together with my deaf friends. When we're together, then that Deaf part of me comes out. People always tell me, You sign like you're deaf. Well, I was, I am Deaf. I was in another lifetime until I was told it wasn't nice for a hearing person to play deaf. But I wasn't playing. I really was. I really am Deaf.

Hearing children of deaf parents appear to be people without culture—straddling a land between the Deaf and the Hearing. Their family experiences include both the normalcy of deafness and the normalcy of hearing, the stigma of deafness and the tyranny of hearing. Yet their dilemma of identity also illustrates the fallacy of cultural dichotomization: you must be Deaf, or you must be Hearing. As one informant told me:

> I'm not deaf, but I'm not hearing. [Signs, *"I don't know, I'm not deaf or hearing. Both, I guess."*]

Braroe (1975) suggests that "to be 'between two worlds' forces individuals into conflicts of choice and produces casualties among those who cannot embrace either the old or the new ways exclusively" (pp. 7–8). These informants' narratives have highlighted a prevailing American ethos, a "flight from ambiguity," as Levine (1985) describes it. The security of categorization, uniformity, and dichotomization characterizes both Hearing *and* Deaf cultures.

Even anthropologists have fallen prey to this world view. The myriad relationships between people with apparent differences and those "others" around them embody a search that has remained fundamental and yet elusive in anthropology: understanding "the other." Can a better understanding of this distant other ultimately provide a better understanding of ourselves? Yet culture, too, is not a category but a continuum: not a dichotomization between ourselves and that infamous Other, but a dialogue between self and group. Hearing children of deaf parents are not only on the margin of one culture or the other; they are also at the center. This is the paradox not merely of these informants' lives, but of that enigmatic framework we call "culture." We are different *and* we are also the same. We are not deaf. We are not hearing. We are neither deaf nor hearing. We are both deaf and hearing.

Hearing children of deaf parents move the schism between those who are different and those who are not to its ultimate setting. Here, the confrontation and the dialogue are not between those separated by geographic boundaries or political allegiances, between parent and child, or between Deaf and Hearing. Here, the drama of belonging and of being different unfolds within oneself. It is a reminder that we must understand not only the contents and meanings of each side of the equation, but also that the dichotomy itself is a social creation. All along, as Robert Murphy (1990) so eloquently recognized, this so-different, so-distant "other" has included ourselves as well.

Now, instead of being interpreters between the Deaf and the Hearing, we speak with blended and broken voices—neither completely deaf nor completely hearing, neither exclusively in sign nor exclusively in spoken words. We speak to hearing parents and hearing educators who never fully understood or accepted deafness, to deaf parents who were shut out of a Hearing world and learned to reject and mistrust Hearing ways, and to the vast majority of others who may learn from our struggles at finding out who we are.

Epilogue

When my mother was two years old the babysitter forgot to strap her into the baby carriage. My mother fell out, hitting her head on the sidewalk. The concussion broke both her eardrums and she lost her hearing. My mother jokes that maybe the fall caused her to lose a little sense as well. My grandparents took her to specialists all over the country, but it was no use. Their only child, perfect in every way, was changed forever.

My mother would tell me the story of the time she was pregnant with me. My grandmother had discouraged her from having children. When my mother became pregnant, my grandmother even suggested having an abortion. My mother wasn't sure why her mother was so adamant. Maybe my grandmother thought a deaf woman would have a hard time raising a child. Maybe, because my mother was an only child, my grandmother thought her daughter wouldn't hold up under the drudgeries of motherhood. Yet from the day I was born my grandmother doted on me. My mother figured that my grandmother's sudden change of heart had something to do with mellowing out.

Within the past few years, my mother discovered that she had an older deaf aunt and a younger deaf cousin: three generations of deaf relatives who had never met. Each of their families had kept them secret from each other. It now appears more than likely that my mother was born deaf. The story about falling out of the baby carriage probably wasn't true at all.

Had my grandparents actually known their daughter was born deaf? It's hard to know for sure. My grandmother died many years ago. This piece of family history leads to a dead end. Sometimes I wonder if my grandmother worried that if my mother had a deaf child, the family secret would have been discovered. I don't know if my grandmother knew it as a statistical risk—not measured in numbers, only in fear. When I was little, I remember my grandmother telling me how proud and how happy my grandfather would be if he were only alive to see me. Now I wonder if she meant something more than nostalgia for her dead husband. Maybe it was because I turned out hearing. A generation later, if I had been born deaf, the truth might have unmasked a lifetime of secrets.

When I was growing up in rural Illinois, my grandmother would visit us almost every weekend. She slept on a cot in my room. Sometimes there would be a bond between us as we both huddled in the darkness, in the silence made into a family. We would both listen to the noises of the clock in the living room or the wind outside. What she never knew was that although we were both hearing, the sounds in the night were different for each of us. She had come before the deafness. I had come after it.

Higgins (1980) briefly mentions that being the hearing son of deaf parents had a profound impact on his research on deaf people. He does not, however, talk about how his research affected him. Agar (1980) points out that "it is just such a concern with the intersubjective breaches between ethnographer, informant and audience that helps explain the recent interest in hermeneutics in anthropology" (p. 231). Toward the end of these interviews, one informant asked me about listening to all these stories: "Do you think it has changed you at all?" He had cut right through to the heart of the matter. Wasn't I, too, answerable to the question: How did having deaf parents make a difference in my life, in who I am? And how did the research itself affect my own sense of self and of my parents?

I first recognized one of the difficulties of being an inside researcher when I went home to visit my parents. My mother innocently asked whom I was going to see. Had I seen the Zeplaks' daughter yet, and what was she like? Was I going to see the Meehans' son? He must be in his forties by now. And both of my parents wanted to know what people were telling me. In *Hunger of Memory,* Rodriguez (1982) laments that the more he identified with the academic world, the greater was his sense of alienation from his father: the more he learned, the more his father shrank. My parents grew during the process of writing this book. They abided by the rules of confidentiality and anonymity, which appear strangely impersonal and distancing in the Deaf world. They allowed me to use their personal stories in the preface and the epilogue. And, finally, without knowing the potential renown or shame such public disclosures might bring, they gave me permission to write this book as I saw fit. Unlike any of my informants, my name would unavoidably be public, and because of the intimate and interactive network within the Deaf community, my parents would share in my uncertain recognition.

A frequent part of the interview process was a reciprocal exchange of family histories: mine for theirs. These men and women wanted to hear about my parents, about my life—not as a condition of being interviewed, but largely out of trying to learn about their own lives and history. I struggled to keep the focus on the informants' experiences so that I would not bias or distort their perspectives. Yet some degree of personal sharing was both affirming and reciprocal. I also recognized that my attempt to maintain researcher detachment was how a hearing person would have done it. I abandoned my early attempts to keep myself totally anonymous during the interviews, and became more relaxed about talking about myself. If my initial research methods reflected a Hearing bias, there were also aspects of fieldwork that meshed quite well with Deaf ways: open-ended conversations, questions, lengthy and detailed explanations, and just plain old storytelling. Although most informants did not know me or my parents, often memories of my own family history surfaced as they told me of theirs. Until these interviews, I had never told anyone about the times I had faked phone calls on behalf of my parents. I had forgotten the time when one of my grade school teachers assigned me to give a class presentation on "Deafness" while all the other kids got topics like "Baseball," "Sewing," and "Pets."

One aspect of being an anthropologist is that you don't keep your distance. In trying to learn another's point of view, you become as fully absorbed as possible into the hearts and minds of those around you. The line is different for each anthropologist—according to the particular circumstances, the anthropologist's own comfort level, and critical decisions regarding ethical standards. The process is one of enmeshing, mirroring, reflecting, and, temporarily, losing one's identity. Being an inside researcher intensified this experience. Among this group of women and men, I lost a certain sense of individuality. The mark of distinction that I hold among most other people was no longer unique.

Distance is also important in anthropology. From the synergy of temporary insider as well as the eventual return to your own culture come insights about yourself and those who have been studied. But what about those of us who began as members of the group? How does our intimacy affect not our entry, but our leaving? How do you create distance in order to explain these experiences to outsiders? For myself, distance was sometimes measured by intervening periods of travel, by geographic distance, by births, by deaths. Leaving, of course, is a misnomer. I can never leave being the hearing son of deaf parents. It is part of who I am. I also have a very faraway place within myself—I am also hearing. It is my dual heritage which I draw upon to tell this story.

Glossary

Although the following terms may have additional meanings, all definitions are given here within the context of deaf people and the Deaf community within the United States.

American Sign Language (ASL): The native language of most lifelong deaf people in the United States. O'Rourke and colleagues (1975) have estimated that at least 500,000 deaf people and an unknown number of hearing people use ASL in this country. Following Spanish, ASL is the second most frequently used non-English language in the United States. ASL is not a visual representation of spoken English nor a way of pantomiming using gestures; it has distinct structural and morphological characteristics like other languages. ASL has a historical association with French Sign Language going back to the mid-eighteenth century, but Woodward (1978) and others argue that ASL developed naturally on its own and merely absorbed some French signs. For a more detailed description and history of ASL, see Wilbur (1979) or Padden and Humphries (1980).

Black American Sign Language (BASL): BASL developed largely in state schools for Black deaf children. A number of states in the Southeast maintained separate residential schools for White and Black deaf children until the 1960s. BASL shares much of the same basic vocabulary and overall structure as ASL.

caption(ing): In film and television, transcription from spoken language into written language—usually at the bottom of the screen. An increasing number of television programs are now captioned through the National Captioning Institute. Special home devices called decoders are available which unmask the captioning normally invisible on the television screen. Federal law has mandated that all television sets will have built-in decoders by 1994. Although a significant improvement in access to the media, television captioning presumes a certain degree of fluency in English as well as the ability to read quickly. Captioning is also not without flaws, frequently resulting in garbled or erroneous translations.

Cued (Speech): Developed by Orin Cornett in the 1960s, Cued Speech uses eight distinct handshapes near the mouth to clarify certain English sounds that might not be discernible by lipreading. These handshapes have no relationship to fingerspelling, ASL, or other synthesized sign systems.

day school: A school (for the deaf) which is not residential; students go home daily. Many day schools are actually classrooms for deaf students within a regular hearing school. Some deaf students remain exclusively in the class with other deaf students; others attend one or more classes with hearing students—sometimes with, often without a certified interpreter.

Deaf club: In rented church basements, local taverns, or Deaf-owned buildings, Deaf clubs have been *the* gathering place for members of the local Deaf community. Depending on the local community, such clubs meet nightly, weekly, or infrequently, and could be informal or organized around specific events (such as a dinner or holiday). Particularly before the widespread usage of TTYs and captioned television, Deaf clubs were the chief source of news for most deaf people. For a highly entertaining and insightful look at a Deaf club, see Bernard Bragg's "Tales from the Club Room."

decibel (dB): A unit for measuring the relative intensity of sounds on a scale from zero for the lowest perceptible sounds to 130 for sounds so loud they can cause pain. Someone with average hearing has between 0 and 20 dB loss. Someone with profound deafness has a 90 dB or greater loss (usually bilaterally).

decoder: *See* captioning.

disability: Although "disability" and "handicap" are often used interchangeably, a number of authors and individuals with disabilities have attempted to make a conceptual distinction. "Disability" is the functional limitation that results from a particular condition (for example, not being able to see, not being able to walk). A "handicap" is the external barrier(s) a person experiences—whether physical or attitudinal (for example, not being able to get information because it is only available in printed English, or being deemed unemployable because of fear of contracting AIDS). The distinction between disability and handicap places the locus of responsibility for limitation on the physical environment and sociocultural attitudes—not on the individuals themselves. Most deaf people, however, disavow both terms, and consider only other people with disabilities to be disabled or handicapped. Deaf people consider themselves deaf.

fingerspelling: A sign system in which words are spelled out using a particular hand configuration for each letter of the alphabet. Currently in the United States, each letter is made using only one hand. Several other countries use a two-handed method of fingerspelling. Fingerspelling appears in ASL and other sign systems when occasional words are fingerspelled. The Rochester Method was an educational approach in which *all* words in a conversation were meticulously spelled out. For some older Deaf people, the Rochester method became their primary communication system.

handicap: See disability.

hard-of-hearing: A term usually indicating someone with a slight hearing loss. Padden and Humphries (1980, pp. 39 ff.) note the culturally dependent nature of being hard-of-hearing. Among most hearing people, someone who is *very* hard-of-hearing is considered to be almost completely deaf. Among many deaf people, however, someone who is *very* hard-of-hearing is considered almost hearing. Hard-of-hearing persons are often suspect in the Deaf community because they generally have better spoken English, and have more often been socialized and educated in the Hearing world—at least peripherally. Like hearing children of deaf parents, hard-of-hearing persons confound the cultural dichotomization as Deaf or Hearing, and often feel themselves in between both cultures.

hearing-impaired: A blanket term popularized in the 1970s to include all people with any degree of hearing loss—from slight to profound. Most deaf people find the term stilted, even offensive, and one generally used only by hearing people.

home signs: Highly idiosyncratic signs and/or gestures that were developed within the home. Although home signs were more likely to be used between hearing parents and deaf children, a number of informants in this study reported using home signs—especially those who were not proficient in or did not use ASL.

interpreter: Historically, interpreters for the deaf were hearing children of deaf parents or other people who volunteered their time. Paid positions developed from a growing demand for qualified interpreters along with federal legislation that mandated interpreters in educational and, later, employment settings. There are now a number of interpreter training programs throughout the United States. Interpreters are certified through the national

Registry of Interpreters for the Deaf (R.I.D.), or, in some cases, by local or state consumer-based groups. Because of the diversity in methods and systems, interpreters often need to be conversant in several different sign language systems as well as oral methods.

lipreading: Observing the lips and mouth movements of a speaker in order to understand his or her speech. Because many English sounds and words appear similar when lipread, it is estimated that even the best lipreader can understand less than one-third of all spoken words. This proficiency can be improved by inference and by what Sacks (1989) calls "inspired guesswork," or decreased by environmental factors such as poor lighting and distance from the speaker.

mainstreaming: In the 1970s, "mainstreaming" was heralded as a panacea that would offset the presumed deprivations of residential schools. Deaf children were enrolled in regular hearing schools and hearing classes in their own home communities. These children could now mingle with hearing peers and reside at home with their own families. Unfortunately, most school systems and teachers were not trained to work with the deaf—having neither the educational background nor a knowledge of ASL. In practice, mainstreamed deaf students were often poorly educated and socially isolated. Mainstreaming has more recently fallen out of favor.

Manual English: A synthesized sign and speech system developed at Washington State School for the Deaf in the 1970s. Like other artificially developed systems, Manual English incorporates certain signs of ASL in an attempt to create a visual representation of English syntax.

oral/oralism: A communication method that espouses lipreading and spoken English. Traditionally, oralism has opposed the use of any sign language. The minority of deaf people who use this method are referred to as "oralists." Oralism is a highly charged issue within the Deaf community. Proponents see oralism as a means to communicate with and be included in the wider English-speaking world. Critics point out that very few genuinely deaf people are successfully oral—not because of differences in intelligence or endeavor, but because the central premise of oralism is ultimately flawed: you cannot make a deaf person be a hearing person. For many deaf adults, oralism is also a reminder of years of educational oppression and stigmatization. After years of being forbidden to use signs or gestures, those deaf children who were not successful at speaking or lipreading were demoted to classrooms that used signs as a last resort. These deaf students (who were ultimately the majority of students) were often felt to be less educable and, ultimately, less socially redeemable.

Pidgin Sign English (PSE): An admixture of ASL and other signed English systems. PSE typically develops "in situ" between someone who uses ASL and someone familiar with signed English. PSE has some structures from ASL or English, and some from neither.

postlingually deaf: Someone who has lost his or her hearing *after* the acquisition of language (generally age 2 or 3). "Language" almost always refers to English. The terms "postlingually deaf," "prelingually deaf," and "prevocationally deaf" (see below) are used in Deaf Education and Rehabilitation programs—almost never by members of the Deaf community.

prelingually deaf: Someone who has lost his or her hearing *before* the acquisition of language (generally age 2 or 3). "Language" almost always refers to English.

prevocationally deaf: Someone who has lost his or her hearing before mid- to late adolescence. "Prevocational" has replaced the "prelingual" and "postlingual" markers as a more significantly consistent threshold in terms of social outcomes. Those who are prevocationally deaf are much more likely to be members of the Deaf community, marry other deaf people, and use ASL.

relay: Relay services are available to allow deaf people to talk with hearing people who do not have a TTY. A third party ("relay") uses a TTY with the deaf person and voice with the hearing person. An increasing number of states and communities are providing relay service.

residential school: A school for the deaf at which most students live on campus. Depending on distance, cost, and preference, students may travel home weekly, monthly, or annually. Almost every state has at least one state-wide residential school; there are also a few private residential schools. Although a handful of these schools continue to use the oral method, most residential schools now conduct instruction in spoken English and sign—although it is more often a synthetic sign system rather than ASL.

SEE: The acronym used for either Seeing Essential English or Signing Exact English. Seeing Essential English was developed by David Anthony in the 1960s, and Signing Exact English was derived from it by Gustason and colleagues in the 1970s. Like Manual English and Signed English, both SEEs are synthetic sign systems based on spoken English. SEE was intended to provide a grammatical sign language—ignoring the fact that ASL, in fact, already has grammar and syntax, and that deaf children skilled in ASL have highly developed and transferable language skills. Although many SEE signs were borrowed from ASL, sign characteristics were often altered or modified to mirror English syntax. In a number of cases, signs were invented which do not follow expected structural and morphological characteristics of ASL, often resulting in highly artificial and constrained pseudo-words.

sign (or sign language): A broad term which includes any of a number of sign languages used with and among the Deaf (such as ASL, SEE, finger-spelling, Manual English). However, when used by most deaf people, "sign" usually means ASL.

signed English: This is a confusing term because it can mean either (1) a more general term for any of the English-based systems (such as SEE or Manual English) or (2) a specifically developed sign system: "Signed English."

Sim-Com: Simultaneous Communication. Often used interchangeably with "Total Communication," Sim-Com emphasizes the combined use of speech, signs, and fingerspelling.

TDD: Telecommunication Device for the Deaf. See TTY.

Total Communication: In a more global sense, Total Communication is a philosophy that encourages the use and acceptance of whatever sign language, sign communication, or oral method works for an individual deaf person. Practically, Total Communication was an educational method developed in the 1970s which stressed using *both* sign language and spoken English. Historically, Total Communication represents an important shift from denigration to recognition and inclusion of sign language within an educational setting. However, Total Communication maintains an insidious bias, since only synthetic sign languages such as SEE or Cued Speech can actually be paired with spoken English. Trying to pair ASL and spoken English is little different from trying to speak English while simultaneously writing in another language (for example, Russian).

TTY: Tele*type*. Initially, old Western Union teletype machines were adapted for telephone use among deaf people. When both parties have a TTY, they can type their conversation back and forth using standard phone lines. TTYs are now manufactured in a wide range of models. Although "TTY" and "TDD" are synonymous, TTY is viewed as the term that deaf people historically used, while "TDD" is seen as a more officious term promoted by Hearing people.

Notes

Preface

1. "Mother father deaf" is the verbatim English equivalent of three signs which, depending on context and accompanying facial expressions, can be variously translated—such as, "My mother and father are deaf" or "Are her mother and father deaf?" Yet the English phrase "mother father deaf" is often recognizable even among those who use American Sign Language. Because of the diverse possible language orientations of deaf people and their hearing children, this signed identifier is often accompanied by mouthed or spoken words. Thus, this hybrid expression can be understood by those who exclusively use ASL as well as those who use only spoken English.

1. Introduction

1. All names of informants have been changed and many identifying characteristics have been minimized in order to ensure anonymity.
2. In describing many women's experiences, Ortner writes: "For it would seem that, as a conscious human and member of culture, she has followed out the logic of culture's arguments and has reached culture's conclusions along with the men" (1974, p. 169).

2. Interpreting Our Lives

1. To those familiar with Deaf history, one of the most ironic occupations for a hearing child of deaf parents is that of insurance salesman. Although this is no longer true, insurance companies denied deaf drivers insurance for many years. This prejudice occurred despite driving records that were and remain far better than those of hearing drivers. One hearing informant recalled that

he, too, had been unable to obtain insurance because his father had no insurance.

2. Deafness can be defined according to four interrelated features: the measured degree of hearing loss; the age of onset of hearing loss; present level of functioning; and/or self-identification. Consequently, estimates of the deaf population in the United States vary from 250,000 (only those individuals who are profoundly prelingually deaf) to 28 million (which includes the profoundly deaf as well as individuals with mild, adventitious, or progressive hearing losses).

3. The only major demographic study of the U.S. deaf population is that of Schein and Delk (1974). They found that of the children born to couples where at least one spouse was deaf, 88 percent had normal hearing. This decreased to 81 percent when both parents were congenitally deaf.

4. There are no available figures on the number of hearing children of deaf parents who have a deaf child. Among all 150 informants in my study, eighty-one had at least one child. Of these eighty-one, four had one deaf child; one informant had more than one deaf child. The likelihood of a hearing child of deaf parents himself having a deaf child varies according to the etiologies of parental deafness. For most adult hearing children of deaf parents, the likelihood is no greater than in the general population.

5. Of approximately two million profoundly deaf Americans, it is estimated that 400,000 are prevocationally deaf—the most common profile for members of the Deaf community.

6. 90 percent of deaf children are born to hearing parents. Although this statistic is approximately the same as the percentage of hearing children born to deaf parents, these percentages are unrelated.

7. Although national figures are unavailable, data from smaller-scale studies indicate that it is highly probable that a prevocationally deaf person will marry another prevocationally deaf person. Of those persons deaf before age six, 83.5 percent of women and 91.9 percent of men will marry another deaf person. These figures drop dramatically for those who become deaf after age twenty—only 5.6 percent of men and 2 percent of women will marry another deaf person (Schein and Delk 1974).

8. Almost every country and political or historical region has a separate and often unique sign language—regardless of its spoken language. A good example of sign language differences occurs in Australia, England, and the United States. Although all three countries are English-speaking, deaf people in each country use a distinctly different sign language.

9. Several informants also had additional cultural influences from particular ethnic or racial groups.

10. Although the term "sign language" is generally used in this book as a synonym

for ASL, it occasionally includes fingerspelling, homemade signs, and other English-based sign language systems. Informants were inconsistent as a group in their use of this term; also, some individual informants were not able to specify the particular type of "sign language" being discussed.

11. See the Glossary for a more detailed description and explanation of "oralism."

12. Woodward (1972) began the convention of distinguishing functional hearing loss (deaf) from someone who identifies himself or herself as part of a cultural community (Deaf).

13. Although a few informants had mild hearing losses, none of them referred to themselves as "deaf."

14. American Sign Language is unique to the United States, and even here regional dialects and variations exist. See the descriptions of ASL and Black American Sign Language in the Glossary.

15. Some studies show a higher incidence of abuse toward children with disabilities who, in turn, may inflict abuse on their own children.

16. Informants who worked with deaf people were far more likely to meet and know other adult hearing children of deaf parents.

17. In 1993, CODA had approximately 350 paid members and over 1,000 names in its database.

18. There are also many articles written by hearing children of deaf parents. See T. Bull's annotated bibliography, "Hearing Children of Deaf Parents," published by the National Information Center on Deafness, Gallaudet University, 1993.

19. A classic example of this approach is outlined by Victor Turner. In *The Forest of Symbols* (1967), Turner proposes a hierarchy of data: (1) those which are external and observable; (2) those interpretations offered by laymen and specialists; and (3) those worked out by the anthropologist.

20. These include: Interpreters of Deaf Parentage (IODP); Hearing Children of Deaf Parents (HCDP); Deaf Parented Family (DPF); Hearing Adolescents of Deaf Parents (HADP); and Adult Hearing Children of Deaf Parents (AHCDP).

21. Millie Brother, who founded CODA, has said that she initially used the musical term "coda" because of its metaphorical parallel with hearing children of deaf parents: a concluding musical section that differs from the main structure.

22. A total of 297 mothers and fathers were described as primary caretakers. (Three parents were deceased or absent from the time of the informant's birth or shortly thereafter.) Of this total, 142 mothers and 137 fathers were described as "deaf," 4 mothers and 5 fathers were identified as "hard-of-hearing," and 3 mothers and 6 fathers were described as "hearing."

23. Notable exceptions to this are Native American populations that have a higher incidence of otitis media, and rubella epidemics that create sharp increases in the incidence of deafness among the general population.
24. In addition to using pseudonyms, I sometimes deliberately avoid specifying an informant's gender.
25. Although I met with informants in twenty-four different states, the informants themselves considered thirty-two different states their principal residence.
26. Harlan Lane (1989) provides a scholarly and detailed account of educational and social changes toward deaf people in *When the Mind Hears: A History of the Deaf.*
27. See the Glossary for descriptions of "TTY" and "decoder."

3. Invisible and Profound

1. When asked about the hearing or deaf status of their parents, nine informants identified one parent as "hard-of-hearing." Yet transcripts show that six of these nine more frequently used the term "deaf" when referring to that parent.
2. A more recent threshold for age of onset is "prevocationally deaf." This correlates with data which show that significant hearing loss before or during adolescence will most likely have lifelong social consequences for that individual.
3. Two signs are used to express this: "strong" + "deaf." A related expression can be found in an alternative sign for "deaf." In ordinary usage, the sign for "deaf" is made by touching the index finger to the ear and mouth. An alternative sign begins with the index finger at the ear, but shifts to the sign for "closed" (made with both hands and often with a dramatic flourish). This latter sign indicates someone who is *profoundly* deaf and/or strongly *identified* as deaf.
4. Two different signs illustrate the subjective nature of being deaf or hearing. (1) A pejorative sign for someone who *thinks* like a hearing person: the sign for "hearing," ordinarily placed on the mouth, is placed on the forehead. (2) A favorable sign for someone who *feels* like a deaf person: the sign for "deaf," ordinarily placed at the ear, is placed over the heart.
5. Davis (1961) describes similar interactions between persons with other types of disabilities and those not disabled.
6. At face value, the term "adult child" recognizes the lifelong relationship of a child to his or her parents. Yet current usage and connotations of this term demonstrate cultural assumptions of causality as well as culturally specific norms for children and parents. The adult child is often characterized as an

adult whose present identity is indelibly linked to and explained by his or her family experiences as a child. In the popular psychological literature, the term suggests an incomplete synthesis—a problematic linkage in which vestiges of childhood memories and roles preclude or conflict with the assumption of adult identity. This connotation suggests that the child's successful socialization has been compromised by parents who are unwilling or unable to adhere to familial standards within their sociocultural group.

7. "Marriage partners" here includes legally sanctioned as well as common-law relationships between two people regardless of gender or sexual orientation.

8. Alba (1990) states that "because of the intimacy of marriage and its implications for family networks and children, it remains a sensitive device for detecting ethnic boundaries, or social boundaries of any sort" (p. 291).

9. Only 9 of the 150 informants had one deaf and one hearing parent. Because I used a combined network and randomized approach to recruit potential informants, this number would have been even smaller if I had not specifically solicited for a subsample of informants with one deaf and one hearing parent.

10. Out of 141 informants with two deaf parents, only 6 parents had divorced (4.3 percent). Out of 9 informants with one deaf and one hearing parent, 6 parents had divorced (67.0 percent).

11. Of the 112 informants who are currently or have ever been married, only 4 are/were married to a deaf person.

12. The most frequently mentioned reasons given by informants for not marrying a deaf person were the following: anticipated communication difficulties between partners; each partner would belong to very separate cultures/worlds; not wanting to repeat childhood roles of interpreting or caretaking.

4. Views from the Other Side

1. Of the total 288 deaf mothers or fathers of informants, 260 (90.3 percent) were born to hearing parents, 3 (1.0 percent) were born to one hearing and one deaf parent, and 25 (8.7 percent) were born to two deaf parents.

2. Informants identified the causes of their parents' deafness as follows: unknown or uncertain (124); born deaf [unspecified] (52); spinal meningitis (47); German measles (22); scarlet fever (13); genetic (13); an accident (10); and miscellaneous (7).

3. Because many informants were uncertain about the causes of their parents' deafness, it is unclear how many of them actually carried a genetic marker for deafness. However, genetically caused profound childhood deafness is mainly autosomal recessive, and determined at any one of over 100 different chromosomal loci; most of these genetic forms of deafness are rare. An

informant who did carry a specific genetic marker for deafness would have to find a partner with the exact same genetic marker in order to have a deaf child.

4. See the Glossary for definitions of and distinctions between "disability" and "handicap."

5. Mori 1983; Bristor 1984; Fortier and Wanlass 1984.

6. Interpreting between parent and grandparent did not occur among all informants. More often, this fell to the eldest child or to only children (see Chapter 6). Nevertheless, younger siblings frequently reported a similar sense of separation between their parent(s) and grandparents.

7. See the Glossary for a more complete description of "Total Communication."

5. The Alternate Family

1. There are two common signs used for these residential schools: "school" and "institution." "Institution" does not have the pejorative connotation that it does in English, but rather indicates that it was a residential school.

2. Of the total 288 deaf mothers and fathers, 123 mothers and 112 fathers primarily attended residential schools; 9 mothers and 12 fathers attended day schools; 2 mothers and 1 father attended regular hearing schools; 12 mothers and 7 fathers attended a combination of schools (at least four years at any one type of school).

3. This contrasts with current trends in deaf education. "Approximately one-third of school-age deaf children attend private or public residential schools . . . The rest live at home and attend day programs in schools for the deaf or special day classes . . . or are mainstreamed into regular school programs." "Deafness: A Fact Sheet from Gallaudet College and the National Association of the Deaf" (Washington, D.C.: Gallaudet University, 1991).

4. Padden and Humphries (1988) observe: "In the informal dormitory environment children learn not only sign language but the content of the culture" (p. 6).

5. Most deaf parents had some contact with their families as children: a few went home weekly, many only occasionally throughout the year. Many informants reported that their parent(s) preferred to stay at school rather than going home to face minimal interaction and frequent isolation within their hearing families.

6. Deaf people's associations with public schools are markedly evident in the sign used for "public" (school)—the identical sign for "hearing."

7. Lipreading is often inaccurate; it is estimated that the best lipreader can understand only one-third of spoken speech without other contextual clues. Although there are a number of English-literate deaf people, English reading

skills among many deaf adults average between fourth and sixth grade levels. This discrepancy limits access to printed information as well as to closed-captioned television programs.

8. See the Glossary for a description of a Deaf club.

9. Ablon (1984) describes a similar dynamic among dwarfs attending Little People of America conferences.

10. Out of 142 informants who had no deaf siblings, only 14 described any regular or significant contact with deaf children while they were growing up.

6. Imperfect Mirrors

1. Fifty-eight informants had one sibling, 33 had two, 19 had three, and 13 had four or more siblings; 27 informants were only children.

2. The most common method of communication between family members who did not use American Sign Language or an oral English method was "home signs" (see the Glossary).

7. A Song You Never Heard Before

1. Shore (1989) suggests that the meanings of cultural symbols change how a child thinks, speaks and feels—depending upon the specific cultural modes of language, competence, and interpersonal relations.

2. Very little cross-cultural research exists on the comparative value of sound in other cultures. My own brief studies in other countries (Australia, Italy, Mexico, Israel, Ecuador) indicate that spoken language is the preferred although not necessarily the exclusive mode of communication.

3. This does not extend to other sign systems (such as SEE or Signed English) which are based on spoken English. These artificial systems are not used conversationally among most deaf people.

4. Sontag passionately demands that disease be stripped of historical and literary fabrication and become, not a euphemism, but a factual description of biological conditions and processes. Yet Sontag reclaims the myth of reductionism: viewing disease merely as the organization of irreducible biological phenomena.

5. Deaf people actually can and do communicate in the dark. There are several methods of doing this, including fingerspelling into the other person's hand or placing the other person's hands on your hands as you sign. These and other techniques are also used by deaf-blind individuals.

6. In *The Interpretation of Culture,* Geertz (1973) proposes various possible meanings of a wink—depending on the immediate situation as well as the particular cultural context.

7. This did not apply to public *Deaf* events, in which most informants were unconcerned about their parents' voices.

8. Hall (1959) included two additional dimensions of human communication: space and time. Despite the title of his work—*The Silent Language*—Hall's explorations surprisingly did not include sign language.

9. When deaf parents' communication preferences as children and as adults were compared, there was a significant shift toward the use of sign language. As children, 131 of the informants' mothers and fathers were described as primarily communicating through sign language (including ASL as well as other sign systems); 86 parents were primarily oral; and 71 used both signing and oral methods. As adults, 259 parents primarily used sign language; 9 used oral methods; and 20 used both.

10. Lane (1984) chronicles how professional acceptance of sign language in America gradually shifted after the 1880 Congress of Milan, an international conference on educational methods for deaf people. Lane describes the unrealistic and often deceptive claims that were made for the benefits of oralism at this conference.

11. Groce (1985) similarly reports acceptance of sign language in the nineteenth-century community of Martha's Vineyard, which had a high incidence of deafness. Her research supports a normative view of deafness when it is a commonplace condition and not ostracized because of communication preferences.

12. The designation of a language as the first or primary childhood language does not necessarily correlate with fluency, adult usage, or attitudes toward that language.

13. Almost three-fourths of this group of informants learned sign language as adults.

14. Gardner and Lambert (1972) found that mastering a second language depends not so much on a person's intellectual capacity or language aptitude but rather on the person's attitude toward the other linguistic group and his or her willingness to identify with that group.

15. Wilcox (1989) discusses the overfocus on hands in studies of sign language. He describes hands as a modality rather than the language itself: "Signing is not a language but only a means of producing (utterances of) a language" (p. 182).

16. DiPietro (1977) defines code-switching as "the use of more than one language by communicants in the execution of a speech act" (p. 8).

17. According to Ervin-Tripp (1973): "Finally, quite aside from such mediational effects, it is possible that a shift in language is associated with a shift in social roles and emotional attitudes. Since each language is learned and usually employed with different persons and in a different context, the use of each

language may come to be associated with shift in a large array of behavior" (p. 58).

18. I do not discuss how different sign languages compare. Just as different values were evoked by hearing and speaking, so too different values were attached to different sign language systems.

19. Larry compared his method of signing with that of his sister: "I was raised [pantomimes signing with tightly closed mouth]—my dad does not use his voice and I sign like my dad, ASL [repeats signing with mouth pressed closed]. No [pantomimes mouth movements]. Nothing! Just closed mouth. That's it! My sister was raised more like my mother. She [mother] would talk and sign at the same time. She does to this day. And, so, we're quite different."

20. According to the transcripts, 87 of the 150 informants spontaneously used at least one sign during the interview.

8. Inside Out or Upside Down

1. "Stand-and-pray" interpreting contrasts with the simultaneous method in that the interpreter motionlessly attends to what is being said—perhaps with head bowed and hands clasped—and eventually repeats or summarizes what has been said up to that point. Although the term "stand-and-pray" describes a technique used by professional interpreters, it evokes the style of childhood interpreting described by several informants: summarizing at certain points rather than interpreting simultaneously.

2. Brim (1968) states: "The final outcome of the ever-growing influence of the child on the parent is the gradual inversion of the relationship between the two, as it shifts from the initial position in which the parent has complete responsibility and authority to the reverse, at a later period, when the child has come to assume these same responsibilities of the parental role toward his aging and less able parents" (p. 214).

3. Deaf peddlers are considered pariahs by most other deaf people because they are thought to perpetuate negative stereotypes to hearing people. During my fieldwork, I interviewed two adults whose parents worked as peddlers. In both cases, this disclosure came late during the interview because these informants were reluctant to admit such discrediting information. One of these informants pointed out, however, that his parents "were enterprising enough to make the best of it" despite living in a society that denigrated and economically restricted most deaf people.

4. *Love Is Never Silent* is the 1985 television movie based on Joanne Greenberg's 1970 novel *In This Sign*. Set during the Depression, the story concerns the hardships of a working-class deaf couple and their hearing daughter.

9. The Heritage of Difference

1. Page (1984) distinguishes between embarrassment, shame, and stigma. Embarrassment is seen as particularistic—a specific moment in a specific situation. Shame is the individual's acknowledgment of failing to meet socially acceptable standards in one or more social roles. "Those experiencing stigma may feel that their whole identity is tarnished because of a particular attribute. Such feelings may be intense; experienced in many situations; and persist for long periods of time" (p. 18).

2. In *Stigma* (1963), Goffman focused on three major types of stigma: "abominations of the body" (such as the physically disabled); "blemishes of individual character" (such as alcoholics or the unemployed); and "tribal" (those of specific ethnic or racial groups).

3. Goffman writes: "One can therefore suspect that the role of the normal and the role of the stigmatized are parts of the same complex, cut from the same standard cloth" (1963, p. 130).

4. Goffman's four learning patterns are as follows: (1) those with an inborn stigma who simultaneously learn the standards of the normal and of the stigmatized; (2) those with a stigmatizable condition who are initially protected by family or community from stigma; (3) those stigmatized as adults—either through circumstances or through awareness that they have always been discreditable; and (4) those socialized in an alien community.

5. Higgins (1980) describes how hearing family members and friends are more likely than deaf people to tell others off if they stare (pp. 129–130).

6. Ablon (1988) writes that "expectant parents everywhere characteristically await the birth of the 'perfect child'—a beautiful baby with all the attributes that their society values" (p. 1).

10. Hyphenated Lives

1. Turner (1967) outlined the attributes of liminality, of "threshold people": "[They] are necessarily ambiguous, since this condition and these persons elude or slip through the network of classifications that normally locate states and positions in cultural space. Liminal entities are neither here nor there; they are betwixt and between the positions assigned and arrayed by law, custom, convention, and ceremony. As such, their ambiguous and indeterminate attributes are expressed by a rich variety of symbols in the many societies that ritualize social and cultural transitions" (p. 95).

2. Meadow (1981) notes that the first question deaf children and teenagers ask a visitor to their school is, "Are you deaf or hearing?"

3. Padden and Humphries (1988) underscore this oppositional definition.

4. Padden and Humphries (1988) describe a deaf girl who corrects her younger

deaf sister's mistaken notion that someone can be deaf *and* hearing. The younger girl is chastised for not yet learning the way of the world: "No one is ever both Deaf and hearing at the same time. One is either Deaf *or* hearing" (p. 13; emphasis added).

11. Identity on the Margins of Culture

1. I have adapted Alba's definition of "ethnic identity" (1990, p. 25).
2. This includes five informants who were currently students in a degree or training program for one of these occupations.
3. Wilbur and Fristoe (1986) found an even higher proportion of respondents in their study who were in occupations related to deaf people: 69.9 percent used their sign skills on the job, including 59.6 percent who worked primarily with deaf people.
4. This correlation is particularly noteworthy in a large, heterogeneous, and mobile society. In smaller and more homogenous cultural groups, parity between childhood environments and adult occupations may be more likely.
5. Levine (1985) proposes that a major characteristic of contemporary America is its inflexibility and uncomfortableness with ambiguity.
6. The most common sign for "hearing" is an index finger placed horizontally against the lips; the index finger then makes a small outward circle. The speaker's accompanying facial gestures and style of hand movement can convey a range of connotations from a matter-of-fact description to one of indignation.
7. Although I have borrowed "people without culture" from Rosaldo (1988), I use the term differently. Rosaldo used the phrase ironically to point out the ethnocentric presumption that dominant white Americans have no culture: only other people have culture because *they* are different. I use the term more literally: people who are disenfranchised or separated from their own cultural heritage.
8. Although "coda-talk" takes its name from the organization CODA, its usage was not officially endorsed nor was it presently used by a majority of members.
9. Coda-talk is more like a glossed and often literal version of ASL than a translation of ASL. For example, a person using coda-talk might simultaneously sign and say, "Feel fork in throat." Ordinarily, the same ASL sentence would be translated into English as "I'm feeling stuck."
10. I have not included the many signs and body language that Rachel also used while telling her story. Videotape would have been a far better way of presenting coda-talk.
11. Although I have not included these data in the present study, I did meet

informally with adult hearing children of deaf parents from several other countries. In general, each adult felt that his or her family experiences were more like those of other hearing children of *deaf* parents (regardless of country of origin) than like those of peers with hearing parents from their own country.

12. "Explanatory model" refers to an organizing pattern of assumptions which (loosely or rigidly) structures ideas, perceptions, and understandings.

13. During the past few years, John Bradshaw has had several series on public television concerning "dysfunctional" families—a general characteristic that he feels applies to most contemporary American families. Using a populist forum and simplified psychological explanations, Bradshaw focuses on people's experiences and their ways of dealing with having been raised in a dysfunctional family. In addition to his television broadcasts, Bradshaw has also given lectures across the country as well as published several books.

References

Ablon, J. 1977. Field methods in working with middle class Americans: New issues of values, personality, and reciprocity. In *Human Organization* 36 (1): 69–72.

────── 1984. *Little People in America: The Social Dimension of Dwarfism.* New York: Praeger.

────── 1988. *Living with Difference: Families with Dwarf Children.* New York: Praeger.

Adler, M. 1977. *Collective and Individual Bilingualism.* Hamburg: Helmut Buske Verlag.

Adorno, T., et al. 1950. *The Authoritarian Personality.* New York: Harper.

Agar, M. 1980. Stories, background knowledge, and themes: Problems in the analysis of life history narrative. In *American Ethnologist* 7 (2): 223–239.

Ainlay, S., G. Becker, and L. M. Coleman (eds.). 1986. *The Dilemma of Difference: A Multidisciplinary View of Stigma.* New York: Plenum Press.

Alba, R. 1990. *Ethnic Identity: The Transformation of White America.* New Haven: Yale University Press.

Ambron, S. 1975. *Child Development.* San Francisco: Rinehart Press.

Andersson, Y. 1987. Culture and subculture. In *Gallaudet Encyclopedia of Deaf People and Deafness,* ed. J. Van Cleve, pp. 261–264. New York: McGraw-Hill.

Ariès, P. 1962. *Centuries of Childhood: A Social History of Family Life,* trans. R. Baldick. New York: Vintage Press.

Arlow, J. 1976. Communication and character: A clinical study of a man raised by deaf-mute parents. In *Psychoanalytic Study of the Child* 31: 139–163.

Bank, S., and M. Kahn. 1982. *The Sibling Bond.* New York: Basic Books.

Barbarin, O. 1986. Family experience of stigma in childhood cancer. In *The Dilemma of Difference: A Multidisciplinary View of Stigma,* ed. S. Ainlay, G. Becker, and L. Coleman, pp. 163–184. New York: Plenum Press.

Barth, F. (ed.). 1969. *Ethnic Groups and Boundaries.* Boston: Little, Brown.

Basow, S. 1986. *Gender Stereotypes: Traditions and Alternatives.* Monterey, Calif.: Brooks/Cole.

Bateson, G. 1936. *Naven: A Survey of the Problems Suggested by a Composite Picture of a New Guinea Tribe Drawn from Three Points of View.* Cambridge: Cambridge University Press.

Becker, G. 1980. *Growing Old in Silence.* Berkeley: University of California Press.

Bellah, R., et al. 1985. *Habits of the Heart: Individualism and Commitment in American Life.* Berkeley: University of California Press.

Bellugi, U., and S. Fischer. 1972. A comparison of sign language and spoken language. In *Cognition* 1 (2–3): 173–200.

Bertaux, D. 1981. *Biography and Society.* Newbury Park: Sage.

Bienvienu, M. 1989. An Anthropological View of American Deaf Culture. Presentation at Sacramento State University, Sacramento, California, March 10, 1989.

Black, C. 1982. *It Will Never Happen to Me.* Denver: Medical Administration Company.

Blauner, B. 1972. *Racial Oppression in America.* New York: Harper and Row.

Bonvillian, J., M. Orlansky, and L. Novack. 1983. Developmental milestones: Sign language acquisition and motor development. In *Child Development* 54: 1435–1445.

Bowlby, J. 1969. *Attachment and Loss.* Vol. 1: *Attachment.* New York: Basic Books.

Braroe, N. 1975. *Indian and White: Self-Image and Interaction in a Canadian Plains Community.* Stanford: Stanford University Press.

Brim, O. 1968. Adult socialization. In *Socialization and Society,* ed. J. Clausen. Boston: Little, Brown.

Bristor, M. 1984. The birth of a handicapped child: A holistic model for grieving. In *Family Relations* 33: 25–32.

Buchino, M. 1988. Hearing children of deaf parents: Personal perspectives. Unpublished doctoral dissertation, University of Cincinnati.

Bull, T. 1993. *A Bibliography of Hearing Children of Deaf Parents.* Washington, D.C.: National Information Center on Deafness, Gallaudet University.

Bunde, L. 1979. Deaf parents—hearing children: Toward a greater understanding of the unique aspects, needs, and problems relative to the communication factors caused by deafness. Washington, D.C.: Registry of Interpreters for the Deaf.

Chan, L., and B. Lui. 1990. Self-concept among hearing Chinese children of deaf parents. In *American Annals of the Deaf* (October 1990): 299–305.

Charlson, E. 1989. Social cognition and self-concept of hearing adolescents with deaf parents. Unpublished doctoral dissertation, University of California, Berkeley, and San Francisco State University.

———— 1984. The social construction of narrative accounts. In *Historical Social Psychology,* ed. K. Gergen and M. Gergen. Hillsdale, N.J.: Erlbaum Associates.

Gilligan, C. 1982. *In a Different Voice: Psychological Theory and Women's Development.* Cambridge, Mass.: Harvard University Press.

Glickfeld, C. 1989. *Useful Gifts.* Athens, Ga.: University of Georgia Press.

Goffman, E. 1955. *Presentation of Self in Everyday Life.* Garden City, N.Y.: Doubleday.

———— 1963. *Stigma: Notes on the Management of Spoiled Identity.* Englewood Cliffs, N.J.: Prentice-Hall.

Goode, E. 1978. *Deviant Behavior: An Interactionist Approach.* Englewood Cliffs, N.J.: Prentice-Hall.

Gorman, M. 1980. A new light on Zion. Unpublished doctoral dissertation, University of Chicago.

———— n.d. Anthropological reflections on the HIV epidemic among gay men. Working paper (mimeo), Medical Anthropology Program, University of California, San Francisco.

Graham, H. 1984. *Women, Health, and the Family.* Brighton, Sussex: Wheatsheaf Books.

Gravitz, H., and J. Bowden. 1985. *Recovery: A Guide for Adult Children of Alcoholics.* New York: Simon and Schuster.

Greenberg, J. 1970. *In This Sign.* New York: Holt, Rinehart and Winston.

Groce, N. 1985. *Everyone Here Spoke Sign Language: Hereditary Deafness on Martha's Vineyard.* Cambridge, Mass.: Harvard University Press.

Grosjean, F. 1982. *Life with Two Languages.* Cambridge, Mass.: Harvard University Press.

Hahn, H. 1988. The politics of physical differences: Disability and discrimination. In *Journal of Social Issues* 44 (1): 38–47.

Hall, E. 1959. *The Silent Language.* Garden City, N.Y.: Doubleday.

Hallowell, A. 1955. *Culture and Experience.* Philadelphia: University of Pennsylvania Press.

Hareven, T. 1986. Historical changes in the family and the life course: Implications for child development. In *Monographs of the Society for Research in Child Development,* Serial No. 211, vol. 50 (40–45): 8–23,

Harkness, S. 1980. Child development theory in anthropological perspective. In *New Directions for Child Development* 8: 1–5.

Hastorf, A., and I. Bender. 1952. A caution respecting the measurement of empathic ability. In *Journal of Abnormal and Social Psychology* 47: 564–576.

Henderson, J. 1976. Writing. In *The Encyclopedia of Anthropology,* ed. D. Hunter and P. Whitten, p. 409. New York: Basic Books.

Henry, J. 1973. *Pathways to Madness.* New York: Vintage Books.

Higgins, P. 1980. *Outsiders in a Hearing World: Sociology of Deafness.* Beverly Hills, Calif.: Sage Publications.

Hockett, C. 1960. The origin of speech. In *Scientific American,* September 1960.

Hoffmeister, R. 1985. Families with deaf parents: A functional perspective. In *Children of Handicapped Parents.* New York: Academic Press.

Homans, G. 1961. *Social Behavior: Its Elementary Forms.* New York: Harcourt, Brace, and World.

Hooyman, N., and W. Lustbader. 1986. *Taking Care: Supporting Older People and Their Families.* New York: The Free Press.

Hsu, F. 1972. American core value and national character. In *Psychological Anthropology,* ed. F. Hsu, pp. 241–262. Cambridge, Mass.: Schenkman.

Jackson, B. 1987. *Fieldwork.* Urbana: University of Illinois Press.

Jacobs, L. 1974. *A Deaf Adult Speaks Out.* Washington, D.C.: Gallaudet College Press.

Johnson, R., and C. Erting. 1984. Linguistic socialization in the context of emergent deaf ethnicity. Wenner-Gren Foundation Working Papers in Anthropology, June 1984.

Jones, E., R. Strom, and S. Daniels. 1989. Evaluating the success of deaf parents. In *American Annals of the Deaf* (December 1989): 312–316.

Jones, M., and S. Quigley. 1970. The acquisition of question formation in spoken English and American Sign Language by two hearing children of deaf parents. In *Journal of Speech and Hearing Disorders* 44 (2): 196–208.

Kaufert, J., and W. Koolage. 1984. Role conflict among culture brokers: The experience of native Canadian medical interpreters. In *Social Science and Medicine* 18 (3): 283–286.

Kaufman, S. 1986. *The Ageless Self: Sources of Meaning in Later Life.* Madison: University of Wisconsin Press.

Kessen, W. 1979. The American child and other cultural inventions. In *American Psychologist* 34 (10): 815–820.

Kirshbaum, M. 1988. Parents with physical disabilities and their babies. In *Zero to Ten: A Bulletin of the National Center for Clinical Infant Programs,* Vol. VII, No. 5, June 1988.

Kleinman, A. 1988. *Illness Narratives.* New York: Basic Books.

Klima, E., and U. Belugi. 1979. *The Signs of Language.* Cambridge, Mass.: Harvard University Press.

Konner, L. 1987. I was my parents' radio. In *Glamour Mazagine,* May 1987.

Korbin, J. 1981. *Child Abuse and Neglect: Cross-Cultural Perspectives.* Berkeley: University of California Press.

Krieger, S. 1983. *The Mirror Dance: Identity in a Women's Community.* Philadelphia: Temple University Press.

LaFontaine, J. 1986. An anthropological perspective on children in social worlds. *In Children of Social Worlds: Development in a Social Context,* ed. M. Richards and P. Light. Oxford: Polity Press.

Lakoff, G., and M. Johnson. 1980. *Metaphors We Live By.* Chicago: University of Chicago Press.

Lane, H. 1989. *When the Mind Hears: A History of the Deaf.* New York: Vintage.
——— 1992. *The Mask of Benevolence: Disabling the Deaf Community.* New York: Knopf.

Langer, E., et al. 1976. Stigma, staring, and discomfort: A novel-stimulus hypothesis. In *Journal of Experimental Social Psychology* 12: 451–463.

Levine, D. 1985. *The Flight from Ambiguity: Essays in Social and Cultural Theory.* Chicago: University of Chicago Press.

LeVine, R. 1989. Cultural environments in child development. In *Child Development Today and Tomorrow,* ed. W. Damon, pp. 52–68. San Francisco: Jossey-Bass.

Lévi-Strauss, C. 1967. *Tristes Tropiques,* trans. J. Russell. New York: Atheneum.

Lewis, J., and B. Meredith. 1988. *Daughters Who Care: Daughters Caring for Mothers at Home.* New York: Routledge.

Lifton, R. 1970. *History and Human Survival.* New York: Random House.

McLaughlin, B. 1978. *Second-language Acquisition in Childhood.* Hillsdale, N.J.: Lawrence Erlbaum.

Mahler, M., F. Pine, and A. Bergman. 1975. *The Psychological Birth of the Human Infant.* New York: Basic Books.

Markowicz, H., and J. Woodward. 1978. Language and the maintenance of ethnic boundaries in the deaf community. In *Communication and Cognition* 11: 29–38.

Mauss, M. 1967. *The Gift: Forms and Function of Exchange in Archaic Societies.* New York: Norton.

McCrae, M. 1979. Bonding in a sea of silence. In *American Journal of Maternal Child Nursing* (January/February): 29–34.

McCrae, R., and P. Costa. 1982. Aging, the life course, and models of personality. In *Review of Human Development,* ed. T. Field et al., pp. 602–613. New York: Wiley and Sons.

McLain, R., and A. Weigert. 1979. Toward a phenomenological sociology of family: A programmatic essay. In *Contemporary Theories about the Family: General Theories and Theoretical Orientations,* vol. 2, ed. W. Burr, pp. 160–205. New York: The Free Press.

Mead, G. 1934. *Mind, Self and Society.* Chicago: University of Chicago Press.

Mead, M. 1953. National character. In *Anthropology Today,* ed. A. Kroeber, pp. 642–667. Chicago: University of Chicago Press.

Meadow, K. 1981. Deaf children and the social process. Keynote paper presented at Washington Regional Conference of Educators of the Hearing Impaired.

Meadow-Orlans, K., et al. 1987. Interactions of deaf and hearing mothers of deaf and hearing infants. Paper presented at the meetings of the Tenth World Congress of the World Federation of the Deaf, Helsinki, Finland, July 24, 1987.

Messerschmidt, D. (ed.). 1981. *The Anthropologist at Home in North America.* Cambridge: Cambridge University Press.

Miller, G. 1992. Quoted by R. Rymer in Annals of Silence, *The New Yorker,* April 13, 1992, pp. 41–81.

Minturn, L., and W. Lambert. 1964. *Mothers of Six Cultures: Antecedents of Childrearing.* New York: Wiley.

Mitchell, R. 1991. Secrecy and disclosure in fieldwork. In *Experiencing Fieldwork,* ed. W. Shaffir and R. Stebbins, pp. 97–108. Newbury Park, Calif.: Sage Publications.

Moores, D. (ed.). 1990. Editorial: Deja vu. In *American Annals of the Deaf* 135 (3) (July 1990): 201.

Mori, A. 1983. *Families of Children with Special Needs.* Rockville, Md.: Aspen Systems.

Murphy, R. 1990. *The Body Silent.* New York: W. W. Norton.

Murphy, R., et al. 1988. Physical disability and social liminality: A study in the rituals of adversity. In *Soc. Sci. Med.* 26 (2): 235–242.

Neville, H. 1990. Intermodal competition and compensation in development: Evidence from studies of the visual system in congenitally deaf adults. In *Annals of New York Academy of Sciences* 608: 71–87.

Niesser, A. 1983. *The Other Side of Silence.* Washington, D.C.: Gallaudet University.

Ochs, E., and B. Schieffelin. 1987. *Language Socialization across Cultures.* New York: Cambridge University Press.

Ogbu, J. 1981. Origins of human competence: A cultural ecological perspective. In *Social Organization* 52: 413–429.

O'Rourke, T., et al. 1975. National Association of the Deaf Communication Skills Program Hand. April 27–30. Silver Spring, Md.: National Association of the Deaf.

Ortner, S. 1974. Is female to male as nature is to culture? In *Women, Culture, and Society,* ed. M. Rosaldo and L. Lamphere, pp. 67–89. Stanford: Stanford University Press.

Padden, C., and T. Humphries. 1988. *Deaf in America: Voices from a Culture.* Cambridge, Mass.: Harvard University Press.

Page, R. 1984. *Stigma.* Boston: Routledge and Kegan Paul.

Park, R. 1950. *Race and Culture.* Glencoe, Ill.: The Free Press.

Perin, C. 1988. *Belonging in America: Reading between the Lines.* Madison: University of Wisconsin Press.

Phillips, D. 1971. *Knowledge from What? Theories and Methods in Social Research.* Skokie, Ill.: Rand McNally.

Piaget, J. 1965. *Moral Judgments of the Child.* New York: Free Press.

Pietrulewicz, B. 1975. Environmental influence of deaf parents on personality of hearing children. In *Psychologia Wychowawcza* 18 (2): 242–249.

Pi-Sunyer, O. 1980. Dimensions of a Catalan nationalism. In *Nations without a State: Ethnic Minorities in Western Europe,* ed. C. Foster. New York: Praeger.

Plotnicov, L. 1990. *American Culture: Essays on the Familiar and Unfamiliar.* Pittsburgh: University of Pittsburgh Press.

Poizner, N., et al. 1981. Representation of inflected signs from American Sign Language in short-term memory. In *Memory and Cognition* 9 (2): 121–131.

Pope, C. 1984. Disability and health status: The importance of longitudinal studies. In *Social Science and Medicine* 19 (6): 589–593.

Redfield, R. 1960. *The Little Community.* Chicago: University of Chicago Press.

Reiss, D. 1981. *The Family's Construction of Reality.* Cambridge, Mass.: Harvard University Press.

Rienzi, B. 1990. Influence and adaptability in families with deaf parents and hearing children. In *American Annals of the Deaf* (December 1990): 402–408.

Riley, M., and R. Abeles. 1982. Life course perspectives. In *Aging from Birth to Death,* ed. M. Riley, R. Abeles, and M. Teitelbaum, pp. 1–10. Boulder, Colo.: Westview Press.

Rodriguez, R. 1982. *Hunger of Memory: The Education of Richard Rodriguez.* Boston: D. R. Godine.

Rosaldo, R. 1988. Ideology, place, and people without culture. In *Cultural Anthropology* 3 (February 1988): 77–87.

Sacks, O. 1985. *The Man Who Mistook His Wife for a Hat.* New York: Summit Books.

———— 1989. *Seeing Voices: A Journey into the World of the Deaf.* Berkeley: University of California Press.

Sahlins, M. 1976. La Pensée Bourgeoise: Western society as culture. In *Culture as Practical Reason,* ed. M. Sahlins, pp. 166–221. Chicago: University of Chicago Press.

Sapir, E. 1917. Do we need a "Superorganic"? In *American Anthropologist* 19: 441–447.

———— 1924. Culture, genuine and spurious. In *American Journal of Sociology* 29: 401–429. Reprinted in D. Mandelbaum, *Selected Writings of E. Sapir.* Berkeley: University of California Press, 1951.

Sattler, J. 1970. Racial experimenter effects in experimentation, testing, interviewing, and psychotherapy. In *Psychological Bulletin* 73: 127–160.

Schein, J., and M. Delk. 1974. *The Deaf Population of the United States.* Silver Spring, Md.: National Association of the Deaf.

Schiff, N., and I. Ventry. 1976. Communication problems in hearing children of deaf parents. In *Journal of Speech and Hearing Disorders* 41 (3): 348–358.

Schlesinger, H., and K. Meadow. 1972. *Sound and Sign.* Berkeley: University of California Press.

Schuchman, S. 1988. *Hollywood Speaks: Deafness and the Film Entertainment Industry.* Urbana: University of Illinois Press.

Seidel, J., R. Kjolseth, and E. Seymour. 1988. *The Ethnograph.* Littleton, Colo.: Qualis Research Associates.

Shengold, L. 1989. *Soul Murder: The Effects of Childhood Abuse and Deprivation.* New Haven: Yale University Press.

Shore, B. 1989. Meaning. Paper presented at the Psychological Anthropology Conference, San Diego, California, October 6–8, 1989.

Sidransky, R. 1990. *In Silence: Growing Up Hearing in a Deaf World.* New York: St. Martin's Press.

Simpson, G., and J. Yinger. 1972. *Racial and Cultural Minorities: An Analysis of Prejudice and Discrimination.* New York: Harper and Row.

Sommers, T., and L. Shields. 1987. *Women Take Care: The Consequences of Caregiving in Today's Society.* Gainsville, Fla.: Triad.

Sontag, S. 1977. *Illness as Metaphor.* New York: Vintage Books.

St. Clair, R., G. Valdes, and J. Ornstein. 1981. *Social and Educational Issues in Bilingualism and Biculturalism.* Washington, D.C.: University Press of America.

Stern, D. 1985. *The Interpersonal World of the Infant.* New York: Basic Books.

Stokoe, W., D. Casterline, and C. Croneberg. 1965. A Dictionary of American Sign Language on Linguistic Principles. Washington, D.C.: Gallaudet College Press.

Takanishi, R. 1978. Childhood as a social issue: Historical roots of contemporary child advocacy movements. In *Journal of Social Issues* 34: 8–20.

Tannen, D. 1990. *You Just Don't Understand.* New York: Morrow.

Taska, R., and J. Rhoads. 1981. Psychodynamic issues in a hearing woman raised by deaf parents. In *The Psychiatric Forum* 10: 11–16.

Turner, V. 1967. *The Forest of Symbols.* Ithaca, N.Y.: Cornell University Press.

Vernon, M. 1991. Historical, cultural, psychological, and educational aspects of American Sign Language. In *Perspectives on Deafness: A Deaf American Monograph,* pp. 148–154. Silver Spring, Md.: National Association of the Deaf.

Volkan, V. 1988. *The Need to Have Enemies and Allies.* Northvale, N.J.: Jason Aronson.

Vygotsky, L. 1978. *Mind in Society,* ed. M. Cole et al. Cambridge, Mass.: Harvard University Press.

Wagenheim, H. 1985. Aspects of the analysis of an adult son of deaf-mute parents. In *Journal of the American Psychoanalytic Association* 33 (2): 413–435.

Wagner, D. (ed.). 1983. *Child Development and International Development: Research and Policy Interfaces.* New Directions in Child Development Series, no. 20. San Francisco: Jossey-Bass.

Walker, L. 1986. *A Loss for Words: The Story of Deafness in a Family.* New York: Harper and Row.

Walter, V. (ed.). 1990. Deafness in the Family. Special edition of *Gallaudet Today,* Fall 1990.

Weber, M. 1968. *Economy and Society.* New York: Bedminster Press. (Originally published 1922.)

Werner, E. 1982. Child nurturance in other cultures: A perspective. In *Child Nurturance,* vol. 2: *Patterns of Supplementary Parenting,* ed. M. Kostelnik et al. New York: Plenum Press.

Whiting, B., and J. Whiting. 1975. *Children of Six Cultures: A Psychocultural Analysis.* Cambridge, Mass.: Harvard University Press.

Whittaker, E. 1992. The birth of the anthropological self and its career. In *Ethos* 20 (2): 191–219.

Whorf, B. 1956. *Language, Thought, and Reality.* New York: Wiley.

Wilbur, R. 1979. *American Sign Language and Sign Language Systems.* Baltimore: University Park Press.

Wilbur, R., and M. Fristoe. 1986. I had a wonderful if somewhat unusual child-hood: Growing up hearing in a deaf world. In Papers for the Second Research Conference on the Social Aspects of Deafness, ed. J. Christiansen and R. Meisegeier. Washington, D.C.: Gallaudet University Office for Research.

Wilcox, S. 1989. Breaking through the culture of silence. In *American Deaf Culture,* ed. S. Wilcox, pp. 180–228. Silver Spring, Md.: Linstok Press.

Woodward, J. 1972. Implications for sociolinguistics research among the deaf. In *Sign Language Studies* 1: 1–7.

——— 1978. Historical bases of American Sign Language. In *Understanding Language through Sign Language Research,* ed. P. Siple. New York: Academic Press.

Zola, I. K. 1982. *Missing Pieces: A Chronicle of Living with a Disability.* Philadelphia: Temple University Press.

Acknowledgments

It is not possible to do something of this magnitude or this depth of heart without the support of others. In the Deaf world, you not only thank with words. You show your gratitude with a bear-hugging embrace.

I had many doubts about whether these stories should be told. Sometimes I wondered why I was doing this at all. Joan Ablon, my mentor and friend, pushed me on. She convinced me that what I was doing was important—not just in an academic sense, but in a human sense. She challenged me to pursue the convictions that I often knew in my heart but sometimes struggled to convey. As a teacher, researcher, and writer, Joan has been a tireless crusader. I can only hope to emulate her concern for the dignity and humanity in all people.

One day during the middle of my fieldwork, I sat in Gay Becker's office, exasperated, bewildered, and fatigued. Trying to explain what this research was like, I signed to her *"mirror."* I was thinking of a sentence I had written in my diary the night before: How long can you stare in the mirror before you go crazy? And Gay nodded in agreement: "Yes . . . it's that close." I realized that in signing to her, I was holding up my open "mirror" hand not at arm's length (as it is usually placed) but pressed up against my face. It was *this* close. Gay has written about the Deaf community and helped me bridge the gap I sometimes feel when trying to go back and forth between two worlds. She shares a knowledge of our history and our culture. I owe Gay many thanks for her hours of listening and suggesting.

One of the benefits of working in a multidisciplinary field like medical anthropology has been the wide range of scholarship available to me at the San Francisco and Berkeley campuses of the University of California. It has been an honor to work with and learn from the writings and suggestions of the following colleagues and faculty members: Judith Barker, Jim Billings,

Margaret Clark, George DeVos, Chris Hatcher, Judith Justice, Linda Mitteness, Aiwa Ong, Nancy Scheper-Hughes, and Carol Stack. I am also indebted to two tireless department secretaries—Priscilla Ednalgan and Effie Meredith—who provided ongoing ballast in the daily routines of university life.

Early on, I asked my partner, Tim Lukaszewski, for help—and I almost never ask for help. I remember telling him that my fieldwork would take me to the farthest edge of the universe: I was going home. Tim provided me with refuge from the immersion. He would take me camping, off to a Sunday flea market, or out to a movie. As the silent partner in a seemingly endless enterprise, Tim has been my most meticulous critic and my most ardent supporter.

Through many days, months, and years of my research and writing, my friends patiently put up with my persistent ramblings and dogged questions: Did this ever happen in your family? Why do you think this happened? What do you think of this idea? I am especially grateful to those who overlooked occasions of my lax friendship and gave me much-needed support and encouragement. Harry Binder, Jim Burgess, David Correia, the Dawson family, Peter de Ruyter, Linda Dodge, Marguerite Fernandes, Judith Flory, Karen Kashkin, Peggy Kenney, Jane Louie, Birdie Lukaszewski, Karen Morebeck, Polly Quick, Erica Spalding, Jill Strachan, Anthony Tusler, and many others contributed greatly to this endeavor and to my personal well-being.

It has been an honor to have this book published by Harvard University Press because the Press has been one of the preeminent publishers of research on Deaf culture. I would especially like to thank Linda Howe, Angela von der Lippe, and my editor Mary Ellen Geer, each of whom has contributed technical expertise and solid advice in guiding this book from early manuscript to final publication.

Finally, I wish to express my heartfelt gratitude and respect for my informants. These women and men have literally made this long journey possible—through their generosity in time, meals, lodging, and moral support. They have been the backbone and the soul of my research. These informants have taken risks by sharing their history and their sense of themselves. As hearing children of deaf parents, we rarely allow others to watch us because it is an uncomfortably familiar place. Along with our parents, we were often stared at because of our difference. We are guarded with our family stories because it is too easy to stand apart, to judge, and to misunderstand. Only within our families are we free to acknowledge and to share our difference. More recently we have begun to explore not just the difference that we share with our parents, but how we are different from them. During the five years I worked on this project, I witnessed a tremendous burgeoning of creative activity by those with deaf parents: novels, plays, short stories, art, music. National and international conferences developed from informal meetings and sporadic newsletters. I am privileged to be able to share this story and this history with them.

Index